A Couple of Miracles

One Couple.
More than a Few Miracles.

Praise for *A Couple of Miracles:*

"I would add to Joyce and Barry's number of miracles ... this book! When two health professionals, despite our training, can open their minds and consciousness to the truth of life, miracles can happen. Read this book!"
—**Bernie Siegel, MD**, author of *Love, Medicine & Miracles*

"*A Couple of Miracles* is an amazing book by two amazing humans. Reading it, I feel inspired to be a better human myself. Being the intimacy experts that they are, Barry and Joyce tell their life story in such an intimate way. They are wonderful story tellers. And what a privilege to be let into their world with such care, humor, sincerity, and vulnerability. I was brought to tears many times. I do love to cry when I am emotionally moved, but it is rare for me to experience this while reading a non-fiction book. I urge you to read this book cover to cover. I don't want you to miss a word of this outstanding book. I would not be at all surprised if it became an international best-seller."
—**Susan Campbell, PhD**, author of *Getting Real*

"A truly inspirational story that can open our hearts to appreciate the many miracles that can come through love, compassion and wisdom. A real page turner!"
—**John Gray, PhD**, author of Men are from Mars, Women are from Venus

"The Vissells' latest book, *A Couple of Miracles*, will bring tears to the eyes of readers: tears of joy, tears of compassion, tears of heartache, and tears of laughter. It's got everything! Readers who are skeptical about miracles should be warned that this book could turn you into a believer! Read this book if you're looking for a jolt of pure inspiration!"

—**Linda Bloom, LCSW** and **Charlie Bloom, MSW**, authors of *101 Things I Wish I Knew When I Got Married*

"Reading *A Couple of Miracles* by Joyce and Barry Vissell is like taking a warm bath in a tub filled with bubbles of love. I both laughed and cried as Joyce and Barry shared episodes from their lives together. Their 57 years in a relationship brought lessons that resulted in them both becoming powerful spiritual teachers. Reading their book is sure to make people happier, more effective, and better at all their endeavors. I absolutely loved reading it, and didn't want it to end."

—**Tolly Burkan**, Founder of the Global Firewalking Movement

"Joyce and Barry Vissell bring the healing power of love to a whole new level of experience. My wife, Carlin, and I have attended their couple's retreats and they practice in their own lives what they teach to others. Now they share their personal journeys in this heart-felt and helpful true story. Whether you are married or single, looking for love or already have it, you will find great enjoyment and practical wisdom in this wonderful book."

—**Jed Diamond, PhD**, author *The Enlightened Marriage: The 5 Transformative Stages of Relationships.*

A Couple of Miracles

One Couple.
More than a Few Miracles.

by Joyce Vissell, RN, MS &
Barry Vissell, MD

A Couple of Miracles
One Couple, More Than a Few Miracles

Copyright © 2024 by Ramira Publishing
www.SharedHeart.org

ISBN: 978-0-9612720-9-8

All rights reserved. No part of this book may be used or reproduced in any manner whatsoever without written permission, except in the case of brief quotations in articles or reviews.

Also by Barry and Joyce Vissell:

The Shared Heart: Relationship Initiations and Celebrations
Models of Love: The Parent-Child Journey
Risk to be Healed: The Heart of Personal and Relationship Growth
Light in the Mirror: A New Way to Understand Relationships (also published as *The Heart's Wisdom*: A Practical Guide to Growing Through Love)
Meant To Be: Miraculous True Stories to Inspire a Lifetime of Love
A Mother's Final Gift: How One Woman's Courageous Dying Transformed her Family
{ *To Really Love a Woman*
  To Really Love a Man }
Heartfullness: 52 Ways to Open to More Love

Acknowledgments

To all our teachers, the ones in this book, and the unseen ones who have continued to help us, we give thanks.

To John Drew, for your thorough editing.

To Penelope Salinger, Linda Woods, Dianea Kohl, Liliana Cartagena, Heidi Kranz, and Jenny Capella for additional editing.

For our parents:

Louise and Hank Wollenberg and
Helen and Michael Vissell
Always loving us from beyond

our children:

Rami, Mira, and John-Nuriel
How proud we are of all three of you

and our grandchildren:

Skye and Owen
Keeping our hearts wide open

Contents

Introduction 1
Prologue: 1989 Santa Cruz, CA 2
Chapter 1: Earthquake! 1989 Santa Cruz, CA 6
Chapter 2: The Voice of Guidance 26
Chapter 3: The Mystery Man from Hartwick 33
Chapter 4: Two Different People 57
Chapter 5: A Close Call on the New York Subway 62
Chapter 6: Separation 67
Chapter 7: And Another Separation 73
Chapter 8: Operation Meharry 77
Chapter 9: Nashville 1968 90
Chapter 10: Serving the Poorest of the Poor 94
Chapter 11: Los Angeles 1970 104
Chapter 12: Betraying Joyce 111
Chapter 13: The Mysterious Hospital Chaplain 125
Chapter 14: Be Here Now 130
Chapter 15: Portland 1972 136
Chapter 16: Mexico 1973 151
Chapter 17: Kern River Miracle 162
Chapter 18: Initiated by John Lawrence 166
Chapter 19: Pir Vilayat Khan 169
Chapter 20: Hari Das Baba 1974 181
Chapter 21: The Cosmic Mass 190
Chapter 22: Rami 1976 196
Chapter 23: Pearl Dorris 213
Chapter 24: Ram Dass 228
Chapter 25: The Bokie Test 235
Chapter 26: Mira 1982 238
Chapter 27: The Shared Heart Miracle 243
Chapter 28: The "California" Book 248

Chapter 29: The Shy Public Speaker 255
Chapter 30: Kriya and the Coyotes 261
Chapter 31: Falling in Love with a New Man 265
Chapter 32: A Heavenly Vision 269
Chapter 33: The Miracle of Fatherhood 273
Chapter 34: Anjel 1986 278
Chapter 35: John-Nuriel 1989 291
Chapter 36: The Intruder Miracle 303
Chapter 37: The Lost Dog Miracle 2001 308
Chapter 38: My Near-Death Miracle 2009 310
Chapter 39: The Hand upon My Head 316
Chapter 40: Miracle on the River 2012 318
Chapter 41: Miracle at Poggio Bustone 2013 323
Chapter 42: Miracle on Lake Tahoe 327
Chapter 43: An Answered Prayer 331
Chapter 44: Two Blondes in the Back Seat 333
Chapter 45: Angels on the Road 336
Epilogue 340

Introduction

The following story, our story, strings together miracle after miracle. Some may be hard to believe, but they are all true. As they say, "Truth may be stranger than fiction."

Our previous nine books also contain miracle stories, some about us and some about other people. In all these books, the miracle stories illustrate teaching points to help the reader grow in awareness and love. This, of course, is wonderful, but we have longed to tell our whole story, to let our story be a teaching in itself.

We write our story, not only to entertain you, our readers, and certainly you will be entertained, but more so to inspire you. One thing we have learned after seventy-five years in these bodies, living on this earth, is that all of us have lives filled with miracles. We sincerely hope you will look at your own lives with new eyes, and discover the miraculous in so many of your own stories. Like Einstein said, "There are two ways to live your life. One is as though nothing is a miracle. The other is as though everything is a miracle."

Miracles are events that cannot be explained by our limited minds. We may try to explain them, but we seem to always fall short. The mind simply cannot believe in miracles, while the heart doesn't have to believe. It knows! The mind craves explanations, while the heart transcends explanation. The mind seeks smallness, while the heart is open to vastness. To be open to miracles is to be open to a spiritual dimension of life.

Enough said about this book. Now please immerse yourself in one true miracle story, as well as a love story...

Prologue: 1989 Santa Cruz, CA

Shortly after 5 pm on October 17, 1989, I went into the bathroom where Joyce was in the bathtub with our five-month-old son, John-Nuriel. I started the after-bath ritual by spreading a towel on the floor next to the bathtub. Joyce handed me our precious little dripping bundle and I laid him on the towel. At 5:04pm, as I was reaching for the corners of the towel to dry our baby, the house began rocking violently.

Joyce and I have weathered other earthquakes. Nineteen years before, when we moved to Los Angeles in 1970, and I started my third-year as a medical student at USC, we rented a tiny one-bedroom upstairs apartment for $89 (including utilities). It was certainly a different era. I remember gas costing 19 cents a gallon.

There was one potential problem. There was a train track immediately behind the apartment, perhaps thirty feet from the building. I asked the owner, "How often does the train pass by?" His answer, "Hardly ever. You won't even notice it."

We moved in. That first night, at precisely 3am, a passing train shook the whole apartment. Joyce and I shot up in bed, and I announced definitively, "Tomorrow, we move! There's no way I will spend even one more night in this place!"

The next morning, Joyce reasoned with me, "How about we give it one more night?"

I reluctantly agreed.

The next night, or rather early morning, again at 3am, the train rumbled by, shaking the apartment. This time, we were barely aware of the commotion, and quickly fell back asleep.

Like clockwork, the train came by every night at the exact same time, and we slept through it from then on. So much for the human ability to adapt.

Not long afterward, we woke up early one morning as pictures fell off the walls, dishes crashed in the kitchen, and we heard a thunderous roar outside as a bridge collapsed a block away. My first reaction was that the train had derailed and was crashing into our apartment. We leapt out of bed to scramble for safety. Then all the noise and shaking stopped. There was no train in our apartment, or in the backyard. We had just been initiated into our first major earthquake.

In those first few seconds in our Santa Cruz house, it felt much like the other rolling earth waves we had experienced. But this one got worse by the second! The house lurched with a deafening roar. I glanced out the bathroom window and saw to my horror that the trees seemed to be moving to the left. Then I realized that the trees were not moving … the house was moving to the right. Built on the topside of a ridge, the house was clearly beginning to slide downhill. I had the awful image in my mind of riding an out-of-control house down a steep hill while it crashed into trees and broke apart.

Joyce suddenly screamed from the bathtub, "Barry, pick up the baby!"

I bent down to grab our son, but the bouncing of the house threw me against the sink. I desperately tried again to reach for John-Nuri, but this time was nearly thrown into the bathtub with Joyce. Half the water in the tub poured over our infant son, while he helplessly screamed and sputtered on his water-logged towel.

Past where our baby lay, the toilet lifted into the air as if some malevolent spirit was pushing from below, and the broken pipe sent water splashing off the ceiling and walls. Between the moving, bouncing, and breaking apart of our house, and the splashing of the water everywhere, the sounds were deafening! It was like the growling of some hidden monster below our house.

After an eternity that turned out to be somewhere between fifteen and twenty seconds, all became eerily still, except for the barking of many frightened dogs echoing across the valley below us.

I quickly picked up a thoroughly soaked and crying John-Nuri, and tried my best to comfort him. With the power out and the water lines pulled apart, the pump stopped and so did the splashing.

Our ordeal had only just begun. There was a new sound, scarier than any other. Just outside the open bathroom window, the gas line from our newly-filled, 250-gallon propane tank was sheared off by the moving house. The tank's unobstructed outlet valve was aimed straight for our open bathroom window. With a roaring whoosh, a thick white cloud of propane gas was pouring in through the window. Our naked bodies were being coated with propane as the bathroom filled with gas. I was aware that the tiniest spark could set off a blazing inferno in that tiny space.

I knew I needed to turn off the valve at the tank, but first I had to close the bathroom window. I ran to the window, and quickly discovered that it would be impossible to close it. The frame was bent, and the window wouldn't budge.

It was definitely time to leave the bathroom! Still holding our baby, I yelled, "Joyce, quick, we gotta get out of here now."

I turned toward the bathroom door, but debris from the cupboards and the cupboard doors themselves blocked our exit. I handed John-Nuri back to Joyce in the bathtub and fought my way through the clutter to the door.

I pulled on the doorknob. Nothing! The door was stuck solid. We were trapped in a bathroom filling with propane gas, with its peculiar, skunk-like smell. I knew we didn't have long before we would succumb to the effects of breathing the toxic fumes....

Chapter 1: Earthquake! 1989 Santa Cruz, CA

Our family had been excited when our third child was born on May 1, 1989. All four of us pitched in with full enthusiasm for his care. Yet after five months, Barry, Rami, Mira, and I were growing weary. John-Nuri did not easily or gracefully adjust to his life on earth. He cried and screamed just as much as he smiled and giggled. At age forty-three, I was a mature and seasoned mom, but I was not up to the rigors of this latest infancy. John-Nuriel, his official name, weighed ten pounds at birth and was hungry from the start. He nursed almost constantly during the day, and was up several times at night. I had a series of eight painful breast infections during the first two months.

In my fatigue and discouragement, I started neglecting my family's emotional needs. Barry had to take complete responsibility for our business and work, and became stressed with all the problems that emerged. Rami had turned thirteen, and was beginning to act aloof from the family. Mira, our eight-year-old middle child, was having trouble getting attention from anyone. I yearned to be able to spend more time alone with her. An insidious distance was spreading between all of us.

Then the slipping of the San Andreas Fault shook us so violently that we have never returned to that place of uncaring, neglect and distance…

Tuesday, October 17, 1989 dawned bright, sunny and hot. The girls wore shorts to school. I kissed them as they went off, longing for more time with them. Barry went down to his home office, which was located in an already crowded laundry room, just off the kitchen. (We had an office in town, but he preferred working at home.) He seemed particularly absorbed in the difficulties of our business that day.

I was tending to John-Nuriel. Today, he was full of smiles. He loved being all alone with me, content to nurse the hours away. I sang songs to him, read to him and kissed his little hands. He nursed, so happy to be close to his mama.

As I nursed, I looked around our little, old rented farmhouse. We had lived here for fourteen years. All three children were born here. Our first three books were written and published here. All five of us loved living here. The two-bedroom house was too small for our growing family. About fifteen thousand of our books stored in the garage made it

seem even smaller. Rami had the other half of the laundry room, which just fit her bed and little altar with all her special feathers, rocks, and other sacred items. It was separated from the rest of the laundry room by a curtain. Barry had cut out and installed a window for her that looked out onto the bird feeder and garden. In her artistic way, she had made it into the most magical room of the house.

Barry's desk was squeezed opposite the washer and dryer. On the floor by his feet sat four bowls of kibble and water for our dog and the cats. He only complained when we piled laundry on his desk, or when I had to run the washer or dryer while he was on the phone. He disliked when we spilled the animals' water so his stockinged feet got wet. On those occasions, he would complain in a bigger way. Mira once announced, "Daddy, I'm going to call you 'Mr. Feety.'" And the name stuck, much to Barry's dismay! I often smiled to think of him in that laundry room office, with water puddles on the floor, doing work that was so important to both of us.

The outside of the house was rundown, and hadn't been painted in twenty years, revealing in many places the original graying wood underneath. The faucets leaked, the front door didn't lock (it didn't even close properly), and some windows couldn't be opened. But we loved that house dearly. The rent was cheap, $270 a month, and we felt we could put up with the inconveniences.

The living room was large and we kept it totally empty. We had all kinds of events here: workshops, Easter services, Christmas pageants, children's plays, weddings, baby blessings and various other celebrations. Week after week, twenty to eighty people crowded into our living room. Our home felt charged with the love and beauty of all who came to us. The healing quality of our work seemed to always pervade the atmosphere. Everyone who entered could feel the energy. Even Dave, the UPS driver, looking in from the front door, said, "What goes on here? I feel hit by a wave of peace whenever I come to your door."

The best part of the house was the land around it. One look out the dining room window revealed why we loved living here so much. A gorgeous 120-acre ranch spread below — a grassy valley with groves of redwoods poking up through the live oaks, and the blue of the Monterey Bay on the horizon. Except for an elderly Texan couple, Norris and Marie, down the hill, who were the caretakers, we were the only people around. To say that we loved living there is perhaps an understatement — we adored it!

Barry: Now, about that elderly couple living below us... Even in paradise there are problems. Norris did not like all the "spiritual" events at our house. He especially didn't like that he had to thread his way through parked cars to get down the hill to his house. Once, when some late arrival at one of our events partially blocked the road, he barged into our house in the middle of a quiet meditation and angrily shouted, "Who's blocking the road? This is not a church!"

Then there was the time Norris couldn't find Ears, their two-year-old, fifteen-hundred-pound bull. He knocked loudly on our door. Luckily, it wasn't in the middle of one of our gatherings. When we opened the door, he said, "I can't find Ears." Then he added, in a not-so-subtle accusatory tone, while obviously looking past us into our house, "Have you seen him?"

I said no, but I wanted to laugh. It seemed like he suspected us of hiding a huge bull in our house, perhaps keeping it as a house pet. Here, Ears, come snuggle with us on our bed!

Norris's son, Mike, later that day, found Ears in a steep gulley in the valley below their house. He had apparently fallen in and couldn't get out. It took Mike's horse and a stout rope to finally pull him out. Ears was fine, just very hungry and thirsty.

One evening, Joyce and I had a big argument. I was so upset that, even though it was close to midnight, I stormed out of the house, got into my old truck with a camper on it, and drove down the hill. My goal was a pretty little pond below us on the ranch. I wanted to spend the night there, away from Joyce. However, I would need to drive right past Norris and Marie's house. Still fuming with anger, I ignored that little detail. I didn't notice the lights going on in their house after I passed it. Going down the hill, I did notice the headlights in my rearview mirrors. I thought, "Uh oh, this could be trouble!"

I made a foolish decision and sped up, driving a little recklessly on the dirt road to the pond. When I got there, I parked and turned off the lights, hoping I had lost my pursuer. No luck. The headlights were rapidly approaching. Norris and Mike roared into the clearing and jumped out of their truck, each armed with shotguns.

Norris yelled, "WHO ARE YOU?"

I timidly called back, "Norris, it's me, Barry."

"Barry? What the *&%# are you doing down here in the middle of the night?"

I decided to tell him the truth. They both just shook their heads, got back into their truck, and drove off.

Other than this occasional unpleasantness, we loved living there.

That old red ranch house was not love at first sight. When we drove up the hill and saw the dilapidated condition of the house, we almost turned around and left. Two things kept us from leaving. First, we both remembered driving up this road when we first moved to Santa Cruz County a few years before. In fact, at that time, Joyce was surprised when I suddenly turned off the main road, Freedom Boulevard, onto this tiny private road.

She said, "Barry, what are you doing?"

I answered, "I have no idea why I'm doing this. Something is pulling me up there."

I drove the half-mile to the top, then came back down, still not having a clue why I did it.

It was the beginning of 1976, and we were pregnant with our first child, Rami. We were discouraged with living in a rented house under the redwoods. It was perpetually cold, even on sunny days. Our counseling clients arrived in shorts and short-sleeved shirts, carrying their down coats to put on inside our house. We longed to live in a warm, sunny house, with lots of privacy and nature around us. But day after day, there was nothing like this in the newspaper.

The second reason we didn't leave presented itself in the form of an old woman, Mrs. Woods, walking up to my side of our VW van.

She smiled and said, "I know what you're thinking, and you're right. The house is not much to look at." Then she pointed behind her and added, "Park your car and go for a walk on this trail. You'll see what I mean."

Next to that little red house was a sixteen-acre piece of land. This property had a magical trail that ran its length, with a gorgeous view south across a wooded valley with the sparkling blue waters of the Monterey Bay in the distance. We felt so at home on this land that we decided to go ahead and rent the house. Every day, we walked that special trail, finding power spots for meditation. Not once did we ever see anyone else hiking there. The land began to feel like ours, and we took care of it accordingly.

Since 1974, during our retreat in the French Alps with Sufi teacher Pir Vilayat Khan, Joyce and I have nourished a vision of a place where people could leave their busy environments to come into an atmosphere of love, acceptance and healing. There, they could discover their own inner wisdom, either in a loving supportive group or alone in nature.

Soon after we arrived in Santa Cruz County, we saw an ad in the newspaper for twelve acres of land for sale. The line that really caught our attention was, "bordered by one quarter mile of creek." We immediately went to check it out. It was gorgeous! It was steep, on a hillside of tanbark oaks and redwoods, with the small creek at the bottom. It was a warm day in the middle of the summer, with dappled sunlight lighting up the dense forest floor. I remember my joy, walking on the bank of the creek, imagining the trail I would build, and the tidy little A-frame sleeping cabins for our retreat participants. In my mind, I could see little rock dams, creating small waterfalls and pools along that whole 1200 feet, with the nurturing sound of falling water soothing the souls of everyone who came to this land.

We purchased the property for $18,000! We hired a bulldozer to put in a road down the hillside to a homesite just above the creek. Even though switch backed, the road was still steep. We brought in crushed granite base rock to make it more drivable.

A friend drew up, with our guidance, plans for our home, with a large living room for gatherings, and a large deck overlooking the creek and wrapping around a large, native maple tree.

Then autumn came, and the sun began to dip below the trees. Then it was gone. Not a drop of sun all day long. And it got cold without any sunlight.

The final clincher was the backhoe operator who drove down to dig a test hole for septic approval. I will never forget the comment he made, thinking I was a hired worker and not the owner. "I've put in a lot of septic systems in all kinds of places in this county, but what kind of fool would want to build something down in this hell-hole."

That evening, with a heavy heart, I told Joyce what this man said. We sat a long time in silence pondering his words. Finally, I spoke, "Joyce, I feel we made a mistake." And Joyce sadly agreed. Then we held each other and cried.

We sold the land, with its new driveway down to a cleared building site, to a young man who was thrilled to have a forested hideaway.

Three years later, during a particularly severe winter storm, the hillside above the building site gave way, covering the site with mud and debris. Luckily, nothing was built there. Any home on that site would have been demolished.

That backhoe operator, although crude and humorless, was nevertheless sent by angels to deliver his message.

During the fourteen years before our rented home was destroyed, we dreamed of someday owning the sixteen acres ourselves. Winter and summer, there was always abundant sunlight.

We found out the property was an investment for a wealthy lawyer who lived near San Francisco, and had only seen it once — the day he bought it. Every year, we sent him what we felt was a fair offer based on current market value. Each time, he wrote back asking for approximately twice what we'd offered. Our offers went higher and higher. His counters kept doubling our offers. It was clear he had no urgency to sell. Finally, we gave up making offers, but we could not give up our feeling that this was sacred land. We continued to care for the property and meditate in special places. Okay, without permission, I kept making new trails and improving on the old ones.

A friend at the time once meditated with us on the knoll with the most beautiful view. Deeply inspired, he announced, "I just felt the nature spirits in this place. They all want you and your family to live here." His statement only confirmed what we already felt.

Joyce: Barry and I loved this special piece of land that was close by our rented house. Access was across a corner of land belonging to a couple named Lois and Carl Woods. Lois was the woman who urged us to walk on this land when we first came to look at the house to rent. We often walked it several times a day, always going through the Woods' land. They were seldom there as they had a home an hour away. Mrs. Woods was a very loving and generous person. She knew how much we wanted to buy the land next to hers, and she also knew that the owner did not want to sell it, even though he never came to see it. She always wished that we could buy that land, and she felt annoyed at the owner for keeping the property only as an investment.

One day, I was going to take a walk by myself on the land. As I was walking through the Woods' property to get there, I suddenly saw Mrs. Woods. But it was not Mrs. Woods in the body. Rather, she was lighter, more floating than standing. After a few seconds, while pointing to the land that we loved, she clearly said to me, "You will be able to own that land, and you will enjoy it very much." Then she disappeared.

I found out the next day that Mrs. Woods was hit by a car and had died a short time before she appeared to me. I had never seen a ghost before or since, but I am convinced that Mrs. Woods came back in her soul-body to deliver an important message to me.

Barry looked at many other pieces of property and even fell in love with a large piece of land that had streams. But ever since Mrs. Woods' message to me, I only wanted to buy the special piece of land near our rented house.

Barry: On the morning of the earthquake, October 17, 1989, I started out for my usual walk onto "our" trail, surprised to see a woman coming toward me on the trail. She said she was a realtor, and then announced that the property was in escrow. Someone was buying "our" land. I can still remember the sick feeling in the pit of my stomach as I returned to our house and sat down on the girls' swing hanging from a large oak. This just couldn't be happening. It didn't feel right. I carried a feeling of sadness the whole day.

Joyce: I looked at our little John-Nuri, still nursing and gazing up at me with his gentle brown eyes. I was reminded of something disturbing — that during my pregnancy, I'd had an unpleasant premonition that he might die before he was six months old. Whenever I would share this feeling with others, they got upset, saying I shouldn't project outwardly such a negative thought. It was a fear I therefore kept within.

Our last baby had died when I was six months pregnant. Perhaps that was the cause of my fear. Barry understood, perhaps because he shared a similar fear. Of course, we had no rational reason to support this feeling. We just had a sense that he might not live past six months of age.

Before John-Nuri was born, our favorite little six-month-old kitten, Mr. Sweet, was killed by a large roving dog. As I held his little dead body, I had the thought that I might also be holding the dead body of my baby at six months old.

John-Nuri sat up from his nursing and gave a loud burp, bringing me back from my reverie. He laughed. Burps always made him laugh. I hugged him tightly. He was a huge baby, weighing almost twenty pounds, strong and healthy. My love for him moved within me like the vast ocean.

"We've made it a long way, little guy," I told him as I tickled him. Only thirteen more days to go, I thought to myself, remembering my awful premonition.

The day progressed uneventfully. I had an eye appointment so, in the afternoon, Barry took the three children to the beach. It was so hot that they swam in the ocean, taking turns watching John-Nuri on the beach. A school of dolphins surprised them by joining in the fun, frolicking nearby.

I came home from my appointment early and had the house to myself. Normally, I would be ecstatic to have time alone. Not today. I worried about my family, eager to have them return. I felt a strange tension in my body, as if I was about to explode. The air felt hot and still, but that wasn't the problem. It was an eerie, nameless feeling. With each minute that ticked by, I felt worse. I longed to be with my family.

They returned at 4:30, exuberant and all talking at once about the dolphins! Even John-Nuri seemed thrilled, pointing his fingers and jabbering away. Their mood of lightness and joy sharply contrasted with mine.

I laid John-Nuri in front of the bookcase, thinking I would make dinner. Perhaps being busy would ease the mounting tension within me. The massive wooden bookcase that Barry had made, stretched to the ceiling, holding six shelves, and hundreds of pounds of heavy books, including Barry's medical texts. This was one of John-Nuri's power spots. He loved lying there, looking up at all the colorful books. We used to laugh and say he was studying and absorbing their contents.

When I walked away from John-Nuri toward the kitchen, the strange feeling within me intensified so much that I felt horrible. There seemed to be no reason for me to be feeling this way, but I did. I walked back to John-Nuri and picked him up.

"Let's have a bath, fella," I said, deciding to postpone the dinner preparation. Baths were a favorite activity for John-Nuri. As soon as I picked him up and moved him from below the bookcase, the tension within me eased to a tolerable point.

While John-Nuri and I were in the bath, Mira came in to ask for help with homework. "Go ask Rami," was my reply at approximately 5pm. Rami was standing by the door leading to the laundry room. She was reading directions for her own homework assignment. She looked at Mira as her younger sister asked for help with her homework. Rami was all set to say no and continue standing there, when she felt a wave of love for Mira and walked the three steps up to the kitchen to help her.

While they stood together in the middle of the kitchen, the earthquake struck. They started screaming as the entire contents of the kitchen cupboards emptied all around them.

Barry: Meanwhile, back in the bathroom, Joyce holding John-Nuri in her arms right behind me, I attacked the wedged door with a vengeance, knowing with certainty that we had only minutes before we would all pass out from breathing the propane gas pouring in through the broken window. We were NOT going to die in that bathroom!

Finally, with superhuman effort, I managed to pull the door free and the three of us made our way over the crazily uneven floor to the living room. Our bodies, coated with propane gas residue, smelled like we had been sprayed by a skunk. In the living room, we met up with Rami and Mira, their faces white with fright. The kitchen was the worst mess in the whole house. Rami's legs were bleeding from half a dozen small cuts from flying pieces of glass. Blood was dripping from a thankfully small cut on Mira's head, where she'd been hit by a falling plate. It was like a bomb exploded in the kitchen, and our girls had been hit by shrapnel.

Kitchen/dining room chaos

Our family reunited, we made our way over loose bricks that had exploded out of the fireplace into the living room, and through thick clouds of dust that were still settling. I'll never forget the smell of destruction, of broken concrete and torn apart wood. I noticed that the floor and ceiling were separated from the walls, but it wasn't until we got to the front door that we realized the full extent of damage to the house. It was then we knew with shocking certainty that we would never live in this house again.

Outside the open front door, where a concrete porch used to be, was now a chasm. We had to jump across this chasm to our porch. I went first, then held out my hand to grab each member of the family as they jumped. From the porch we could see that the house was five feet off the crumbled foundation, leaning precariously. By the grace of God, the roof had not caved in upon us all.

We helped each other out to the dirt road to view what had once been our home. The house and almost everything in it at that moment appeared totally destroyed. Rami started screaming. John-Nuriel was still coughing and choking on the bathtub water. Eight-year-old Mira cried and asked, "Are we in the heaven world now?" And I imagine that, to a child, it could have easily looked like the end of the world.

Joyce: Barry suddenly threw up his hands in ecstasy, shouting, *"We're alive! We're alive!"* We stood in a circle, thanking God and shouting, *"We're alive!"* We kept hugging each other with the deepest sense of appreciation.

In that moment, as we stood naked on our dirt road, not knowing if we could recover anything of our material world, we were made aware of what is most important in life. Our home and possessions had been taken from us in twenty seconds, but we had each other. Standing among ruins, we found we had gratitude and appreciation for the most

House is barely standing

important things of all — our lives and one another.

We stood there, naked and holding each other. Actually, I was not completely naked. I had on a shower cap.

After a few minutes, we heard the sound of a motorcycle roaring up our hill. Approaching us was a tough-looking biker dressed in black on a Harley. He pulled right up to us and stopped. It would have made a very interesting photograph, this rough-looking person with slicked back hair and a large black beard, and Barry and I completely naked except for my shower cap.

I don't know what I expected him to say, but his words surprised us.

"Are you folks all right? I was down the road when the earthquake hit, and thought I'd better come up the hill and check if anyone needs help." He didn't seem to even notice our nakedness.

We thanked him and sent him past us and down the hill to check on Norris and Marie, whose old and poorly-built house was also destroyed by the quake.

Barry ran around the house and turned off the gas, then returned and checked the girls' cuts. When we saw that the house was not about to cave in, we very cautiously ventured back inside. Once there, we realized how close we had all come to either serious injury or death. John-Nuri's "power spot" by the bookcase was a huge pile of fallen books and shelf boards. We shuddered at what might have happened if I had left him in that spot when the earthquake hit. Perhaps this could have been the source of my morbid premonition.

The door Rami had been standing near, before she went up to help Mira with her homework, had sprung off its hinges and bizarrely shot across the laundry room and lodged itself halfway out the window. Rami would have been in the path of that door had she remained standing there.

The kitchen floor was covered with broken glass and dishes, appliances and spilled food. Barry had, the day before, purchased a case of spaghetti sauce in glass jars. Twelve quarts of sauce covered the kitchen floor and even splashed up on the walls, looking like a crime scene. There was nothing in any of the cupboards or on the counters except, bizarrely, a vase of flowers on the middle of one of the counters, still standing peacefully in the midst of all the destruction.

Had the earthquake lasted even a few seconds more, the house would probably have slid down the hill. The roof was close to collapsing in several places.

It's an absolute miracle that all five of us survived the earthquake with only minor cuts and bruises. It's a miracle that we are alive to tell about the experience. We are convinced the angels were working overtime.

The silent distance that had been creeping into our family vanished, leaving in its place gratitude and appreciation for one another's presence. We couldn't look at each other without realizing how close we had come to dying and how precious was our time together. The fatigue, discouragement, moodiness and acting out that had begun to separate us, now seemed trivial and unimportant. All that mattered to each one of us was the gratitude that all of us were alive. After the earthquake, we could not say enough how much we appreciated each other.

It was twenty-four hours before news from Santa Cruz reached beyond our town. Friends and relatives were frantic. When I was finally able to reach my parents in Buffalo, New York, my mother told me that many people had figured out how to contact them on our behalf from information in our books. Her voice choked with emotion as she told me how much love was being poured out to our family. She said, "Your dad and I and Barry's parents have often wondered why a medical doctor and nurse would choose work with so little financial reward. But today, I understand where your wealth is. It is in the gratitude and appreciation of all these many people you have helped. You have chosen the greatest of wealth."

And it's true. The greatest investment we ever made was to fully share our hearts with others. Now, we needed to draw upon that investment. We decided to follow through with our plans for a weekend couples' retreat starting Friday evening, three days after the earthquake. Ten of the twenty couples still wanted to come. We brought our children and allowed everyone to bathe us in love. The girls were having difficulty sleeping at night because of dreams of the earthquake.

We gave everything we had at that retreat, but more than ever before, we *received*. At one point on Sunday morning, I was not able to hold back the tears, and Barry asked everyone to hold us. John Astin sang, *"Blessings on your journey ... on your way back home ... just carry the light within you."* As the tears flowed, we once again realized that home is just a feeling. We felt how much help is available to us at all times. We felt the presence of the angels and the illumined ones who have never stopped helping and guiding us. We felt how much everyone was willing to help us ... and we needed a lot of help. We were so grateful for the outpouring of love from our beloved sisters and brothers. In that moment, we gazed into one another's eyes and rededicated ourselves to doing divine work — the work of continually opening our hearts to giving — *and receiving from others.*

Although we were aware of the hand of God in this disaster, we still had the human feelings of grief, loss and sadness. With each aftershock, and there were many, we relived the earthquake. Sometimes it seemed like a bad dream from which we would soon awaken. This was especially true when we returned to the house, a little part of us hoping to find it intact. More than once, we wistfully thought of the miniature aliens in the movie, "Batteries Not Included," who miraculously fixed anything that was broken.

Gratitude and appreciation were the tools that saw us through a year of tremendous change, stress and difficulty. When the feelings of grief, loss and sadness threatened to overwhelm our family, we remembered that we still had one another, and gave thanks to the Light.

Barry: Joyce and I have experienced many gifts and blessings from the Loma Prieta Earthquake. It has helped us to more deeply understand the divine workings behind the scenes of all seeming adversity.

In geology, as the years of built-up pressure between the earth's continental plates is suddenly released as an earthquake, the region becomes more stable afterwards. True, the pressure may again slowly build over the next twenty to thirty years, or it may not. No one knows for sure. After a major earthquake, however, there is a new stability, a new beginning, a fresh chance. Here's how this played out in our lives:

Months after the earthquake, while in a rented house we did not like, our thoughts and feelings returned to the sixteen acres that we still loved. We were reminded again of our vision for it. For all we knew, someone had bought it and was by now planning to build. We called the old owner anyway and were told it was still on the market. He seemed friendlier. We learned that shortly after the earthquake, unknown to us, the new buyer had come up our hill. He saw our destroyed house, along with five other badly damaged homes on the road, must have panicked, and promptly dropped out of escrow. He hadn't known how poorly our house was built, with a totally inadequate foundation.

After the earthquake, a lot of people were leaving Santa Cruz County. Homes and land were flooding the real estate market. Prices were plummeting. The owner agreed with us on a price for "our" property that turned out to be much lower than our offer of several years before. This was yet another important lesson on how loss often turns into gain. After hearing our story, people teasingly blame us for causing the earthquake so we could afford to buy this land.

During our years in the old red farmhouse, as we said before, we treated the sixteen neighboring acres as our own. I kept all the trails clear. I built new ones. And, years before, we had placed an old yellow metal folding chair in the most beautiful spot with gorgeous views. On that chair, we sat gazing at the expansive views, we meditated, and we worked on our books. Once, when our friend Michael Stillwater saw this chair, he announced, "I hereby declare you, as the owner of this chair, which has been here for years, as official 'squatters.' Because this is your chair, and you have sat on it faithfully all these years, you are hereby entitled to 'squatter's rights. You will be entitled to sit on this chair as long as you live." He had us rolling on the ground in laughter.

We are now living on the sixteen acres, a bit more than squatters, in a home that has been built to withstand a much greater earthquake than the one in 1989. We call it our "HomeCenter," because it is equally a home and a center for our workshops and retreats. The center of the large living room/meeting room is built directly over the spot where the yellow chair sat. It has always been a power spot for us. Now it is a power spot for many people.

Chapter 2: The Voice of Guidance

Joyce: I was born May 18, 1946, into a family of mother, father and older brother. My mother had lost twin boys at birth two years earlier, so I was regarded as a miracle by my parents. My birth was also celebrated by my six aunts, who were like mothers to me, as well as my uncles and fourteen cousins, all of whom lived a short drive from our home. My parents, brother and I lived in a small house in Buffalo, New York, that they bought for $3,000.

My dad played games with me when he returned from work each evening, and read me stories as I was going to sleep. He also carefully arranged all of my stuffed animals in

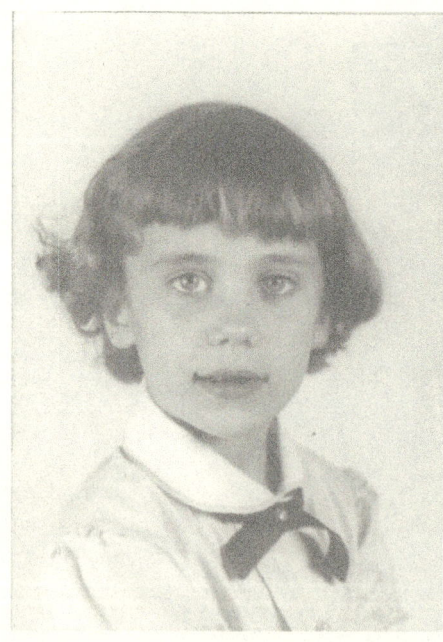

a circle around my bed in the order I liked. I still have my stuffed "Squirrely," although all his fur has been lovingly rubbed off over the years. My mother took good care of me during the day and baked homemade bread, cookies and pies as well as good meals. In other words, I was blessed by a small nuclear family and a large extended family.

Yet there was an undeniable sadness that

could always be seen in my eyes. I have many pictures of family gatherings, which occurred whenever someone had a birthday, there was a holiday, or someone simply felt a need to gather. Amid pictures of all this joy and love, I always had a faraway look of sadness. Even with everything seemingly right, there was something important missing.

One of my earliest childhood memories occurred when I was four years old. I had trouble sleeping and had the vague memory of another home, which I now know to be the heavenly home from which I came. I remember thinking to myself, "I don't like this place that I live. I love my mother and father, but I miss my other home very much. I want to go back to that home."

In my childlike mind I reasoned that if I had been able to come into this body, then surely I could also leave. Seeking an exit, I thought about each part of my body. "There must be a way out of here!" I tried to find the door out through my hands, then my feet, my eyes, my heart, my stomach, the top of my head, my mouth, my nose. Nothing worked. There was no door to allow me to go back out. "I am in a prison," I desperately thought to myself.

When I could find no way out, I let out a piercing scream of anguish. My father was at my side in an instant. Sobbing, I told him I wanted to go back to my real home and I couldn't find the way out to go there.

My father was an engineer and saw things from a practical viewpoint. He told me I was just having a bad dream, and told me I could just change the channel and find a good dream. He then lovingly picked me up and brought me in bed to lie between him and my mother. I felt comforted, but not free. Gradually I returned to sleep. These experiences happened perhaps several times a year for several years until I was nine years old.

At the same time, our pediatrician, Dr. Jacobson, was concerned with what he referred to as my "failure to bloom." My mother was doing her best to feed me well-balanced meals, yet I had little interest in eating. I had plenty of friends, activities, and fun in my life. And yet something just wasn't right in my heart. I was missing something I couldn't exactly name.

Dr. Jacobson finally told my worried mother, "She hasn't quite decided if she wants to be here. I suggest you get her a pet." My parents went right out and found a small dog named Nicky, plus a cat and goldfish. The pets gave me great joy, yet they did not take from me this faraway sadness that kept me from nourishing my body and being truly happy.

When I was seven, Dr. Jacobson decided I needed a tonsillectomy. "This will help her to bloom," he told my mother with confidence. As much as I honor this man for his wisdom and compassion, this was not a good plan. The operation and overnight stay were the most traumatic experiences of my young life. The tonsillectomy gave me a horrible sore throat that seemed to go on forever. The nighttime experiences of feeling trapped in my body grew in intensity. I lost weight and, rather than blooming, faded a little bit more. The doctor told my mother to give the tonsillectomy a bit more time to work its magic. It never did!

One aspect of my family life that I did not like was my brother's teasing. My brother is a genius in intelligence and humor, and could captivate an entire family gathering with his wit. I generally thought he was funny until he made me the object of his jokes. I was sensitive, and my feelings were easily hurt. When my brother would tease me, my eyes would fill with tears. My parents said I was too sensitive and couldn't take a joke. I was told to go to my room if I needed to cry. Once sent to my room, I would feel lonelier and more hurt than ever. Other people laughed when he teased me, but I could find nothing funny about it. It felt mean to me and actually hurt my heart.

His teasing grew in intensity, and I continued to be sent to my room for my tears. "You can't be happy in your life until you learn to not be so sensitive," my parents would say in exasperation. "Learn to take a joke. You are too sensitive, and you will not make it in this world until you can learn to laugh off things."

My parents meant well and were sincerely seeking to help me learn how to brush off teasing, mean remarks. However, they were giving me the message that my sensitivity was a handicap, and I felt that I was as handicapped as much as a person who is deaf or blind.

During one of these times of being sent to my room, something happened that changed my life forever. I was nine years old. As usual, I went to my bed and cried as a growing despair grew within me. Suddenly, I felt myself enfolded by loving arms. No one was with me, yet I felt a strong loving presence speak to me in my heart.

"A boy right now is growing up and is meant to be with you. He will understand your feelings, will love your sensitivity, and will hold you when you cry. You will recognize him as a tall, dark-haired young man who will become a doctor."

Through the energy of this loving guidance, I felt instantly connected to this boy who was to come into my life. I did not doubt for an instant that what was spoken to me was true. I relaxed deeply for perhaps the first time in my young life. What had been missing had been promised to me. The sadness was no more.

I began to gain weight. My cheeks flushed with color and health. Dr. Jacobson was convinced the tonsillectomy finally started to work, even though it had been two years.

My life went on as usual with typical childhood joys and sorrows. My brother continued to tease me, and I was still sent to my room for crying, but I never again felt totally alone. I felt connected to my tall, dark-haired, doctor-to-be, special friend who would understand my tears and sensitivity. He was in the process of growing up too, and we would meet when the time was right.

This knowledge gave me untold peace, especially throughout adolescence. While my girlfriends dated and were asked out to proms, and my mom worried about my lack of social life, I was seldom concerned that I was seemingly alone. I had an ever-growing awareness of my connection to my future beloved.

My first boyfriend was short, blond, and wanted to be a teacher. I enjoyed the thrills of holding hands, kissing, and going out on dates. When he suddenly dropped me for another girl, I was not hurt at all. I had never taken the relationship seriously. Obviously, he was not the one.

Feeling the loving arms of the unseen being, and hearing the still voice in my heart, led me into a very spiritual life. I rose early in the morning to read inspirational books and to pray. My mother, who is a very spiritual person, was a constant source of reading material and inspiration to me. Half of my life seemed to be spent in church, going to services, Sunday school, youth groups and choir. Though my mother was a Presbyterian, she wanted me to be open to great leaders of other faiths. Gandhi was one of her heroes, and she exposed me to many of his teachings. This introduction to other spiritual views has profoundly affected my life. It also opened the door to meeting my beloved.

I had been a good student in high school, with high SAT scores. I could have gone to any college I wanted. Looking past the prestigious east coast schools, I settled on Hartwick College. "Why Hartwick?" my peers wanted to know. No one had ever heard of it. My minister's sister had gone to Hartwick and described it as a small, Protestant college in the Catskill Mountains of upstate New York. Something clicked inside me, and it was the only school I applied to. It was one of those decisions that felt right, but had no rational explanation.

In the fall of 1964, I arrived at Hartwick College to begin my freshman year. Though I missed my parents and family very much, I felt a joy almost bursting inside of me. I was so happy, I literally skipped wherever I went and shouted greetings of hello or have a nice day to everyone I passed. My enthusiasm was so great I began to be criticized for it. People thought I was faking it or just putting on a show. I consciously tried to tone down my joy. Sometimes I would question myself with, "Why are you so happy? People think you're weird. Why are you behaving this way?" I didn't know why. I just knew that I'd wake up filled with mounting excitement.

Chapter 3: The Mystery Man from Hartwick

Barry: For as long as I can remember, I have always wanted to be a doctor. Perhaps my desire was inspired by the tall, kindly pediatrician, Dr. Schmidt, who came to our home when I was very sick with the measles. Perhaps it was simply an innate knowing.

I knew Joyce's story of hearing an inner voice at age nine. She was clearly told that she would recognize me as "tall, with dark hair, and would become a doctor." Once, while visiting my mom many years ago, I asked her, "Mom, do you by any chance remember when I decided to become a doctor?"

Without even a moment's hesitation, she said, "It seemed to come out of the blue one day when you were nine years old."

Of course, it might not have happened like this, but I like to think that I made the decision in the same moment Joyce was receiving her instructions.

The number nine seems to have a prominent place in our lives. I was born nine days after Joyce (although Joyce was on time and I might have been nine days late). Joyce was born on the 18th of May (1 plus 8 equals 9). I was born on the 27th of May (2 plus 7 equals 9). In Numerology, number 9 is the number of universal love, eternity, spiritual awakening, service to humanity, leading by positive example, and interestingly, romance. Pretty auspicious!

Like many people, I found the deepest peace in solitude. I considered myself lucky to move from Brooklyn at the age of six and spend the rest of my childhood growing up at the edge of a neighborhood in Elmsford, NY, in a house bordering a vast area of farmland and woods. I loved playing with

older sister Donna, Barry (age 13), and younger brother Richard

the kids in the neighborhood, but most of all I loved wandering the open spaces for hours by myself, making up stories about being a pioneer doctor.

At the age of eighteen, in my senior year at Sleepy Hollow High School in Tarrytown in 1964, I finally started noticing girls, especially one particular girl. I went out with Becky for three months. Although it was puppy love, it was still my heart's first awakening, my first time kissing a girl, and holding hands in public, proclaiming to the world that I was now in a relationship.

At the same time, I was waiting to hear back from the colleges to which I had applied. I must admit, I was not that great a student. I only excelled when a subject interested me (or a teacher made the subject interesting, like dear Mr. Pace, my earth science teacher). The process of applying to colleges felt unimportant to me. In fact, and this is embarrassing for me to admit, I had so little motivation that my mother ended up doing most of the work for me, researching schools and filling out applications.

I have to also admit that I was a bit of a juvenile delinquent. Perhaps more than a bit. I have done some things that could have landed me in a detention facility. I stole from stores. I did some potentially dangerous, even though quite creative, pranks. Luckily, no one ever got hurt. I'll share one of my most creative ones.

There was a drive-in theater just down the hill from our neighborhood. We could actually watch the movies, albeit without sound, right from our house. It was approaching July 4, Independence Day, and I was well-stocked in fireworks. I dreamed up a major prank, a prank of epic proportions. Armed with a backpack filled with rockets, I believe they were called Roman Candles in those days, and wearing dark clothing, I silently crept around the drive-in theater behind the screen. Below the screen, amid the support structure, I was in the dark where no one could spot me.

I began my work, securing groups of the Roman Candles, each one had perhaps ten or twenty rockets of different colors, to the infrastructure, pointing to all the cars, where hundreds of people were innocently watching the movie. To each cluster, I inserted the fuse into a cigarette. No, I didn't smoke. This was my only use for cigarettes.

I took a moment to inspect my sinister, but creative, handiwork. All was ready. I lit all the cigarettes and ran for all I was worth. From past experience, I knew I had approximately twenty minutes for the cigarettes to burn down to the rocket fuses, ample time to circumvent the theater and run up Beaver Hill Road to my yard, where I could watch the mayhem.

And mayhem it definitely was! The rockets started igniting, blasting out from under the screen. From where I was watching, it looked like the cars were under attack, rockets streaking through the air, some even bouncing off car windshields. People starting panicking, running from their cars in terror. Of course, nowadays, with the real threat of terrorism, this kind of prank would take people's feelings to a whole other level. But it was the early 1960's, a very different, even innocent, time.

Even though I learned from the news later that no one was hurt, I deeply regret scaring all those people. If, by some miracle, someone reading this book was there that night, I sincerely apologize for this invasion of your evening. For this act, and for all the others, I have done much work on forgiving myself, and feeling God's forgiveness. I wish I could have channeled my creative energies in a healthier direction.

Back to the spring of my senior year of high school. I waited anxiously to hear back from colleges. And I enjoyed my new girlfriend. Then, only a few months into my brief relationship, Becky announced she didn't want to be my girlfriend anymore. I didn't get it until the next day, when I saw her in school walking down the hall hand-in-hand with another boy. That sight really drove home the fact that the relationship was over. Up to that point, I held out the hope that she didn't really mean what she had said.

I was heartsick. I remember lying in bed with an awful empty feeling inside and wished good old Dr. Schmidt had a remedy for my heartache.

Not long after Becky broke up with me, I was cut from the baseball team. The pain and rejection were enormous, even greater than my broken heart. Baseball was my passion. When I wasn't wandering the woods and fields by myself, I was organizing a baseball game with as many kids as I could round up from the neighborhood.

I even slept with my baseball glove; it was such a deep part of me. Not long ago, when a man heard about this in a talk we were giving, he yelled out, "That's probably why your girlfriend broke up with you!"

To make matters worse, one after another rejection letters started to come in from prospective colleges. It didn't seem to make any difference to me -- I already felt hopelessly rejected. Then came the rejection letter from the last college, my safety choice, the one I felt surely would accept me.

It was the final blow. My dreams of becoming a doctor seemed far away now. Yes, I hadn't made the baseball team, but I survived that. I could still play baseball. Yes, I lost my girlfriend, but I could survive that too. Somewhere deep within me, I knew there was someone somewhere waiting for me. I had gotten a taste of love, a feeling of connection with another. It had awakened in me a deeper yearning to travel to even higher places of joy and love, to experience that wonderful feeling of being at home with another.

But now all these college rejections. It was just too much for me to take. It wasn't even that I wanted to go to these particular colleges. It was more the picture I had in my mind (since age nine) that I would be a pre-medical major in college that next fall. It was so confusing to have such a clear picture inwardly that didn't match what was happening on the outside.

I became depressed. While my friends were whooping and congratulating each other on their college acceptances, I was forlornly wandering the school halls between classes, head hung low, trying to avoid seeing Becky and her new boyfriend, my college-bound friends, and the members of the baseball team.

It was precisely at one of these moments, while trudging in a fog of self-pity from one class to another, that I heard the voice of God. Keep in mind that the voice of God that Joyce heard at age nine, true to her nature, was a quiet inner voice. For me, the heavenly voice needed to be a little different to fully get my attention. While everyone in the high school was out in the halls, the school's loudspeaker crackled to life.

"BARRY VISSELL," said a booming voice, "REPORT TO THE PRINCIPAL'S OFFICE IMMEDIATELY!"

My immediate reaction was one of fear. My mind was reeling! What had I recently done that might have caused a call to the principal's office? Were the police waiting for me there? As I walked quickly to the office, and all eyes were on me, my mind was running through the list of possibilities, the pranks that might have been discovered, perhaps a witness who had seen me running from the drive-in theater, or something even worse.

I felt at my all-time lowest point, and now it might get even worse. I might be kicked out of high school. I might be going to prison. I stopped myself from thinking about even more possibilities.

I rounded a corner and almost bumped into Becky and her boyfriend. She had obviously heard the announcement, and looked embarrassed to see me, but mouthed a barely audible, "I'm sorry," obviously meant to help me feel better. It didn't work.

Nearing the principal's office, I felt immensely relieved to see the principal standing there smiling at me. Whew, I thought to myself, I'm not in trouble. He then ushered me into an inner office, where I was welcomed by a neatly-dressed, smiling man whom I remember was distinctly older. He appeared to be in his thirties. I remember his short hair and a thin tie. He shook my hand and said he was representing Hartwick College in Oneonta, NY. I'd never heard of Hartwick College. I'd never even heard of Oneonta. Apparently, it was a few hours north in upstate New York.

He took probably one minute to tell me about the school, and then pointed to some papers on the table behind me.

"This is an application for admission to Hartwick College. With the help of your school officials, we've filled it out with information from your school records."

There on the table was, indeed, an application to Hartwick filled out with all my personal information. Next to it were all my high school records and transcripts, pathetic as they were.

I was beginning to feel dizzy. Had I been watching too many episodes of "The Twilight Zone?" Was this some kind of joke to get even with me for all the pranks I had played on others? First, my mother did most of the work applying to colleges that end up rejecting me. Now, this strange guy was filling out another application to a college I'd never even heard of.

I didn't have much time to ponder these things. This "older" man next pulled a shiny pen out of his sport coat pocket and extended it to me. "If you'd like to join us next fall at Hartwick, sign here," he said, placing a finger of his other hand next to a line at the bottom of the application.

I didn't know what to do. If this was for real, I would potentially be signing away four years of my life, to go to a school I knew nothing about. Maybe I needed to do a little research about this college.

"Can I have some time to think about this?" I stammered. "It seems like such an important decision."

"Sure, sure," he answered in a very reassuring tone, "Take a minute."

I had hoped he would have offered me a few days.

I paused probably fifteen seconds, solemnly took the pen from him and proceeded to sign away four years of my life. Something just simply felt right about all of this. In my naïve eighteen-year-old mind, I reasoned, "I suppose colleges travel around, looking for high school students who didn't get accepted, even with mediocre grades, then fill out their applications for them. What did I know?"

He retrieved his pen and thanked me with an almost uncomfortably warm yet genuine smile. His final words as he walked me out of the office, while he was clapping me briskly on my back, still ring in my ears: "I promise you. You'll never regret this decision."

"How does he know?" was my thought.

But somehow, I felt at peace. Driving home on my old Vespa motor scooter, I felt a joy and lightness bubbling up from within me, feelings I had almost forgotten about. It felt like my old Vespa had wings. I had the feeling that someone was taking care of me.

Upon arriving home, I remember the incredulous look on my mother's face as I triumphantly announced, "Mom, I'm going to Hartwick College next fall."

Her startled reaction was, "Where's Hartwick College?"

It's funny about youth. I gave no real thought to who that man was or how he found out about me. I just accepted it as a matter of course and showed up that next fall at Hartwick College in the rolling Catskill Mountains of upstate New York.

Now a college student, I tried, for a few months anyway, to be the person I thought I should be. I fell in with Alpha Delta Omega fraternity which, at the time, had a reputation of being the "partying" fraternity. I tried to convince myself that "sophisticated" girls were the ones to date. The word in 1964 was "cool," as in *West Side Story*.

I saw Joyce for the first time at a soccer game on a very cold day later that fall. I was sitting on the bleachers with some of my "cool" dorm buddies. I was in college now, and I wanted to show everyone that I was an adult. That meant controlled laughter ... not too loud ... and controlled body movements ... never anything that could be judged as childish. After all, I was eighteen years old and all grown up.

There was a loud outburst of almost hysterical laughter a few rows above me. I turned to see who could be making such an immature display of emotion. It was an attractive female freshman with large blue-green captivating eyes, sitting with her friends and laughing the "wrong" way ... way too loud, uncontrolled, obviously immature, and worst of all, not caring at all what people must be thinking of her – in other words, "not cool." How dare she act so childish! But I couldn't stop looking at her. My mind was repelled by her, but my heart, which I scarcely understood at the time, was irresistibly attracted to her. I was having minimal fun. Joyce was having all the fun she wanted. I was dampening my joy. Joyce was freeing hers, living up to her name. I was hiding my childlikeness. Joyce was in no hurry to grow up, exuberant in her innocence.

    I forced myself to look back at the soccer game, but my curiosity overwhelmed me. I kept sneaking glances over my shoulder. Who was this girl who cared so little about being cool? She was simply allowing herself to have an outrageously good time. Her joy was innocently and unselfconsciously bubbling over. I, on the other hand, was caught in a world of social conformity, a world of play-acting to get the approval of others. I felt shame, then embarrassment, and looked away again. I had a feeling of insecurity deep inside me ... that this girl would never willingly have much to do with me.

    For the next several weeks, I tried to get the image of this girl out of my mind but I couldn't. Then came the first snowstorm of the year. Someone in our boy's dorm had the idea to attack the girl's dorm and challenge the girls to a snowball fight. We bundled up and ran, whooping and hollering, across campus. Outside the girl's dorm, we started throwing snowballs at the windows, and yelled out challenges. The girls wasted no time in hurriedly dressing and rushing out of the dorm to meet our challenge. I was ready with snowball in hand. I spotted a good target, a girl standing about a hundred feet away with her back to me. I launched my projectile with the practiced arm of a baseball player, then watched in horror as the girl turned around. Almost in slow motion, and helpless to stop the arcing trajectory, I watched the snowball heading right for her face, and recognized the face. It was the girl from the soccer game, the girl I felt so attracted to, and so conflicted about.

Too late, I saw the snowball smash into the middle of her head. I heard her startled scream. For a moment, I didn't know if she was hurt. And I didn't dare announce my guilt.

Suddenly, she burst out laughing, bent over to grab a bunch of snow, and took off after some boys. They saw her racing toward them with such wild abandon that they turned and ran in fear. All I could do was gawk at her boldness. I was deeply impressed, and I still didn't even know her name.

A short time later, I applied at the school cafeteria for a job as student-waiter to help with college expenses. Dinners were a bit of a formal affair, with sit-down dining for the students. The job paid a whole dollar an hour. For some reason, boys and girls were paired up to work as a team serving a row of tables. And who did I happen to be assigned with? You guessed it, Joyce.

I was thrilled – and uncomfortable at the same time. I don't think I ever felt quite that uncomfortable around a girl. Perhaps it was the combination of my profound attraction, bundled with my fear that she wouldn't like me. And what if she found out that it was my snowball that hit her head.

Meanwhile, Joyce had noticed me almost from the beginning of the school year. She and her friends referred to me as "the boy who dressed weird." You see, I had very little awareness of clothes. My mother had bought all my clothes and, to tell the truth, she had very poor taste in clothes. I guess I stood out from the crowd, but not in a good way. And that's probably why Joyce had noticed me.

Now we worked together. And I wore a uniform as a waiter, so I suppose I looked better.

Joyce: The waiter assigned to work with me was a tall dark-haired boy. I didn't take much interest in him. He was very skinny, shy, and looked so boyish. At the end of our shift, we were cleaning the tables together when, to be polite, I asked him his name.

"Barry," he said with a nervous smile.

"Do you have a major?" I asked.

"Pre-med," was his reply.

In that moment, a shiver ran through my body. I looked at him more intently. Not my type, I decided, looking at his boyish face and remembering his weird way of dressing. I also couldn't help glancing again at his dark hair and height. Hmmm...

Barry: I asked Joyce out, a bit awkwardly I remember, for the following Friday night. She said yes, and inwardly I rejoiced. So far, so good.

Friday came around and, seeing me walking along to class, she approached me and asked what time I would be picking her up for our date. I did the unthinkable. With a perfect deadpan expression on my face, I answered, "What date?"

To this day, I have no idea why I said that. Perhaps I thought it would be a clever joke. My sense of humor at that time needed some tweaking.

Joyce looked shocked and humiliated. Our beginning relationship, precarious as it was, now appeared to be over.

Somehow, I managed to apologize for a very bad joke, and she, miraculously, accepted my apology. We were still on for that evening. Perhaps being tall, with dark hair, and studying to be a doctor put me higher on the list than I even knew.

I took her to see the movie, *Tom Jones*. I actually have no memory of what the movie was about. I felt so attracted to this girl, Joyce. Sitting next to her in the movie theater, all I wanted to do was hold her hand. I gingerly reached my hand toward hers. When it touched her hand, she made my life so much better by opening her hand and taking mine. A joy filled my heart, just holding her hand for the rest of the movie, whatever it was about.

Then we walked up the hill to the campus in a frigid early December Catskill Mountain's evening. I wanted to continue holding her hand forever, but it was just too cold. We needed our hands in our own pockets to keep them warm.

We approached Joyce's dorm, Dewer Hall. There was a ten o'clock curfew and it was approaching that time. Other couples were converging on the dorm at the same time from their dates. We squeezed into the small entry room minutes before ten. The other couples were saying good-bye to one another. A small window framed the face of ancient Mrs. Wilcox, the dorm mother, who was probably in her seventies. She watched with hawk-like eyes to make sure all the couples were behaving appropriately.

With so little time, all I could do was say good-bye to Joyce with the briefest of kisses. I leaned forward and felt my lips lightly touch hers. It wasn't passionate. Mrs. Wilcox, if she saw it, which she probably did, would have fully approved. What she didn't see, what she could never see, was the transmission of energy between two souls at the speed of light. One small kiss, but a powerful recognition of something very big, a love we did not yet realize but could feel clearly in that touch of lips.

We were lost and overwhelmed in that eternal moment, when the door suddenly opened and elderly hands started pulling Joyce away from me and into the dorm.

I remember floating slightly above the frozen ground rather than walking back to my dorm. I had kissed a few girls before Joyce, but this was something else entirely. It was like waking up from an eighteen-year dream sleep. Neither of us had developed the framework for understanding what had happened in that moment. Our minds were both blown, but our hearts were starting to awaken.

Joyce: What a kiss -- my life would never be the same. We were too young and immature to understand the powerful energy that passed between us. I simply thought "Boy, he really knows how to kiss!" I also had the thought, "Maybe he attended some kind of 'kiss school.'"

It was like the kiss upon Snow White's lips causing her eyes to open. In that kiss was the deepest feeling of connection and of coming home. In that moment, I knew why I had been so excited for the three months I had been at college. I had sensed the nearness of this young man.

As innocent children, we probed our way into the mysteries of love. We used to meet secretly every evening in the dark dining room and talk for hours. Finally, I felt I had met someone who understood me completely and was my best friend.

Shortly after meeting Barry, I had one more experience of lying in bed and feeling like I was trapped inside my body. I hadn't had this experience in many years and was surprised by the return of this childhood experience. As I was trying to get out of my body, I again heard the same gentle, guiding voice of my childhood say,

"Now you can feel totally at home here and won't feel the need to leave again."

I had found the tall dark-haired doctor-to-be whom I would love for the rest of my life. And truly he understands me and knows how to hold me in my deepest feelings.

Barry: Working together in the college dining room became a true joy. Serving the students together was a foreshadowing of our later professional lives of serving together.

In time, I found myself laughing just as hard as she did. So much for acting "cool." We had such a fun time serving the students at our tables that it was contagious. It seemed like our row of tables had the loudest laughter in the cafeteria. In Joyce's presence, my heart blossomed, my soul and body loosened up, and most importantly in the ensuing months, I fell in love.

I have to tell you about our second date. I took Joyce out to eat at a favorite Oneonta restaurant, Molly's. Then I proceeded to do something unimaginable to me at the time. I started telling Joyce the most vulnerable, embarrassing, and even shameful details of my life so far. I told her about puberty and first masturbating. I told her about the time when my mother walked into my bedroom and discovered me masturbating, and the horrified look on her face that conveyed a feeling that I was doing something very wrong, even though it felt very right. I told Joyce about my sexual confusion in my early teens, not so many years ago, trying on my mother's underpants.

I couldn't stop myself. I told her things I could never even think of telling anyone else. I felt completely safe with Joyce, a safety I had never experienced before. Everything I had bottled up inside me now came pouring out.

Joyce sat across from me and listened without judgment. She had very little experience with dating. Most of her relationships ended after the first date, when she found out the height, hair color, and career goals of her date. Second dates were uncommon to her. She figured maybe this is what guys do on their second dates, completely spill their guts as some kind of test to see if the girl can take it.

I did, however, notice her occasionally glance around to make sure no one else was listening.

Over the months, our love blossomed. One night, we were at our jobs at the school cafeteria. We finished clearing the tables, turned off the lights, and sank into chairs in the far corner of the cafeteria. We were totally alone. The red exit sign cast a warm glow on our faces. As usual we held hands and, between kisses, talked about our lives before we met.

For some reason, I began telling Joyce about my Bar Mitzvah.

She looked shocked. "Barry, you're Jewish???"

She evidently thought my last name of Vissell was perhaps French. In fact, my father's family name was Levinson. His descendants escaped the Tzar in Russia in the early nineteen hundreds by buying the name, Visakewitz, from a man who already served in the Tzar's army. It was the only way someone could leave the country at that time. After my father married my mother, Helen Lehrman, very few could pronounce her new name. Remember, this was a time when women changed their names after marriage. My mother took matters into her own hands. She took the "Vis" from Visakewitz, and added "L" for Lehrman, creating a new name, Vissell. My father conceded.

I looked into Joyce's beautiful green eyes, "Of course I'm Jewish. Aren't you?"

Even though she didn't particularly look Jewish, I thought her last name of Wollenberg was similar to Goldberg or Rosenberg.

"Barry, this is a Lutheran-founded school. Everyone I know goes to chapel each morning. I'm a Christian."

I was confused and said, "What?"

I didn't know any of this. The "angel," or whoever it was who recruited me, didn't say anything about Lutheran or chapel.

Suddenly, everything got serious and heavy. I wasn't a practicing Jew. I had actually given up on religion soon after my Bar Mitzvah at age thirteen. But since my birth in 1946, not long after the Holocaust, it was drilled into me that I needed to marry a Jewish girl, that it was my responsibility as a Jew.

It was also a cultural shock for both of us. In both our families, it was simply unheard of for anyone to marry outside of the religion. At the time, I had never even heard of a Jew being with a non-Jew. In Joyce's family, one time, someone married a Catholic, and that was a big deal.

These traditional values had a lot of power and hold on us. The question, "And how will the children be raised?" would echo in our minds.

I took Joyce's hands in mine and gravely spoke these words, "We can never marry!"

Joyce shook her head solemnly in agreement.

With those few words, our days of innocent bliss were over. We had entered a very adult world of social consequences and heavy expectations.

But hey, we were only eighteen years old. Even though we both agreed that we would never marry, we could still live in the moment. Why break up just because we couldn't marry? It felt so good to be together. It was settled. We wouldn't think about the future.

Easier said than done. Our religious differences kept coming up, providing fuel for a great many arguments. One moment, we'd be having a great time. The next moment, we'd be trying to change each other, which, of course, was futile.

It wasn't just our religious differences that we fought about. We were both young and immature. Mostly me. Remember, Joyce had an innocent, childlikeness about her that sometimes I had trouble with. I remember one time walking from campus down the hill into the town of Oneonta. Joyce had a way of walking that was the antithesis of the way I wanted a woman to walk. She had too much of a bounce in her step, really enjoying just being alive and walking. Unfortunately, I could not appreciate her way of walking. I was just plain embarrassed. Slowly widening the space between us, I hoped nobody would notice we were together.

Joyce noticed. She stopped walking and asked, "Barry, why are you so far away?"

My lame reply, "Is there any way you can walk like a normal person?"

I could see she was hurt by that question.

Still, she asked resentfully, "Okay then, how does a normal person walk?"

"You know," I tried, digging myself deeper into a hole, "more calmly, without that bounce that makes you look like a kid."

Now, she was mad. "Stop trying to change me! I was walking that way because I was happy to be with you. But now that I'm angry, I can probably walk the way you want. Are you happy now?"

No, I was anything but happy.

Our arguments were often loud and long, in private as well as in public. Our friends wondered why we stayed together, so common was the sight of us arguing. At the end of the school year, we were actually voted "The couple least likely to succeed!" What can I say? We were passionate in all ways, in our loving and in our fighting.

This whole time, imperceptibly, the false was dying and the truth was growing within each of us. After each fight, and I was again alone righteously proclaiming to myself that Joyce was not the right person for me, I would find myself in a state of grieving. The differences between us would lose power and importance, and Joyce would become more and more attractive to me. Her beauty seemed to be emerging more and more, and a respect for her was growing within me.

When Joyce first started dating, her dad took her aside and said, "I don't care who you date as long as he's not Jewish and doesn't come from New York City."

Undoubtedly, he was reacting to one or more bad experiences with New York Jews. Well, here I am: a Brooklyn-born Jew. Somehow, Joyce didn't learn about this until it was too late – she already was in love with me and I with her.

Joyce went home to Buffalo for spring break that first year of college. I was planning to drive there for a visit after a few days at home with my parents who live close to New York City. When her dad found out who she was serious about, and that I would be coming in a few days to visit, he was not pleased.

I telephoned Joyce, and who should pick up the phone – her dad. Because I didn't know about his prejudice, I launched headlong into getting to know this special young woman's father. When it finally came time to get his daughter on the phone, he covered the mouthpiece of the phone and whispered, "Joyce, I really like this young man!"

There was one dance that first year at Hartwick I will never forget. It was a slow dance, and Joyce and I were out in the middle of the dance floor, rocking gently to the music. I couldn't take my eyes off hers. My heart opened wide in love. Time stood still. The music stopped, but we didn't notice it. The band must have taken a break, because all the couples left the dance floor. We were alone on the dance floor, still swaying to the music that kept going inside of us. We were in our own world, our love bubble, oblivious to the stares from those who couldn't comprehend the kind of love we were feeling. It was a long time before we came back down to earth enough to notice our situation. By then it was too late. It seemed like the whole world had seen our love, and we didn't care.

I was unbelievably attracted to Joyce from the very beginning. All I wanted to do was make out with her. After that first kiss, I longed for the sweetness of her lips. Of course, as a healthy adolescent with more testosterone than I knew how to handle, I longed for more than kissing. Joyce, however, held a firm boundary regarding sex. She wanted to wait till she was fully ready, and the time felt completely right.

Remember, I was not that great a student. My study habits were almost nonexistent. I think I was averaging a C grade, not at all good enough to get into medical school. In the evenings, after classes and dinner, I was more focused on getting Joyce out into my old VW beetle than studying. Joyce, meanwhile, was a solid A student.

She made a deal with me. All my studying and homework must be complete before there was any "making out." I reluctantly agreed, and fairly quickly went from a C student to an A student. Nothing like a little motivation!

And oh my, after fulfilling my studies, the sweet times behind the science building in my VW, with windows steamed up from our passion. The feel of Joyce's lips against mine was sublime. Our mutual attraction surpassed the earth's pull on the moon. My hands had a mind of their own, but Joyce held a firm boundary of keeping our clothes on. I suppose it would have been embarrassing to have been discovered without clothes by faculty or security. Still, clothes or no clothes, nothing could stop the fever pitch of our passionate embrace.

When Joyce heard the story of how I got to attend Hartwick College, she said, "Have you tried to find the name of the scout who recruited you, so you could thank him?"

"No," I answered flatly.

"Barry, it's the considerate thing to do."

At the time, I had a lot to learn about consideration. I made my way to Hartwick's administrative offices, spoke with several people who had no idea who this could have been. Finally, I was introduced to the Director of Admissions, who listened with rapt attention to my story.

He said, "Barry, that's quite a story, but I'm afraid I've never heard anything like it. Here at Hartwick, we do have a recruiting program, but we recruit only outstanding soccer players from around the world. We have never recruited a non-soccer player."

With an incredulous look on his face, he shook my hand, apologized that he could not help me, and said good-bye.

When I think about this mystery man who recruited me, I almost always get goose bumps. Was he an angel? Was he an ordinary man who took it upon himself to do a good deed? If I think about it too much, I'll just give myself a headache. In the end, it really doesn't matter who he was. It only matters that someone ... or Someone ... took care of me. And directed me to a small college in the Catskill Mountains where I could meet my soulmate.

Once, after leading our annual couples' retreat in Hawaii, Joyce and I were having a meal with Richard Koob, the founder of Kalani Honua, the retreat center we have used since 1986. He was telling us about the diversity of groups now using Kalani.

"We even have our first college bringing a group here."

"Which college is that?" I asked him.

"Oh, it's a small college. You probably haven't heard of it."

"Try me, Richard. I know a lot of colleges."

"Have you ever heard of Hartwick College?"

I paused, smiling, "Yes, I believe I have."

Then I told him the story.

Now, as I look back, all these decades later, decades of living and loving together, I can see the divine guidance behind all these events—my failed relationship with Becky, the "angel" with the college application, the soccer game, the cafeteria job, the well-aimed snowball, and that kiss. Now, I understand a lot more about the powerful forces helping us every step of the way. Call it God, Universe, Higher Power, or whatever you want, I know we are never alone, never without help. I believe I was destined to meet Joyce. On my own, I tried moving in all the wrong directions. At that crucial time of my life, I clearly needed help, and the help came in the form of a mystery man who pointed me to the school where Joyce was enrolled.

Recently, at one of our workshops, I told this story and someone pointed out, given the work we do, the appropriateness of the name, "Hartwick" College. Joyce and I never thought about this before. I got the image of a wick, like a candle wick. By itself, a wick cannot sustain a flame, but in the candle, it has the ability to channel the fuel up through itself. A "heart-wick" is a conduit for the energies of the heart to burn ever more brightly, lighting up the world with "heartlight." And that's exactly how I feel about the love Joyce and I share.

Chapter 4: Two Different People

Barry and I came from very different types of families. My mother was Swedish, soft-spoken, a good listener, and interested in many things. My dad was German, and he loved making people laugh, but his greatest joy was being with children.

In my family, when someone talked, everyone else listened. There was respectful interest in whatever topic someone brought up. My parents were both early civil rights activists, at a time when this was not a popular thing. They were dedicated to their Presbyterian church, and attended every Sunday. They often invited foreign students from the University of Buffalo for meals. They wanted my brother and me to have an open attitude toward all people of different nationalities. Sunday dinners often included Chinese, African and Japanese students. They also had a best friend who was gay. Though my mother was an excellent cook, food was seldom talked about.

No family is perfect, however. Like I said before, my family had trouble accepting my sensitivity. In addition, feelings in general were not acceptable. When my parents were upset with each other, there was an icy silence at the dinner table. It was painful for me to be the only one to feel their invisible anger.

Barry, on the other hand, came from a loud Brooklyn Jewish family. When I first visited his family at age eighteen, I was shocked to observe that everyone talked at the same time. It was like stepping into the movie, *My Big Fat Greek Wedding*. It seemed to me that no one was listening to anyone. If someone really wanted to be heard during a meal, they simply spoke louder than everyone else. But that rarely worked, for eventually, it seemed to me that everyone was speaking in loud voices, almost shouting. I felt intimidated. I felt like hiding in a closet. Barry seemed to not notice any of this and just sat quietly eating his meal. This was "normal" to him.

In my family, the emotions were hidden. In Barry's family, it felt like they were over-expressed. There was a lot of yelling. Barry apparently coped mostly by withdrawing like a turtle into his shell.

When I first met Barry's father, he didn't ask me the traditional questions like, "Where does your family live? What is your major in college? Do you have brothers or sisters?" Instead, he came down the stairs, shook my hand and asked, "Do you know how to make tuna salad?"

I said, "Yes. My mother was a good cook and taught me from the time I was quite young."

"Please tell me how you make tuna salad."

I felt embarrassed, put on the spot by someone I had just met, but still wanted to impress.

"Well, I mix the tuna with mayonnaise, and maybe add a little salt and pepper…"

I wasn't finished, but he waved his hand dismissively and smiled, "You don't know how to make tuna salad." He then proceeded in the next half hour to explain how he made tuna salad, even demonstrating with an imaginary knife the special way he chopped up the celery, an important ingredient that I "forgot."

That was my first contact and conversation with Barry's dad, and I have never forgotten it. His love for food seemed strange to me at first. His eccentricities were sometimes over the top, but I grew to love these qualities about him. He truly didn't care what people thought about him, a quality that had its positive and negative sides. Barry seems to have inherited this particular quality, and is one of the things I admire about him, unless it embarrasses me.

At the age of fifty, Barry's dad, Michael, was driving to his job as a telegrapher in New York City, when a young man, coming from the opposite direction on the Saw Mill River Parkway, fell asleep at the wheel and crashed head-on into his dad. The young man eventually died. Michael flew through the windshield and landed far in front of the wreckage. During the six months of recuperation from his extensive injuries, Barry's mom bought him a basic set of oil painting supplies, even though he had never expressed any desire for art.

He never went back to work at his job. He became an artist, developing his own style over the remaining years of his life.

One of Michael's favorite things to do was go to the grocery store each morning. He would wake up with a list in his head.

Often, while waiting in line to pay for his groceries, he would look into the shopping carts on both sides of him. Once, he noticed asparagus in a woman's cart, and said to her, "Excuse me, but what are you planning to do with that asparagus?"

She seemed at first surprised by his inquisitiveness, but finally said, "I'll probably just steam them."

Again, the dismissive wave of his hand, and then, "No, not good enough! Here's what you should do with the asparagus." And he'd tell her, in detail, even though it was obvious that she would rather be anywhere but here in line with this strange man.

With Barry's dad, the main subject of conversation during a meal was the next meal! Not only was he overweight, but he had chronic angina pain and hypertension. Barry's mother constantly admonished him about his over-eating. Consequently, he often saw people through the filter of weight. If a particular person was brought up in conversation, his typical comment was one of two choices, "He or she has gained," or "He or she has lost." When Barry and I would visit their home, he'd appraise each one of us, and announce, "You've lost" or "You've gained."

At the time I met Barry, his parents lived in a mostly Jewish world, with most of their friends and neighbors being Jewish. Besides his dad's preoccupation with food itself, the kinds of foods were also strange to me. I'll never forget my horror when we sat down to lunch during that same first visit, and yes, there was tuna fish salad on the table. I watched Barry's dad take a piece of gefilte fish from the jar and slide it into his mouth. With a glint in his eye, he lifted the jar to his lips and drank the slimy gel. "Ahhh," he said, putting down the jar, with the gel still clinging to his mustache, "That's the best part of all." He offered a piece to me, which I politely refused.

Barry's mom had been a first-grade teacher for twenty years when I first met her. She loved children very much, but she sometimes treated her grown children as part of her first grade. The first meal I had at their house, I was politely told, with a voice that sounded like it was addressing six-year-olds, that I must wash my hands first and not to forget to use soap and scrub carefully until they were "squeaky clean." Though surprising at first, this quality became endearing to me.

Both Barry and I came from loving families. But as you can see, they were different, as well as having their own share of dysfunction. It was shocking for Barry to sit at our family table and realize that, when he spoke, everyone else would listen to him. At first, it made him uncomfortable, but he got used to it.

Even from the early age of eighteen, Barry knew that part of loving me was also loving my family. He couldn't change how they were, so he found a way to fit in, just as I needed to do with his family. I never did learn how to make tuna salad as precisely as Barry's dad. At first, I was a little intimidated, then, a few years later, we became vegetarians. No, not because of the experience with Barry's dad.

Chapter 5: A Close Call on the New York Subway

In the spring of 1966, as a naïve, energetic nineteen-year-old woman, I placed my life in extreme danger without even the faintest idea of what I was doing. Strong-willed and stubborn, I was used to setting my will to achieve a goal and pushing aside every barrier that came my way. I always considered myself a spiritual person, but when it came to making decisions and achieving my goals, I depended on my own will power. I sometimes followed the decision with a prayer, but it was always an afterthought.

In my sophomore year at Hartwick College, I decided I needed to get a specialty education so that I could begin working at a good job as soon as I finished college. I chose nursing and selected Columbia University in New York City. I could graduate with an RN and BS.

And yes, there was another reason for leaving Hartwick. I just couldn't see a way to make my relationship with Barry really work. Our religious difference seemed too big at the time.

Saying a tearful good-bye to Barry, I left the security of small-town Oneonta and traveled to New York City for an admittance interview. I had never been to the Big Apple and didn't know what to expect. I set my will, braved buses and subways and arrived at the school in the afternoon.

The interview the next day went well, and I decided this was the next step I would take in my life. I would transfer to Columbia Presbyterian Nursing School in the fall.

That night, I became homesick for all that was familiar, especially Barry. I looked at the bus and subway schedules and realized if I left the dorm at 3:30am, I could catch a 5:00am bus out of Grand Central Station and be back with Barry by 10:00am. After that, the next available bus to Oneonta would arrive in the evening. I set my will; I was getting on that earlier bus.

I got up at 3:00am, quickly packed and quietly crept down to the front entrance of the dorm. The way was barred by a big security guard who was sound asleep in a chair immediately in front of the door.

He woke with a start as I tried to exit, took a moment to focus his eyes on me, and finally said gruffly, "Where do you think you're going, young lady?"

I politely explained my plans to him, "I'm taking a subway to Harlem, then I'll transfer and take a subway to Grand Central."

A look of alarm came across his face. "I can't let you out of these doors!" was his urgent reply. "You're risking your life going to Harlem in the middle of the night!"

"You can't stop me!" was my stubborn reply. "I'm a guest here, not a student." I stood there resolute, completely ignorant of my foolish plan.

To my surprise, his eyes filled with tears as he looked at me and said, "I'm afraid for your life. Please let me say a prayer for you." He took my hands and said a fervent prayer for my protection. My will was so set, however, that I hardly heard his prayer.

I pushed open the door and set out into the night. The early morning air was cool and I zipped my coat up higher. I got on the subway at 168th Street and got off at Harlem.

As soon as I exited the train and stepped onto the litter-strewn platform, the enormity of my mistake hit me. With growing panic, I looked around as the train sped away and saw that I was alone. There were no police. I later learned that the situation in Harlem in the mid-sixties was so dangerous that no policeman would take the subway night shift in the section I was in. I had put myself in a definitely dangerous situation.

A nearby group of young men turned around to gawk at me, obviously taken aback by the audacity – or maybe they felt insanity – of this young woman who had just entered their dark world. One man pointed at me, said something to the others, then they all stood up. For a moment, I thought it was all over. They would come after me, a helpless girl.

To my horror, I realized that my own will power was not going to be enough for this nightmare. I stood frozen with fear, my legs suddenly feeling unsteady beneath me.

My mother's words came to me, "When you're afraid, just repeat the 23rd Psalm and it will give you courage."

In a quiet but urgent voice, I began, "The Lord is my shepherd. I shall not want..."

As I spoke this prayer, which the young men could probably hear, I noticed the one man, obviously the leader, suddenly look nervous, glancing around quickly, almost as if he was afraid of something or someone. He turned to his group, said something seemingly urgent, and they all turned and briskly walked away. It was as if I represented something more powerful than I looked.

I took that as my cue to start walking, shakily at first, but then gaining strength and purpose. I walked past a pair of drunken men, swaying back and forth passing a bottle between them. As if that wasn't enough, I even noticed a young man sitting on a bench injecting something into his arm.

I repeated these soothing words as I walked past a group of men with knives in their hands, past rowdy drunks who stumbled across my path, and past a desperate-looking man shaking so violently he could barely stand. A wine bottle was thrown at me, but fell short, smashing into pieces on the hard, cold subway floor. Terrified, I pretended not to notice this attack.

Two rough-looking men approached me with sticks, or clubs, in their hands. They got within five feet of me, then suddenly stopped and backed off. Although I was still scared, I felt as if I had an invisible wall of protective light around me.

As if in response to the men with sticks, I repeated, "Thy rod and Thy staff they comfort me..." as I climbed stairs filled with the stench of urine. At the top of the stairs, a young man almost knocked me over as he ran past, trying to get away from a second man who was pursuing him. I crossed platforms and, while I waited for the next train, I continued to feel that invisible shield of protection around me, a loving good Shepherd that was bringing me back to safety.

The train finally came, the doors opened, and I rushed in. There were a few conservative-looking business men on the train, absorbed in their newspapers. The doors closed and we left that desolate world behind us.

As the train accelerated, I felt the full impact of what had just happened to me. I could no longer hold back the tears and they flowed down my face. None of the men seemed to notice, but it didn't matter. Something had changed within me. I knew I could never go back to my old way of being. Asking for God's protection and guidance in any situation had become more important than setting my own will. I had learned to trust in God's protection and plan for me as the most important priority in my life. On that dark and gloomy subway on an early spring morning, God, the infinite presence of love, had become primary rather than secondary in my life.

Chapter 6: Separation

That next fall, I started nursing school at Columbia University in New York City and Barry, not wanting to feel left behind at Hartwick, transferred to Boston University, continuing in his pre-medical education. We spent some beautiful times together over the summer and Barry asked if he could drive me to my dorm to say goodbye. In anticipation of our separation, the drive was slow and sad. We were planning on not seeing or talking to each other ever again!

In the lobby of my dorm, we tenderly held hands and, through our tears, spoke soft and loving goodbyes to each other. Our minds were convinced that ending our relationship was the right thing. Our parents, even though secretly happy, still showed compassion and said, "Give the relationship space. Date people of your own religion. Try to forget each other." But our hearts were in deep pain.

Barry entered Boston University where there were plenty of Jewish girls to date. I threw myself fully into life at the Columbia Presbyterian Nursing School. The medical school dorm was immediately next-door and I was suddenly surrounded by medical students of my same religion. Though I dated several wonderful young men, even tall dark-hired young men, that quality of heart connection that I had with Barry was not present. I was trying to follow the direction of my mind's resolve, but it was difficult.

Barry, similarly, dated Jewish girls, but never found that same feeling of "home" that he had with me. After one month, he called. He told me how much he had been missing me. A joy I had almost forgotten filled my being. "Barry, I thought we weren't going to talk to each other," I exclaimed. My surprise turned to pure joy. "I'm so happy to hear your voice."

Joyce at Columbia Nursing

Again, time stood still as we talked for hours on the phone. We made arrangements to see each other. I traveled to Boston and was thrilled to be with Barry again. We realized we couldn't stay apart. Thus began a year and a half traveling back and forth, the physical travel coupled with the travel deeper into our love.

Saying good-bye was always painful. Each time Barry put me on the bus for my return trip to New York City, he watched me find a seat and press my teary face against the window. Not being able to take the sadness of our parting, he would begin to make funny faces. He made me smile despite the sadness.

Thanksgiving, I visiting Barry at his parent's home an hour north of the city. I developed a toothache and needed to have an emergency dental appointment with Barry's family dentist. It turned out to be a large tooth abscess, which he had to open up to drain. He neglected to give me antibiotics. Barry dropped me off in New York City and returned to school in Boston.

The next day, I developed a fever, which quickly escalated to septicemia, a massive infection in my bloodstream. My temperature soared to over 106 degrees. I was quickly admitted into the university hospital, where antibiotics failed to bring down the fever. In a desperate measure, I was wrapped in ice and put in a cooling tent.

To make matters even worse, I had an allergic reaction to the first antibiotic given, Penicillin. My body swelled up like a balloon, threatening to kill me if the infection didn't.

I remember looking up at all the doctors and nurses in the isolation intensive care unit. They all looked so worried as they hurried around me doing various procedures. I remember thinking to myself, "My body feels so terrible. It would be so much easier to just let go and leave this world." I lapsed into a coma.

A doctor called my parents and told them, "If you want to see your daughter alive, you need to come right away. We are not sure she will live."

It was almost December, and Buffalo was experiencing blizzard conditions. There was only one plane scheduled to fly to New York, and there was only one seat on that plane. My parents decided my mother should have that seat.

My mother finished her duties as church secretary and hurried home to get ready for the flight. Another call from the nursing school confirmed that my condition had gotten even worse. My blood pressure had dropped dangerously low due to septic shock. There seemed to be little chance I would be alive by the time my mother arrived.

By the time my mother sat on the plane and buckled her seat belt, she was hit by the full reality of the situation. I might be dead by the time she got to me. She knew she could respond one of two ways. Part of her felt like melting into a puddle of tears, but a stronger part of her knew she must place my life in the hands of God. She bowed her head in prayer and fully entrusted my life to God. She promised to accept God's will for my life. As she did so, she later told me, "I felt as if Jesus himself came and sat down next to me. He told me to not worry. He was right here. For my entire flight to New York, I felt enveloped in the most love and peace I have ever felt."

When my mother arrived at LaGuardia Airport, it was late at night and snowing heavily. There was a line of cabs waiting to take passengers to their final destinations. Columbia Presbyterian Hospital was a shorter ride, and the cab drivers all wanted a long ride to make more money, since the airport was closing. The whole long line of cab drivers refused to take my mother. At the very end of the line, she came to an older black cab driver. My mother had always been a strong civil rights activist, and this was 1966, a time of unrest among the Blacks. This man offered to take her to the hospital and, when he found out I was possibly dying, sang gospel songs and prayed with her. At the end of the ride, he refused to take any money. I sometimes wonder if that man was perhaps an angel in disguise.

The director of the nursing school met my mother's cab and escorted her directly to my hospital room. It felt like I was not in my body, for I strangely remember looking down and seeing every detail of my mother approaching my room, even though the room door was closed. Outside the room, there was a circle of about eight doctors. The hospital had called not only the experts from Columbia University Hospital but also experts from Cornell Hospital.

An older man, probably the attending physician, approached my mother and respectfully said, "We're sorry, Mrs. Wollenberg. We've done all we can and have brought in the top experts in the city. Your daughter is dying and there is nothing we have been able to do about it. Do you want me to walk in with you? Joyce does not look the same way as when you last saw her."

I heard my mother say, "No, I want to go in by myself."

She told me later she was still feeling the same loving presence that surrounded her on the plane. She said, "Though they told me you were dying, this presence of love told me it was not so. I felt full confidence you would live."

When my mother touched the door handle and began to open it, I suddenly came back into my body. As she entered the room, a ray of bright light came into my heart and I was instantly alert, after having been in a coma for over twelve hours. She walked over to my bed and took my hand and simply said, "Hi, Sis. You're going to be all right now."

I weakly replied, "Oh, Mother, I need you so much. Thank you for coming."

I began to get better from that moment on. It took several weeks, but my mother's appearance was the turning point from near death to life. I believe my mother brought me back to life by her total surrender to God's will and a belief in my life.

My mother stayed at my side and helped me to begin eating, walking and all the aspects of starting to get strong again.

After one week, I ordered my mother to go back home. I was not even very nice about it. I felt horrible after she left, and called to tell her I was sorry. I didn't know why I had done that. I believe I had been so uncomfortable about needing my mother so much, I was trying to prove to myself I didn't need her as much as I did. I missed her dearly after she left. As I grew just a bit older, I came to peace with how much I needed my mother's love.

Chapter 7: And Another Separation

By our senior year of college, Barry and I had more fully entered into our adult selves. Our youthful ability to forget our differences was diminishing. The seemingly insurmountable barrier of religion was once again right in our faces. I would never consider becoming Jewish. Christianity was just too important a part of my life. And Barry would never consider becoming Protestant.

Our friends were getting engaged and married. We felt pressure to make a decision about our future. We had no model for a Jewish/Christian couple. Remember, this was the sixties on the east coast, not California. Our parents were urging us to separate. Our friends thought there was no way we could make it as a couple. We did the only thing we understood to do. We broke up once again.

We planned one final day to be together. It was a bittersweet day, filled with love and tenderness, as well as sadness and hopelessness. That evening, Barry returned me to my nursing school dorm. In the lobby, we held each other as we did a few years earlier, cried and expressed our love to one another. We told each other that we would remain in each other's hearts forever. We assured each other that we were doing the right thing. When it was time to go our separate ways, we kissed and held each other, savoring the feel of each other's lips, the smell of each other's bodies. We said goodbye. I went to my dorm room and cried harder and longer that I ever had. My heart once again felt broken.

The following days, weeks, and months passed by like one painful blur. My mind kept saying, "You made the only appropriate choice. You'll feel better soon." I went out on dates with the students at the medical school, especially the tall ones with dark hair. I went to the ocean with my girlfriends, and did every fun thing I could think of. Throughout it all, the pain in my heart grew less and less tolerable.

After three months, I could take it no longer. In the middle of one sleepless night, I took the elevator to the twenty-second floor, the rooftop of the dorm building. I walked over to the edge of the roof. I was all alone, looking down on a magnificent view of Manhattan.

I stayed up there for hours. I got down on my knees and prayed. I prayed longer and more intently than I had ever prayed before. I had always felt a deep and personal relationship with Jesus. When my brother joined a fundamental Christian church his first year of college, he urged me to do the same. Though I loved and honored my brother, his views on Christianity felt too complicated for my simple devotional nature.

For me, Jesus was simply my trusted friend. It was from this innocent place in me that I prayed to Him. I told Jesus that I was willing to sacrifice my relationship with Barry for Him, if this was God's Will. I acknowledged how broken my heart felt. There was a deep, unshakable knowing inside of me that I would never love another man as deeply as I loved Barry. Even given that knowledge, my spiritual path was of greater importance. I saw no way to merge the two.

From the depth of my soul, I cried out, "If there is any way I can be together with Barry, show me the way, give me a sign. Otherwise help me to accept this path of my religion without Barry."

I stayed on the roof until the first rays of sun bathed the Manhattan skyline. I returned to my room and slept peacefully for a few hours.

That afternoon, my friend Sally Bixler had a surprise visit from her mother. Mrs. Bixler was from a small, central Pennsylvania town. Everything about this sweet, older woman spoke of homespun uncomplicated goodness. She had traveled four hours by bus to visit. Sally and I made a fuss over her arrival.

"Why did you come, Mother?" Sally asked, hugging her mother.

With a twinkle in her eye and a smile upon her lips, Mrs. Bixler told her story. "I was sitting for my usual prayer period this morning. I opened my Bible and a little card dropped out. I hadn't seen this card in several years and I fondly picked it up. As I held it in my hand, I heard a voice inside of me say, 'Take this to Joyce today.' I've learned over the years not to ignore this voice, no matter how inconvenient, so I got on the bus to bring it to you, Joyce."

I could scarcely believe that this woman made such a great effort just for me.

She handed me the card. On it was written, from the famous First Corinthians 13, *"Above all else, love is most important."*

When she saw the tears come into my eyes, Mrs. Bixler reached out to give me a hug. As she did so, I felt myself suddenly enfolded in what seemed like the loving arms of an angel. As she held me, I knew the love that I felt for Barry was most important – that love is more important than religion – that love is the heart of religion.

I didn't know how we would make our religious differences work. I only knew that we would. This card and visit from Mrs. Bixler *was* the sign I had prayed for on the roof all that past night.

While Sally and her mother went off to visit, I ran to the payphone to call Barry. Amazingly, he was home. I told him of my tears, my prayers, and of the visit from Mrs. Bixler. He listened to every detail. When I finished, there was silence on the phone and then, in a choked voice filled with emotion, "Joyce ... I love you. All I want is to be with you. My life here in Boston without you has been miserable."

The next morning, Barry got into his VW Beetle and drove into New York City, and into my waiting arms. What a reunion!

Four years previous, we had met in a childlike, innocent way and had ridden on the high of being together. This day, we met as adults who had been heartbroken and overcome the obstacles to love. We were guided back to our hearts by the greatest power in the universe — love. The two struggling fish had finally surrendered to love and were being pulled in. I was reunited with the tall, dark-haired, doctor-to-be of my vision.

Chapter 8: Operation Meharry

Barry: In my last year of college at Boston University, I applied to about twenty medical schools. I got rejected by all but one. I was put on the waiting list at Meharry Medical College, a predominantly black school in Nashville, Tennessee.

Once again, I felt discouraged. First, college rejections. Now, medical school rejections. I wondered if another "angel" would make an appearance and sign me up for medical school.

At least I was on the waiting list for one school. However, the chances of clearing a waiting list and being accepted were slim. I felt like giving up on becoming a doctor.

I began putting more time and energy into playing rock and roll songs on an electronic keyboard that I had recently bought from the keyboardist of a local Boston rock band named "Phluph." Much to Joyce's dismay, I joined up with a local guitarist, bass player and drummer, and we jammed and rehearsed songs late into the night. I remember being particularly obsessed with learning the organ part to "Light My Fire" by my then hero, Ray Manzarek of the Doors.

Meanwhile, at Columbia Presbyterian Hospital in New York City, Joyce was busily involved in her nursing program. One of her patients happened to be a medical student who was injured in a car accident. She told him about me and the waiting list at Meharry. He sat up straighter in bed, although he was in pain, and said, "tell your boyfriend that he can tremendously increase his odds of being accepted by them. They need to know who he is, more than simply a name on a waiting list. Tell him to be more assertive and proactive."

Joyce called me that night and shared her excitement. I caught the flame or should I say, she "lit my fire." Together, we came up with a plan that we named, "Operation Meharry." She said, "Barry, just use your Chutzpah." This is a Yiddish word that means "nerve" or, even better, "balls." That coming from my non-Jewish girlfriend.

The next day, I called Meharry and asked to speak with the president, the dean, the chairman of the admissions department, and several members of the admissions board. I announced my intention to visit Meharry, to get to know more about the school. I made appointments with each of these people and arranged to have a tour of the campus.

Chutzpah? Absolutely!

In each interview, I sold myself as a dedicated and capable medical student-to-be. I was personable, friendly, and yet professional at the same time. I gave it my all.

I found out there were to be one hundred first-year medical students. Ninety percent needed to be black since, at the time, there were only two medical schools in the United States that predominantly served the black community. Ten percent of each class would be non-black. That's ten students. There were two hundred applicants on the waiting list.

I went back to Boston knowing I did my best, yet I was also sobered by the apparently slim odds of getting in.

I graduated in June without hearing any news. I moved back home in Elmsford, NY, intending to live with my parents. I got a summer job as a research laboratory assistant at Sloan-Kettering Institute nearby. Eating my mother's cooking was not the best thing for me. I gained thirty-five pounds in one summer!

Engagement

Meanwhile, for the previous half year, Joyce had been bringing up marriage. She made it clear that, for her, marriage was the next step. I, on the other hand, was content with having Joyce as my girlfriend. Underneath, I was really afraid to choose Joyce for the rest of my life. Marriage seemed too permanent, too confining ... too big a risk for me.

To her credit, rather than asking me to marry her, she made plans to move on with her life. She graduated from Columbia. She applied and was accepted as a nurse to work with Native Americans on a reservation in the southwest, thousands of miles from New York. I remember feeling that she would never leave me. How could she? She loved me too much. So I maintained my stance of inactivity, in a way calling her bluff.

One day she announced, "Barry, I just bought a one-way plane ticket to Albuquerque, New Mexico. I'm really doing this."

In those days, tickets were fully refundable, but I started to get nervous anyway. Joyce really was moving on with her life without me. If I wasn't going to choose marriage, she was choosing a career away from me. My indecision was too painful to her.

I spent a few days examining my deepest feelings. I certainly didn't want to choose to marry Joyce just because she was leaving, yet I did feel sorrow at the thought of losing her. I allowed my mind to play out my life without Joyce. It became unbearable. I felt that losing Joyce would be the greatest mistake of my life. In that moment, in my mind and heart, I chose to spend the rest of my life with Joyce.

The next day, I went out and ordered a diamond engagement ring. It would cost me every penny I had, but I would be choosing Joyce, and that was worth everything. I wanted it to be a surprise, but made the mistake of telling my mother, who was never good with secrets.

A week later, Joyce and I stopped by my family home. As we opened the door and went inside, my mother blurted out in her strong Brooklyn accent, "Barry, the jeweler called. The ring is ready."

Her hand went quickly to her mouth.

"Oops, I shouldn't have said that..."

I saw the beginnings of a smile form on Joyce's lips, but nobody said anything more. I did, however, notice my older sister, Donna, shoot an exasperated glance at my mother.

The next day, I picked up the ring, stowed it safely in my pocket, then drove down into New York City to be with Joyce. From her dormitory, we walked to our favorite place, the George Washington Bridge. We ventured out to the first tower and there, 212 feet above the Hudson River, I took the ring from my pocket and asked Joyce to marry me.

She looked down at the ring in my hand and smiled, but it was a tense smile. I thought her hesitation might have reflected some disappointment at my attempt to ruin her plans to go out west. She actually seemed nervous as well.

She said, "Of course I want to marry you, but please, Barry, put that precious ring carefully on my finger and, whatever you do, don't drop it!"

Now, I realized the cause of her nervousness and hesitation. We were standing on a walkway grate with holes easily big enough for a ring to fall through and be lost forever.

No matter, the important thing was that I chose Joyce to be my wife.

Chastised by my Rabbi

Knowing our plan to get married, my mom made an appointment for us to meet with my childhood rabbi. I naively thought he might give us marital advice, or even offer to marry us. We drove to Temple Beth El in Tarrytown, a place I knew so well, at least until my Bar Mitzvah, after which I stopped going. We entered the temple and found his office. The rabbi shook my hand and said hello to Joyce, and all went downhill from there.

He turned very serious, and said, "Barry, by marrying Joyce, a non-Jew, you are turning your back on your Jewish heritage. You are neglecting your duty and responsibility as a Jew."

In an angry tone, he turned to Joyce and said, "You will never be welcomed inside a temple!"

We have since learned that these were his feelings, and not true of many synagogues. We have since met the most loving and open rabbis, who have welcomed Joyce without judgment.

Finally, he looked at both of us and angrily said, "You have no right to marry each other!"

My rabbi's tirade continued, and we felt worse and worse, and helpless to defend ourselves.

Finally, he was done, his harsh message was delivered, and we shakily got to our feet and managed to leave. Sitting in our car, Joyce and I held each other and cried. We felt abused. In our pain, we needed each other even more. Rather than driving us apart, and making us aware of our mistake, my rabbi's actions had driven us closer together.

Some years later, we heard that this same rabbi's son married a non-Jewish woman. It felt a little like a story from *Fiddler on the Roof*. Even though a part of me was glad, and called it "karmuppence," Joyce and I sincerely hope he had opened his heart to his daughter-in-law.

Joyce : After the meeting with the rabbi, Barry drove me to my dorm back down in New York City. We drove in silence, the rabbi's words hanging in the air between us, "You have no right to get married."

We had a long and very loving embrace before I got out of his car. Our love for each other was very deep. The rabbi could not take that away from us.

I had a very restless sleep and woke up with the thought that perhaps the rabbi had been right. I would do Barry a favor by breaking up with him, and giving him the space to find a Jewish woman. I felt very sad and tears filled my eyes. I looked out my window at the expansive view from my twenty-third-floor room. I gazed across what seemed like all of the West Side.

Then I heard it, a very gentle loving inner voice told me very clearly,

"You do not understand how it will all work out because so many people are telling you it is wrong. I am telling you it will all work out beautifully. Go ahead and marry your beloved Barry. You will be very happy together."

I felt surrounded by the reassuring love of this gentle energy.

Barry: At the end of the summer, one week before Meharry Medical College was scheduled to start, my mother, father, older sister, Donna, and younger brother, Richard, had just sat down to dinner when there was a loud knock on the front door. I opened the door and saw a Western Union courier, who announced in a dry monotone, "Telegram for Mr. Barry Vissell."

My heart rate quickened. In my mind, there was only one thing it could possibly be. I opened the envelope and read, "Barry Vissell (stop) Congratulations on your acceptance into Meharry Medical College (stop) Please be here for orientation in three days (stop)"

I ran back to the dining room to share the news with my family. My mom started screaming with joy. Then she stopped and looked concerned, "Wait, when do you have to leave?"

I thought about it for a moment, then said, "Oops, I have to leave tomorrow morning!"

I called Joyce. She was overjoyed! "Operation Meharry" had been a success!

As I found out later from Dr. Lloyd Elam, the president of Meharry, one non-black slot had opened. When the committee met to decide upon someone from the waiting list, it was a no-brainer for them. I was the only prospective student they had actually met, and I had won them all over.

Just as a bit of a side note, as the last student admitted that year, I felt slightly inferior to the others. To compensate, I dedicated myself that year to studying harder than I ever have. I ended up the top-ranking student in my class at the end of the year. I found out that Pfizer Pharmaceuticals gave a gift of one thousand dollars to the number-one first-year medical student at all one hundred medical schools in the United States. It was a lot of money back in 1969. I bought a state-of-the-art stereo system, among other things. We still have the Lafayette Electronics speakers in our living room today.

I had gone from last to first in one year!

My experience at Meharry was not easy. It was the fall of 1968, Martin Luther King had just been shot the previous April, and the whole country was in a state of unrest. I was naïve. I figured I could fit in and make friends. And I did make a few friends, but I also felt discriminated against. It was painful to walk into a classroom and be hit in the face by a wall of silence that may as well be made of brick.

Later that fall, Joyce came to visit me in Nashville. We missed each other and longed to be together. We spent most of the time in bed, but also we wanted to plan our wedding ceremony. Without any precedent, or even knowledge, we set out to combine what we considered the most important elements of a Christian and Jewish wedding ceremony. We created an original ceremony, something that now is commonplace, but then, well, we were pioneers.

Joyce: After Barry's rabbi refused to marry us, we did not know what to do. My mother spoke to the minister of her church, University Presbyterian Church, right across from the University of Buffalo campus. My mother had attended this church since she was seven years old and rarely missed a Sunday or important meeting. My father often volunteered to do maintenance on the church property. They were well known and loved at that church. I grew up attending church every Sunday, teaching Sunday school, attending youth group, and other events.

My mother told me she asked the minister of her church about marrying us, and he agreed provided that we meet with him first. On the day that we were to meet with the minister, Reverend Davis, we were both filled with trepidation. Would this meeting be the same as with the rabbi?

Fortunately, it was very different. After talking with us for about a half hour, he said, "It's obvious that you two love each other very much and I believe you can have a wonderful marriage together."

This was the first adult who had ever said something this positive to us about our relationship. He was the first person who believed in us as a couple. We were only twenty-two years old and we needed a spiritual guide, someone older who could see good in our relationship.

Reverend Davis then continued, "I'll marry you on one condition. You must promise to honor the differences in each other, rather than try to change each other. It's your differences that complement one another."

Such wise advice! We saw his wisdom and agreed.

He turned to Barry and said, "What can I do to make you feel more comfortable in our church?" Barry thought for a moment and answered, "Would you be willing to learn a Hebrew prayer of blessing for a wedding and speak it during the ceremony?" Reverend Davis promised that he would. We will always be grateful to this man of God for his blessing and guidance.

On the day of our wedding, December 21, 1964, there was a heavy snowstorm in Buffalo, New York. Our wedding was set for seven in the evening. My mother had done so much to decorate the church with many poinsettia plants and candles. The candles came in very handy as the electricity went out during the ceremony, leaving the church romantically lit by candlelight.

I was so happy to be marrying Barry that I hardly noticed the snow. I spent the day in such a delightful way preparing for the wedding and being with my friends. Poor Barry had to pick up his parents at the airport and drive them around. To make matters worse, his best man developed a tooth abscess and Barry had to drive him around to different dentists to get emergency treatment.

Immediately before the wedding was to start, I was upstairs in the church balcony room, in my wedding gown, with my father and bridesmaids present. The atmosphere was charged with happiness and anticipation, when my mother came rushing up the stairs. She had just seen Barry approach Reverend Davis and ask him to remove the cross that was on the altar at the front of the church. Without any hesitation, the minister had simply placed the cross on the floor behind the altar.

It nearly broke my mother's heart to see this "desecration" in the church that she loved so dearly. She rushed over to me and held my arm and urgently whispered, "Joyce, I just saw Barry ask the minister to remove the cross. It's not too late to change your mind and cancel this wedding."

In five minutes, I was scheduled to walk down the aisle with my father. "Mother," I said lovingly, "I'm not changing my mind. With my whole heart, I want to marry Barry."

Obviously upset, but realizing the wedding could not be stopped, she quickly turned, forced a smile, and walked down the stairs, walked down the aisle with my brother, and sat in the front of the church. No one else seemed to notice the absence of the cross and, after the wedding, the minister calmly put the cross back in its proper place.

My father, who was oblivious to the drama that had just occurred, proceeded to walk me down the aisle. Barry and I held candles and took light from one candle that symbolized to us the oneness of all religions. We said our vows to each other. Reverend Davis did keep his promise and spoke a beautiful Hebrew prayer. My brother's wife, Ruth, beautifully sang a prayer that Barry knew so well, "May the words of my mouth and the meditations of my heart be acceptable to thee oh Lord, my light and my redeemer." Looking into Barry's loving brown eyes, I watched tears slide down his cheeks. This was a moment we shall never forget. It felt as if the heavens opened up and poured a great blessing upon our union.

Wedding 1968

Throughout our wedding, Barry's mother cried, and not quietly. I would like to say they were tears of happiness, but I couldn't help feeling that they were tears of mourning, like one would cry at a funeral. Perhaps it was a mixture of the two. It was a big deal for Barry's parents to attend a non-Jewish wedding of their son – and in a church. I was grateful that Barry's parents had chosen to come.

Our mothers certainly redeemed themselves over the years. My mom grew to deeply love Barry. And when we began to meditate, she also took classes in meditation so that she could understand what we were doing. She grew to love meditation and so enjoyed talking to Barry about her experiences. When my mother was dying, and Barry and I were taking turns caring for her in the evenings, she looked up at Barry one evening as he was getting her ready for bed and said, "Barry, you are no longer just my son-in-law. I love you like my own son. I could not have imagined a better man for Joyce."

Barry's mother also changed. When I first met her, she was living in a Jewish world, with all of her Jewish friends. She had a very difficult time accepting that her beloved first son did not marry a Jewish woman and was not going to raise Jewish children. When we decided to get married, she once approached me and announced, "Joyce, it's your responsibility as a woman to convert to Judaism."

I boldly looked into her eyes and said, "I would never do that!" This, of course, created a tension between us.

On the day of our wedding, she handed me a small box and said that I must put it on the door of our home. I barely opened the box when I noticed it was a Jewish symbol, a mezuzah, and I closed it right back up. Barry told me we would not be putting it on our door as it meant a faithful Jewish family lived there.

When I was first pregnant, she handed me a book that said, "How to raise a Jewish child." I saw the book and handed it right back to her and said, "We won't be needing this book."

If I told her how deeply I loved Barry, she looked disappointed rather than happy. Barry called to tell her when our first child, Rami was born. Her first question was, "Whose side of the family does she most resemble?" Of course, she was hoping that Rami looked Jewish. Barry, prepared for this inevitable question, responded with, "She looks just like Joyce!" And with that statement, Barry's mom accepted me. Just like that.

Over time, I began thanking Barry's mom for raising such a wonderful son. Each time Barry spoke to her on the phone, I always got on and thanked her. Soon, she was telling Barry that I was the best thing that ever happened to him, and she continued to say these precious words every visit. We grew to have a deep, very loving and wonderful relationship that lasted throughout the rest of her lifetime.

Barry: We had a lovely, romantic, but way too short honeymoon. We left the wedding reception to spend our first night of marriage at Niagara Falls, just an hour north of Buffalo. The next day, we had a skiing honeymoon for a few days at a ski resort south of Buffalo called, appropriately, "Kissing Bridge." Because we had so little money, and rarely spent money on extravagances like ski vacations, I was determined to get my money's worth. I had us skiing all day long. Then, in the evening, I discovered the indoor swimming pool, and insisted that we have a full work-out swimming laps. After all that activity, we were too exhausted for romance. Joyce complained that this was not feeling very much like a honeymoon. Starting the following day, I slowed my pace, and we actually enjoyed ourselves.

Chapter 9: Nashville 1968

Joyce: Back in Buffalo, Barry and I packed up our car, a 1964 Plymouth Belvedere that was a wedding gift from my parents, and drove down to Nashville.

Nashville at that time was divided by one road into the "white" section and the "black" section. We moved into an apartment on the white side of town (the only place that would rent to us).

We had very little money and an apartment without one piece of furniture. I got the idea to walk the neighborhood, introduce ourselves, and ask if they had any furniture they did not want. Barry wasn't the only one with "chutzpah."

At the first house an elderly man opened the door and said, "Yes, can I help you?"

We introduced ourselves and I said, "My husband is a first-year medical student here in town and we have no money to buy furniture for our little apartment. (I let him assume it was the predominantly white Vanderbilt Medical School.) Do you by any chance have any old furniture you don't need anymore?"

The man's eyes lit up and he said, "Yes, we have two old bedside tables that I really want to get rid of." We took them and kept them for ten years, they were in such good condition.

At another house, a man answered and, when we told him what we wanted, he again was delighted and ran down to get an old lamp that belonged to his wife's mother. Before long, his wife came on the scene, and it became a smorgasbord of free furniture.

We had many delightful experiences that day getting to know our neighbors and, by the end of the day, we had all the furniture and lamps we could use, and some of it was really beautiful.

We had fully furnished our apartment. The only thing we paid for was a new mattress!

Barry: Several years later, in 1972, while we were living in Portland, Oregon, and I was a resident in psychiatry, we had a spiritual teacher named Jack Schwarz. Jack was born in Holland, was captured as a pilot by the Nazis during World War II, and was tortured by them. Partly by necessity, he developed the ability to separate himself from his body, to survive the torture. Later on, he refined this mental control over his body, and became a pioneer in the field of holistic medicine.

In a famous study at the Menninger Foundation, he demonstrated the power of the mind over matter by stabbing a long sail-maker's needle through his biceps without bleeding. He stated that he put the needle through "an arm," not his arm. He was asked by one of the researchers, Dr. Green, to make his arm bleed. At this request, Jack moved his attention from his higher self to his body. His wound opened up like a faucet. He then let go and moved back into the silence of the higher self, and the bleeding stopped instantaneously.

Jack was a gifted spiritual teacher, and we learned much from him. One time, during a private meeting with him, he was studying my aura, the energy field around my body, and said, "Barry, your spiritual rebirth was in January, 1969. Do you remember what happened at that time?"

I glanced at Joyce, then said to Jack, "You probably mean December, 1968, when we got married."

Jack shook his head emphatically, "No, I'm quite clear. It was definitely January of 1969."

Neither Joyce nor I could remember anything truly significant the month after we got married. Jack remained adamant, and we left that meeting still bewildered.

It wasn't until years later that we realized he was exactly right.

On the morning I was to resume classes at Meharry, in January, 1969, I was hit by a feeling of dread as I was saying goodbye to Joyce.

She looked into my eyes. "Barry, what's wrong?"

Joyce knows me sometimes better than I do. She can instantly tell when something's wrong.

I wanted to share with her how difficult it was to be discriminated against, but the only words that came out were, "It's hard to leave you."

In that moment, Joyce felt behind my words to my deepest vulnerability, my true need for her love and protection. She felt me entrusting my scared little boy-self into her care, even though I didn't have the courage at the time to actually speak those words. It was, perhaps, the first time I was openly and honestly vulnerable with another person.

When I finally got up my courage to leave our newly-furnished apartment on the white side of Nashville, and got into our car, I cranked down the window to see Joyce loving me more than ever. She seemed to be looking right through me and said, "Barry, I'm so in awe of your beauty."

It wasn't so much the words she spoke as it was the way she spoke them ... and the way she was looking at me with so much love. She was seeing in that moment my highest self, the real me, which I had not yet discovered. I didn't know what to do or how to receive this enormous gift of love. I lamely mumbled, "Gee, maybe you shouldn't be feeling that way." I'm not exactly proud of that comment. Thankfully, it didn't seem to faze Joyce. She just stood there beaming rays of love to me.

All these years later, I realize my feeling of vulnerability was a great gift of love to Joyce. Showing her my fear and complete need for her love empowered her to rise in love to see me in a deeper, more authentic way.

This moment was, indeed, my spiritual rebirth. Joyce saw my Higher Self because of my naked vulnerability. And, from that moment on, I knew I must grow into this true self, and learn to see myself the way Joyce saw me in that vulnerable moment. I'm still amazed that Jack Schwarz was able to tune in, years later, to that pivotal moment!

I have to say that, after getting married and moving to Nashville, Joyce and I made a serious mistake. Religion had been the cause of so much pain and suffering in our relationship, we threw it all away. But we also threw away our spirituality. It was like throwing out the baby with the bath water. We needed to throw away the outer structures, but we needed to keep our inner search for deeper meaning in life.

This created a vacuum in our lives, which we proceeded to try to fill with alcohol, pot, and later in Los Angeles, psychedelics. Of course, we could never replace spirituality with physical substances, and so our souls and our marriage took a hit.

Chapter 10: Serving the Poorest of the Poor

Joyce: As a graduate from Columbia University Nursing School, I had received an intensely academic training at perhaps the best nursing and medical facility in the United States at the time. My New York City education did not prepare me to be a public health nurse in the poorest of the poor ghettos in Nashville. Perhaps it was because I was new, or maybe the Southern nurses at the time did not appreciate Northerners, but I was given the poorest most difficult section in town.

In my nursing training, they never taught me what to do when the patients do not have doors or windows on their homes, and it is snowing outside. I was never taught what to do when the children were bare foot and shivering, and there was no food to eat or clothes to wear. I had learned charting, treatment plans, anatomy and physiology, medicines, vital signs and listening skills. My public health experience was in the ghettos of New York City, but people still lived in apartment houses. I never dreamed such poverty existed in our country.

I realized how little my fancy Ivy League education had actually prepared me for this real-life drama of poverty. And yet I loved these poor black people with all my heart. I loved them more than the white citizens that lived across town in their very isolated neighborhoods, people who never got to really know a black person, and yet judged them to be inferior human beings. These poorest of the poor could find joy in simple ways, and they treated me with respect.

I walked up and down the rich white neighborhoods asking for clothes and shoes and brought them to these wonderful and simple people. I spent one and a half years helping these precious people and, in the process, my heart opened in love and gratefulness for them. It was not an easy job, but I remain forever grateful for my time there.

Mrs. Monice

One of my favorites was elderly Mrs. Monice, who took in ironing from her neighbors. She heated her antique iron on her only source of heat, a tiny woodstove. She was like a mother to me, so great was her love.

My own mother was the first civil rights activist that I knew. She and my dad loved the black people and felt that they deserved equal rights. From an early age, she taught me to love and respect blacks, gays and all minorities. I never knew discrimination, as my parents made sure that Blacks, Muslims, Gays and other minorities were regular dinner guests each Sunday.

Some of my other relatives were not so tolerant. One uncle, upon hearing that a black family was moving in to their Buffalo neighborhood, took it upon himself to write a petition asking this family to leave, and gathered signatures from other like-minded neighbors. While the family was moving in to their house, this uncle marched up to their front door and knocked. His plan was to give the petition to whoever opened the door.

The door was opened by a huge black man whom my uncle instantly recognized as one of the star players of the Buffalo Bills football team. The frown on his face was immediately replaced by a welcoming smile, and the hand with the petition quickly snuck behind his back. I'm sure my uncle wished he had been holding a fresh-baked pie as a housewarming gift.

Though I knew about discrimination, especially in the South, it was still a complete shock to me to move to Nashville, Tennessee. In the white neighborhoods, people were even prejudiced against us when they found out that Barry went to Meharry Medical School.

Several months after I moved to Nashville, we had the opportunity to march for civil rights. Barry and I, and our new friend, Jim, traveled deeper into the South to a community where whites ruled and the blacks had little or no rights. Before the march, Dick Gregory gave a speech to all who were gathered. The three of us were the only whites present with hundreds of blacks. Mr. Gregory told everyone that there might be violence towards the marchers, and people would be arrested, but he also shared the value of doing this march, the first one in this community.

We marched down the main street of this town and, on all sides, angry white were yelling and swearing at us. Tensions were high!! The police came and started clubbing the marchers. I saw a large, black man being beaten by the police just because of his size. He did nothing to provoke them. People were indeed being arrested. Those in charge of the march told the three of us to leave fast, as we were in even more danger as the only whites. We slipped away and felt totally protected, like there was a Harry Potter invisibility cloak around the three of us.

I often reflect on what a dangerous situation we had put ourselves in, especially after seeing the movie, *Selma*. And yet we had been kept safe, as we had important work to do in this life, and it was not right for our lives to end so soon.

Driving home with Jim, we felt so grateful for the opportunity to participate in something so important. It was small in the overall civil rights movement, but lots of small acts coalesced into a very big movement and change.

The next day, I was called into my boss's office and was told that I could never march again. She had seen and recognized me on a TV news report. The cameras probably zoomed in on the only three whites there. She said that if I did march again, I would lose my job and probably not be able to find another in the city. I had no choice as we needed my salary.

News spread fast and, one by one, the nurses in the office told me I should not have done such a stupid thing. I was never really accepted after that by those nurses in Nashville. I did not march again. But that one civil rights march deepened my awareness of human rights.

I began to have a very strong desire to go back to school and get another degree. I didn't even know what I wanted to study, I just felt that I needed to be back in school learning again. I could hardly think of anything else. Barry and I talked and decided that, when he finished medical school, I would go back to school. We needed my salary, and neither of us could figure out a way for me to return to school and support both of us at the same time. Waiting three more years seemed almost impossible to me.

Our friend Jim invited us to a party and told us we would meet a special professor from USC in Los Angeles. Without much enthusiasm, we went and were not prepared for the force of love that hit us when we met Leo Buscaglia for the first time. Right away, he hugged us. Then, he launched into the deepest appreciation we had ever received. I wish I could remember the beautiful and loving things he said to each of us.

We had never been hugged by anyone other than each other and our parents. It's hard for people to believe but, in the United States in the late sixties, most people did not hug. They shook hands. Leo's parents were Italian immigrants, and Leo learned from them and hugged everyone. In all of our lives, we had never experienced such an open loving man who included all of us in his love.

Throughout that evening, we could hardly stop looking at Leo, and marveling at his ability to reach out, hug and love complete strangers. After that evening, we longed to be around Leo and his amazing energy. We felt changed by our connection with him. The next day, he traveled back to his home in Los Angeles and we stayed in Nashville. Seeing him again seemed very unlikely.

With my urging and desire to leave the South, and with Leo still in the back of our minds, Barry applied for a transfer to two medical schools in Los Angeles, USC and UCLA. And, miracle of miracles, he was accepted by both!

He flew to Los Angeles to choose between the schools. He decided upon USC, the more clinical and less research-oriented school at the time.

Barry: Boarding my flight back from Los Angeles, I walked down the aisle, ticket stub in one hand, carry-on bag in the other, looking for my seat. It was a window seat in a small plane with a two-by-two configuration. I saw my seat, and saw that the aisle seat was occupied by a man quite a bit older than me. He smiled warmly and, when I stowed my bag in the overhead bin and pointed to the seat past him, instead of getting up, he gestured to the seat. It felt a bit strange. Did he expect me to climb over him to get to my seat?

I said, "Excuse me, would you mind letting me get to my seat?"

His response, "Sure. You're a young buck. Just hop over me."

I thought maybe he was crippled and was brought to the seat in a wheelchair.

I said, "Are you able to stand up?"

He said, "Sure, but I just thought it would be more fun for you to climb over me."

I said, "If you don't mind, I'd rather you stood up."

He looked slightly disappointed, but obliged.

I was happy to walk rather than climb to my seat.

I sat down, buckled in, and looked out the window, hoping to avoid any more weirdness.

Then I heard him say, "Hi, my name is Bill. What's yours?"

Cringing inside, I turned away from the window and there he was, smiling and offering his hand. I reluctantly shook hands and noticed that he held my hand a bit longer than was comfortable to me.

Finally, I got it. He was obviously picking up on me. Sometimes, I'm a bit dense. I needed a quick way to change gears.

"Good to meet you. My name's Barry. I'm excited to be going home to my wife in Nashville."

I noticed the briefest flash of disappointment on his face, but he recovered quickly and said, "I'm also going home to Nashville but, alas, I'm single. But it looks like I'll be moving to Los Angeles. I just got a job at USC."

That perked my interest. And it seemed he had let go of me as a possible love interest.

"Wow," I said, "We're also moving. I just got accepted for my final two years of medical school at USC. What's your new job at USC?"

Bill sat up straighter in his seat, letting the conversation change gears, "I just got hired to manage a new master's degree program for a professor there."

"My wife Joyce and I just met a USC professor visiting Nashville who completely blew our minds. His name was Leo Buscaglia."

Bill burst out laughing. "What a small world! That's who I'll be working for!"

My heart nearly skipped a beat. "What an amazing coincidence! (I didn't yet believe in miracles or divine guidance.) What exactly will you be doing for Leo?"

Bill answered, "I've been hired to enroll ten students in a brand-new master's degree program that will last only one year under the direct supervision of Dr. Buscaglia." He continued, "These ten students will be given a full scholarship plus living expenses and take most of their classes with Leo. I've been hired to interview the many students who will apply for this special program and pick out just ten."

I was beginning to wonder if this was really happening or just a dream, but I found my voice, "My wife has an RN and BS, but really wants to go back to school. I think she would be perfect for the program."

Bill closed his eyes and was silent for a few seconds, then opened his eyes and said, "Okay, she can be my first student to be accepted."

Just like that!

I could not believe this great blessing. Not only could Joyce go back to school and have it all paid for, but she would be having most of her classes with this amazing man that we had met in Nashville.

Joyce: Barry returned home to me in Nashville filled with excitement. When he told me what happened on the plane, I thought he was joking. How could anything so incredible come into my life with so little effort? Bill had given Barry an application that I filled out immediately. Not only would I get money for living expenses but, because Barry was my dependent, I would get money for him as well. This blessing was beyond anything I could have even imagined or hoped for. It was clearly yet another miracle in our lives.

When Barry's second year of medical school at Meharry ended, we started preparing to move. It was hard to leave my beloved elderly black patients. I loved them like they were my own family. We had very tearful good-byes, and I took photos of each one. Barry enlarged them for me in his darkroom, and we framed them for our new home. I still have a precious black and white photo of Mrs. Monice holding her ancient iron.

Barry: We decided to have a farewell party at the apartment where we lived. It had a nice swimming pool, and there were often parties. I'll never forget one time, I was standing in the pool visiting with some of the other tenants and, by some miracle or divine prompting, I happened to look down into the water. There, just a few feet to the side of our legs, lay a toddler on the bottom of the pool, motionless. Hoping beyond hope that I was not too late, I rocketed down under the water, grabbed the child, jumped out of the pool with him, and held him upside down. Water poured out of his nose and mouth, and then, miraculously, without the need for CPR, he gasped for air. I was not too late.

His father, who we knew, had been drinking too much, and lost sight of him. The child evidently slipped into the pool without anyone seeing him. How thankful I was to have saved the life of a child. The toddler recovered completely, not even needing a trip to the hospital.

Wanting to have a special time with our medical school friends, we arranged to have a pool party and invited some of the "brothers" (as they called themselves in those days) from the class and their wives.

We were having a great time when I noticed a small, wiry, balding man approach the pool with a grim look on his face. He was the manager of the apartment complex. In each hand was a gallon bottle of bleach. Without saying a word, he began walking around the pool, pouring the bleach into the water as we were swimming and playing. The wordless message was loud and clear. "Get out! You are not welcome here! You are polluting our precious pool!"

Joyce and I stood stunned. One of our black friends turned to me and quietly said, "It's all right. We're used to this kind of treatment. Frankly, it's a miracle we got to be here even this long." Soon, all our friends left.

It was at that point that we knew we had made the right decision to leave the South. The racial discrimination had become too oppressive for us. We had had enough.

Chapter 11: Los Angeles 1970

Barry and I found a very small apartment in Los Angeles that only cost $89/month, including utilities, the one so close to the railroad tracks. This was all we could afford though and so we took it. We found out a week later that this apartment was just three doors down from Leo's house. He lived in a nice house overlooking Sycamore Park in the Highland Park area. The thought of not only having Leo as my teacher but also as our neighbor was almost too good to be true. I hoped he didn't think I was stalking him!

My year with Leo Buscaglia as my teacher and mentor was absolutely amazing in every single way. Leo was perhaps twenty years older than we were. It's sad that he couldn't fully come out as a gay man at the time in 1970, because he would have certainly lost his job.

Leo was filled with love and enthusiasm for life. His classes were all about love and opening to the fullness of life. He loved me deeply, and expressed over and over again how much he appreciated my sensitivity and deep feelings. He spoke words I had needed to hear my whole life. I felt like the luckiest person in the world to have had that year with him, shared only by the other nine people that received the full scholarship. Leo left USC after that year. I sometimes wonder that perhaps he wanted to have us ten students to pour his heart into so that we could carry out his work somehow.

He also taught a hugely popular class for the general student population, "Love 1-A," and I attended it every time. There was a deep hunger inside me that wanted to absorb every single thing that he spoke to me. The lessons from Leo and the books he had us read set me on a new path in my life, one I have never strayed from.

Leo also welcomed us into his home and into his social life. His friends became our friends, most of whom were gay. For the two years we lived in Los Angeles, we were part of a loving gay community, with Barry and me as the only hetero members. The experience of living, knowing and understanding gay men and women so closely has been a tremendous blessing for us.

One of the books Leo had us read was *Why Am I Afraid to Tell You Who I Am*, by a Jesuit priest named John Powell. It was a simple book, with just a few sentences on each page. But that book still influences us to this day. The essence of the book is that, in order to know someone and really understand their heart, you must first open up yourself in a vulnerable way and share what you are feeling. Barry and I have taken this so to heart that, in every workshop, we share about our own vulnerability. Before reading that book, I always assumed it is best to put your strength forward and hide your vulnerability. But the author is stating that the opposite is actually true. This book was written in 1969, and it was a totally new concept for living.

Leo was constantly sharing his vulnerability and encouraging us to do the same. He took himself off the pedestal again and again so that we could see him as a real human being with deep feelings, faults and the ability to make mistakes. Because he did this, we could love him all the more, and love ourselves for our own shortcomings.

Sometimes, I'd watch him yell at someone, "Stop trying to be like me. You'll never succeed. No one can be like me." Then, in a softer voice, he'd lovingly speak, "But no one can be a better you."

Sometimes a miracle occurs just by witnessing something that has a profound effect on you and stays forever in your consciousness. A simple event that I witnessed has stayed with me forever, and I shall be blessed by it for the rest of my life.

During my year as Leo's student, I arrived early one morning at the USC education building the same time as Leo, and we met at the elevator. Leo looked especially enthusiastic as he explained to me that he had set up a very special meeting on the tenth floor of the building. He said that all of the school's top officials were already there, and he was to present a new idea at exactly 9am. He was obviously excited as well as a bit nervous, hoping they would accept his idea.

The elevator door opened and we both got in. USC was a very old school even when I was there, and this elevator must have been there from the beginning. It opened very slowly and closed its door even more slowly. It inched itself up to the next floor. It stopped at each floor even if only one person was in the elevator. Once it reached the top floor, it inched itself down painstakingly slow to the lower basement, 12 floors below. The whole ordeal took an agonizingly long time. Usually, I just ran up the stairs, but Leo had a heart condition that would not allow him to climb so many stairs. He told me, "I've come early so I'll get to the meeting right at 9am. It's important to be on time for the dean of the school."

Finally, having waited forever, the elevator door opened and we both got in. We got talking and, when the elevator arrived at my destination, the fifth floor, we were both so engrossed in our conversation that we both got off the elevator. He walked along with me until he realized he was on the wrong floor. We turned and rushed back only to hopelessly watch the elevator doors finish closing.

Leo, with a sad expression on his face, urged me to go on so I wouldn't be late. Because of the slowness of the elevator, he was now going to be late for his important meeting. I felt awful leaving him standing there, but I did as he instructed and left for my class, the only class I had with another instructor.

I started walking to my class, but I stopped and turned around, feeling deeply concerned about Leo. What I saw was an image that has become permanently imbedded in my mind and heart. I was only a short distance away from him. Leo's back was to me as he faced the elevator doors. He was hugging himself and saying in a quiet but clearly audible voice, *"It's all right Leo. You got off at the wrong floor with Joyce and will be late, but you are still a beautiful person. I love you, Leo, you adorable guy. It's cute how you keep making these funny mistakes."*

I had to smile. I had seen people under similar circumstances swear, throw books on the ground, stomp their feet, and in many other ways act irritated and angry toward themselves for making a mistake. Yet there was Leo, alone in the hallway, knowing how late he would be for his meeting because of his mistake, and he was hugging himself and sending himself loving messages. *I had never seen anyone use a mistake as a chance to give themself love.*

That image has stayed with me over time, and I have tried to do what Leo did whenever I make a mistake. I have used this image in my parenting, and each of our three children know this story very well. Once, I drove our daughter Mira back to the University of California, Santa Cruz, where she was a freshman and living in the dorm. She had been home for Thanksgiving. Normally, the drive takes forty-five minutes, but the traffic was horrible and it took us almost an hour and a half. Our son was too young to leave at home, so he was in the car as well. We got to her dorm room and she checked for her key. Her face went pale as she said, "I forgot my key at home."

I flashed on Leo and told her to get back into the car, that I had a really good story to tell her as we once again made our way back into the traffic.

By the time I was twenty-five, I had been rejected several times by friends who told me that I was too sensitive and so it was hard to be with me. It reminded me of the criticism from my childhood. I took this rejection very hard and blamed myself and felt there was something terribly wrong with me. This rejection rested like a heavy weight on my heart.

During my yearlong study and mentorship with Leo Buscaglia, this heavy weight was lifted, never to return again. He adored my sensitivity, and that's just what I needed. He told me once, "Most people are clueless about the negative energy they are putting out. You, Joyce, feel their energy and respond accordingly. You can't help it. Then you're accused of being too sensitive."

One warm sunny day, I had a private appointment with Leo in his office and I arrived a little early. I wanted to talk to him about his love class. I loved this class so much, and I wanted to thank him for teaching me and hundreds of others so much about love.

His secretary told me that it would be a little wait, and pointed to a chair right by his door where I could sit. She told me that the dean of students and other important officials from USC were there to talk to Leo. I settled my books and purse on the floor, and sat down to wait.

I didn't mean to listen, but the noise coming from the room, even with a closed door, became so loud that I could hear every word spoken in anger, "Leo, you can no longer teach your love class. It's a great embarrassment to the university. Word has gotten out about your popular class, and newspapers and magazines are writing about it. It is not good for our university to have this kind of attention on such a controversial subject like love. This is a long-established academic university. You are ruining our noble image!!"

Leo spoke in a calm voice, "I understand your concerns. I really hope you can also understand why this class is so important. The psychology of love is too often misunderstood..."

He was cut off by a booming voice, "That's the end of this discussion!! You will stop teaching the love class immediately!"

With that, the men all got up, opened the door, and almost tripped on me in their hurry to leave.

I was shocked! How could anyone speak so harshly to my beloved teacher, the best teacher I had ever had in my life? And how could they possibly terminate this most-wonderful non-credit love class to which hundreds of students packed into an auditorium to hear, and more were coming every week.

I walked into Leo's office at the direction of his secretary. I was actually surprised to see him sitting there so calmly.

I said, "I'm so sorry, Leo. I heard the whole thing. They treated you so badly."

I will never forget Leo's words, which have never left my heart, *"Don't be sorry for me, Joyce. Be sorry for them. I have so much love to give, and they don't want to receive it. They're the ones who are losing."*

This was another miracle for me, that I should happen to be sitting right there and hear the entire conversation and, more importantly, to hear Leo's response. Afterwards, I thought about the people who had rejected me, and how much I had suffered over that. Even though I was alone, I said out loud to all these people, "I feel sorry for you because I have so much love to give you, and you're missing out on that." I have used this over and over in my life. Leo's words have been a blessed healing for me.

When Leo left USC, he went on to write many books about love, and he has been the only author to have five books on the New York Times' Bestseller List at the same time. His talks around the country sometimes had 10,000 people in attendance, many of them lining up afterwards for one of his famous hugs. It is largely because of Leo that Americans now hug one another. People received the love that he was offering, and it changed their lives, just like he changed my life.

I reflect often on the miracles in my life, and how God loves me and is taking care of me even when I am totally unaware. In my top five miracles is certainly Barry happening to sit next to Bill on the plane and my being given a full scholarship to spend a full year with Leo Buscaglia.

Oh yes, I even earned a master's degree!

Chapter 12: Betraying Joyce

Barry: In my final year of medical school at the University of Southern California, I was reading a new book, *Open Marriage*, and pressuring Joyce with my "need" to open our relationship to include sex with other persons.

We had a few sexual "experiences" that included other people. It was exciting to me, but Joyce never felt good afterwards. She worried about our marriage, and what would happen if we continued in this direction.

One day, in the living room of our tiny apartment in Highland Park, she tried to address the deeper issues. "Barry, I need your love. Don't you need mine?"

My vulnerability was too deeply hidden. "I love you, Joyce. I don't *need* you."

Then, I went on to new heights of denial, "I can love other women fully, and it won't take anything away from our love. You're being selfish to want me all to yourself."

I was residing, at the time, too much in my head. I was the one being completely selfish, hiding my desires behind some kind of spiritual ideal.

Joyce was in tears from the sheer arrogance of my words. She ran into the bedroom and shut the door....

Leo Buscaglia loved Joyce!! And through Joyce, I had also felt close to Leo, although most of my time was occupied as a medical student at the same university.

He used to say to me, "Whatever Joyce feels is written all over her face. When she's sad, she cries. When she's happy, she smiles. When she's angry, it's visible. When she's at peace, her face is relaxed. I love that about her. What you see is what you get."

With brutal honesty, he'd say to me, "I don't know what you're feeling. You can smile when you're angry or sad. So I can't trust your smile. Stop being phony, Barry!"

He was right, albeit blunt. I *was* hiding my sadness, anger, fear, and every other emotion I considered unpleasant. I had learned all my life, as many of us have, to cover up and ignore my vulnerability. A significant piece of this vulnerability was my human emotional need for Joyce – and for love in general. All this was now about to change.

Joyce's best friend from nursing school, Lita, came to visit us from New York. On the phone a few days before the visit, she told us she was separating from her husband, and needed to be with us.

Our first evening together, sitting in our tiny living room next to one wall which, for some strange reason, we painted a dark red, there was a moment when Lita and I looked at each other for just a little too long ... or with just a little too much warmth ... and it made Joyce feel uncomfortable and excluded. Plus, there had always been a bit of flirtatiousness in Lita and my relationship.

Joyce addressed us both, "I can feel the energy between the two of you right now. I don't like it at all. I'm not feeling real secure at the moment in our relationship, Barry. If the two of you act upon these feelings, I won't be able to handle it." Lita and I looked at Joyce with sympathetic understanding, and nodded in agreement.

The next day, while Joyce was at work and I was free, I took Lita to the beach. The sexual tension between us continued to build. Somewhere between my wanting to prove that I didn't need Joyce, and Lita's need for sex as proof of love, we acted upon our sexual attraction. We crossed a sacred boundary and had sex in the VW van.

To my credit, I had no need to keep it a secret from Joyce. I told her that evening when she came home from work. After I spoke, there were a few seconds of silence as I watched the expression on Joyce's face shift from happy to see me, to shock, to revulsion, to deep pain, to anger, and finally to rage.

She started screaming at Lita and me, **"HOW COULD YOU DO THAT AFTER WHAT I TOLD YOU LAST NIGHT!!! YOU'VE COMPLETELY BETRAYED MY TRUST!!!**

In that moment, she felt enough rage to want to kill us both. Instead, a better part of her prevailed. She ran into the bathroom and locked the door, partly to protect herself from seeing us, and partly to protect us from what she felt like doing to us.

Lita and I sat in the living room in stunned silence. Hours went by, while the screams from the bathroom gradually changed to sobbing. Sometime in the middle of the night, while Lita and I slept on the floor, Joyce crept out of the bathroom, took our golden retriever, Bokie, and left the apartment. She also left our marriage!

When I woke up, I found a note: "Barry, I will always love you. I understand that you need your freedom more than you need me. I now give you all the freedom in the world. You can do whatever you want. Please respect my decision to end our marriage. DON'T try to contact me."

Somehow, I never thought Joyce would ever leave me. Even violating our monogamy, I still thought she would try to understand my "quest" for freedom. I thought her compassionate heart would keep her in the marriage at all costs. I had severely underestimated her inner strength and her inner compass.

I also thought I'd be happy with my newfound freedom but, after Joyce left, my life collapsed. I was alone – with my feelings. And up to the surface they came – agonizing pain, an aching hole of sadness in my heart. I was shocked and surprised by the intensity of these feelings. I had no idea that Joyce's absence from my life would be so debilitating.

As a fourth-year medical student, I had been taking more and more responsibility for patients' care at Los Angeles County General Hospital. I was making important decisions for patients. Unfortunately, I was in no condition to make these decisions. The loss of Joyce was like a weight pushing me to my knees. I could barely function at the hospital. I could barely function anywhere. A dark cloud had settled over my life, and I walked through it heavily like a robot, isolating myself from everyone.

A few days after Joyce left, I realized I didn't want Lita in my life anymore. Despite her protests, I sent her back to New York to sort out her own life. I needed to be alone to find out who I really was.

I tried calling Joyce at her place of work. The secretary there was instructed by Joyce that she did not want to talk to me. In my arrogance, I was convinced that I could talk Joyce into coming back home and accepting that I needed sex with other women, but that I wanted her to live with me. Finally, after calling perhaps ten times in a row, the secretary had pity on me and put the call through to Joyce's office. When I heard Joyce's voice I said, "I want you to come back home. And I now realize that the way I want to live my life is to be able to be sexual with other women. Surely you can handle that for me."

Joyce was very brief, "Barry, don't you ever call me again. As long as that is the vision for your new life, it won't be with me!

She slammed the phone down and, though I called back many other times, the secretary never put me through to Joyce again. I sadly realized that Joyce was not coming back.

One evening, all my feelings rushed to the surface, especially unbearable despair. I found myself lying on the floor in a pitiful heap, sobbing uncontrollably. A word started to emerge from my depths, and soon I was calling it out, "mama … ma … ma!"

I felt just like an infant, completely helpless. In that state, I didn't know where my mother was, just that I needed her terribly. Truly regressed by all the pain, I reached upwards and, in my mind, I could see my own mother's face, how she looked when I was an infant. Then my mother's face morphed into Joyce's face, and I knew how much I needed her, just like an infant needs his mother. This bittersweet feeling continued its evolution. Joyce's face took on a new dimension. She was now the Cosmic Mother, the mother aspect of God. The feeling was overwhelming!

In that moment, I knew I would never be the same. I had discovered a buried child part of myself, a child who unabashedly needed his mother. I could no longer deny my physical, emotional, mental and spiritual need for Joyce … and for mother.

That evening, for the first time in my life, I made peace with a little boy inside me that needed love, acceptance, and nurturing – the part of me that needed Joyce, needed mothering, needed God, needed love. I made peace with my humanity, instead of pretending to be above it. I had been convinced that need and dependence, sadness and fear, and all so-called "negative" feelings, were signs of weakness. Now, I realized the courage and strength it took to feel all my feelings – to be truly vulnerable. I had been convinced that feeling my humanity would prevent me from feeling my divinity. I now knew that feeling my divinity depended upon my feeling my humanity. We are human beings on a spiritual journey, and spiritual beings on a human journey.

The following day, I ignored Joyce's request and tried to find her. I called her friends, and they lovingly but firmly let me know that Joyce did not want to see me – ever!

Desperate, I knew I needed to ask Leo for help. I walked down the street to his door and knocked.

Leo opened the door a crack, saw that it was me, and quickly slid out onto the porch, closing the door behind him. I had no idea that Joyce was staying at his house, and she didn't want me to know where she was. As far as she was concerned, our relationship was over.

Leo looked at me inquisitively. Completely devoid of self-pride, I blurted out my despair, my face and tears finally matching my inner pain. Leo studied me until I finished blubbering. To my utter surprise, a giant smile lit up his face, and he grabbed me in one of his famous hugs. While squeezing me, he excitedly spoke, "Barry, you're finally real … you're finally real!!"

It was a little like Gepetto (another Italian) holding Pinocchio, his puppet, who had miraculously transformed into a real little boy.

Although I didn't share his rejoicing in that painful moment, I knew he was right. My "puppet" days were over. I was no longer hiding my vulnerability. And it did feel good to finally let my feelings out, and be comforted by another human being – and a very loving one!

After being with Leo, and returning to our apartment, I had a bittersweet realization. I had lost my beloved wife, and might carry remorse and regret for the remainder of my life. That was the bitter part. The sweet part was the gift of vulnerability, the gift of a fuller life, with all my feelings and, especially, the awareness of a little boy inside me who needs love. It took my losing Joyce to finally feel my need for her!

Joyce: I thought if I loved Barry enough, he would realize the special bond between us, and know that he needed me just as much as I needed him. It was obvious to me that he needed me just as much, but painful that he could not see it. It was obvious to all of our friends and family as well.

And I needed to change my life as well. I realized my depth of devotion to Barry was bigger than my devotion to myself and to God. I realized I could no longer live this way. It was as if I had made Barry more important than myself. Until now, his desires became more important than my own. Now, I was on a new path, one that made me just as important as Barry, or anyone else for that matter.

A week after I left, Barry got a note to me through a friend of mine. The note simply said, "Can I please just talk with you for fifteen minutes? I had a realization that has changed my life. I am so sorry for what I did."

Through my friend, a time was arranged. Though I was intrigued by his note, I entered the meeting with Barry with a closed and protected heart and mind. My sense of betrayal was so huge that I actually felt done with the relationship, and nothing he could say could convince me otherwise. I was prepared to be strong and keep my boundaries. I was not prepared for how he looked or for the message that he spoke.

Barry did not look good. Gone was the false pride and arrogance. He was pale and had obviously not been sleeping well. He had also lost weight. He was completely vulnerable and it showed on his face. He said, "Joyce, I know I've probably lost you forever because of what I did with Lita. I've finally realized my need for your love. I've been hiding it, mainly from myself, for way too long. If you could ever forgive me, I would like to start over. If not, I'll continue to live by myself and just feel this small child part of me that needs love."

I forced myself to say nothing, although it wasn't easy. I stayed the agreed-upon fifteen minutes and then walked out, just as I had planned to do. I was not ready to open up to him or give him any comfort whatsoever. He had hurt me in the worst possible way. And yet, for another week, I could think of nothing else but his vulnerability and his newfound feeling of needing my love. Even though I was angry and hurt, and I still didn't trust him, I couldn't help also feeling strangely drawn to him.

One Saturday, Barry called me at my friend's house and asked, "Joyce, can we spend this day together hiking in the mountains? It's such a beautiful day!"

Still feeling closed to him, I said, "I doubt if I could enjoy doing anything with you right now."

One thing about Barry, he can be very persuasive. He said, "I know it's hard for you to be with me. I just thought that perhaps we could enjoy the mountains together once more."

Some tender quality in his voice caused me to finally agree. He picked me up and drove me to our favorite trail up in the mountains. He offered, "How about we walk in silence, trying to be aware of our footsteps and the beauty of nature?"

That sounded good to me, so off we went. After about a mile, we came to a slippery spot on the trail. Barry reached out to help me across. I had not allowed him to touch me in several weeks. I held out my hand, and the warmth of his hand, despite my resistance, felt good. I flashed back to the first time he held my hand, on our first date in the movie theater, and how instantly comforting that felt.

I could have dropped his hand after getting across the tricky spot, but I didn't, and he didn't let go either. We continued walking hand in hand.

After several more miles, we were tired and lay down in the lush green meadow grass for a nap in the sun. The angry and resentful thoughts seemed to have gradually slipped out of my mind with each footstep upon the earth. The effort that it took to be closed had become too much, so I opened to the beauty of our surroundings.

As I awoke from my nap, I saw Barry leaning on one elbow, tenderly looking at me. I once again saw my beloved, and we hugged in joy. Nature had once again worked its magic upon us, at least for the day.

Back in Los Angeles, the images of Barry having sex with my best friend returned with a vengeance, and my heart closed again.

I was at Leo's house for one of his earlier and more intimate love classes. Leo knew exactly what was going on between Barry and me. At one point he spoke to the whole class while looking directly at me and said, "Everyone deserves a second chance. People can and do change."

I went into another room and called Barry. He walked the three minutes to Leo's house and brought me back to our apartment. Once inside, we fell into each other's loving and passionate embrace. My mind had its reasons to stay closed to him, but my body and my heart opened wide. In-between urgent kisses, Barry kept saying, "I'm so sorry. I've been such an arrogant fool. I now know how much I need your love."

We began the journey of healing. It took two years before I could fully trust him again. Sometimes, even in the most tender moment, I would flash on an image of Barry in a sexual embrace with Lita, and it would shut me down. I learned to eventually simply tell Barry what was happening, even without anger. He stayed steadfast in his love for me and, especially, his need for my love. And, importantly, in those painful moments, he would say, "I trust in the change within me and I trust that I will never make such a mistake again. I need you too much. I hope someday you will trust me completely again."

Had Barry not approached me with vulnerability, I don't believe we would have made it as a couple. The vulnerability was strong enough to draw me back into his life, even though I was determined not to come back.

Still, though we were back together, we had much healing yet to do. We needed help, but didn't know where to turn. Our relationship hung together by a mere thread. We loved each other but were lacking a very important and yet undiscovered ingredient.

I still didn't completely trust Barry. He needed to be trusted again and missed my love. We each sought out in other people what we needed from each other. Barry spent more time with his male friends, while I chose to be with my best friend, Dawn. I was trying to receive from Dawn what I desperately needed from Barry.

In addition, the external stresses made this healing even more difficult. Barry was involved with finishing medical school. I had my first important job. I was hired to run a residential treatment program for teenage boys who could not function in their homes and schools because of their behavior. Cecil B. DeMille, the famous Hollywood moviemaker, had donated his beautiful three-thousand-acre ranch in the hills above Los Angeles. Since part of my responsibility involved hiring the staff, I naturally hired many of my friends, especially Dawn. Our opening day at Hathaway Ranch was graced by a visit from the famous movie star, Julie Andrews, who warmly thanked me for the important work we were about to do. Julie had also helped to financially support this important project.

The staff of thirty became a warm and loving family not only to the boys, but to me as well. I had never before known such joy in a job, never realized it was possible to laugh and play at work. Since Barry was often busy working at the hospital, I stayed longer and longer hours at work. I found I was happier there than I was alone at home.

I loved being in the mountains in Little Tujunga Canyon, and exploring the wilderness with the boys and my friends. I loved the colorful peacocks that strutted outside my office window, but mostly I loved going to the barnyard with the children to visit the animals. There were five horses available for riding. There was Betsy the pig, Noisy the turkey, Big Ears the donkey, and our favorite, Bertha the calf.

Each day, no matter what bizarre behavior the boys were exhibiting, a trip to the barnyard had a miraculous calming effect upon them. Bertha was always the first to run to meet us, and was usually rewarded with pieces of an apple. The boys would hug her and pet her soft head, then run off to the other animals.

I stayed with Bertha, talking to her and looking into her beautiful, fathomless brown eyes. Bertha became my friend as

A COUPLE OF MIRACLES

well as a helper to me. Some days I was troubled, often about my relationship with Barry, feeling as if an innocence was permanently shattered. It was then that Bertha's calm, peaceful manner and unwavering trust soothed me. When I couldn't fully count on anyone else in my life, except for our beloved Bokie, I could count on Bertha. Her innocence seemed to give hope that Barry and my innocence could be revived.

Through my relationship with Bertha, I was learning about the sensitivity, peacefulness, and intelligence of cows for the first time. I was deepening my relationship with the whole animal kingdom.

One Saturday, one of my days off, I was invited to have a special dinner with the boys. Usually, we were served a rather simple but tasty meal. Tonight, however, we were served an elaborate roast beef. Midway through the meal, the cook came out to ask how we were enjoying the food. The boys raved enthusiastically.

"I'm so glad," smiled the cook. "Our menus seemed so plain lately that we killed and butchered Bertha today."

A dark silence overcame all of us at the table. One by one, we pushed our dinner plates away. One by one, we left the table, absorbed in our own sorrowful thoughts.

It was obvious that, to the cook, Bertha simply meant food.

I went outside and stood by a tree, feeling terrible inside. I felt repulsed that I had just been eating one of my dearest friends and teachers. In that moment, I realized that Bertha represented my kinship with all animals. Just as Bertha was my friend, so were all animals my friends. The life within Bertha was no less sacred than the life within me. She probably was shot in the head without any honor or respect for the beautiful divine creature she was. She most likely had been treated by her killer as a thing, as food, rather than as a sacred living being. I shuddered to realize that, every time I ate meat, I was eating another Bertha, or Noisy, or Betsy. How could I ever eat another friend again?

That night, I returned home and somberly told Barry what had happened. I blurted out in grief, "I feel we should never eat meat again!"

Barry, who also knew and loved Bertha, looked at me intently, obviously weighing my words. He simply spoke, "From now on, we're vegetarians!"

Barry: Joyce felt amazed at how quickly I responded to her plea. She shouldn't have been. As a child, I often refused to eat meat, much to the dismay of my parents. They even brought me to the doctor one time, just because of this. The doctor asked, "So what *does* he eat?"

My mom said, "He eats a lot of peanut butter."

The doctor replied, "He's probably getting enough protein. Don't worry. He'll grow out of it."

I didn't. Not really. As an adult, the only meat I ate was hamburgers and hot dogs. For some reason, if meat needed to be cut with a knife, it turned me off.

Nevertheless, at the time, neither one of us knew how to be vegetarian. We didn't know what a big change was in store for us.

The following day, we had the opportunity to take a much-needed vacation. We traveled to a campground north of LA, right on the wild Pacific Ocean. Because of our vow to become vegetarian, we had stopped along the way to buy salad supplies. This was the only food we were sure vegetarians ate.

We were diligently preparing our salad when an extraordinary-looking young man walked up to our VW van. The side door was open so we were clearly visible. He was dressed in ordinary clothes, yet his eyes were shining. He looked at us for a moment, then at the salad, and said, "I'm glad you've chosen to become vegetarians. This will bring much happiness to your lives."

How did he know we had just become vegetarians just from seeing us with a salad? We smiled at him as he turned to walk away, saying nothing more.

Seconds later, after briefly glancing at each other, we realized that we wanted to ask him many questions, so we jumped out of our van to ask him to come back.

He seemed to have vanished into thin air. There was no humanly possible way for him to have disappeared so quickly. Even if he had run, we still would have seen him. Nothing like this had ever happened in our secure little world of medical student and nurse. There was only one explanation: we had just been visited by an angel, or some otherworldly being, in human disguise. We obviously needed direct confirmation of the rightness of our decision to become vegetarians.

Of course, now, so many years later, our plant-based, whole foods diet has evolved. We still love salads, but have added many more items. We've learned so much about healthy foods to eat. And we've never regretted our decision ... ever!

Our deepest heartfelt gratitude goes out to you, dear Bertha.

Chapter 13: The Mysterious Hospital Chaplain

Joyce: Somehow, I couldn't help letting the power of my job go to my head. I felt not only important, but indispensable as well. Some days, I felt so disconnected from Barry, that my job was giving me more than my marriage. Somehow, I knew I was on the wrong track, but I ignored this knowing.

Finally, one Friday night, after having not prayed in a long time, I asked God for help. The answer to my prayer came the next day in a way I would never have chosen.

It was Saturday, and Barry was free from medical responsibilities for the first time in several weeks. We could be together. Instead, I chose to spend the weekend with Dawn, even though I knew this would hurt him very much. I went to Dawn's house with our golden retriever. Bokie was more like

a child to me than a dog, even more so since the tragic loss of Bertha. Since I felt so insecure in my relationship with Barry, Bokie was a steady loving presence that I counted on. While I still couldn't fully trust Barry, I could completely trust Bokie. He was never far from my side.

Dawn and I were talking and, as usual, Bokie was lying next to me. Dawn's roommate came home and let in her German shepherd. Without warning, the dog instantly attacked Bokie. Bokie was not a fighter and took a thoroughly submissive stance. The German shepherd seemed like he was trying to kill Bokie. I became hysterical and reached for the shepherd's collar to pull him away. This was a bad move. The dog turned and bit deeply into my hand. His owner finally got him outside.

I went to the emergency room and was told it was nothing to worry about. Back home, sixteen hours later, my right hand contracted into a painful, reddened claw. Barry took one look and said, "Let's get you to the hospital right away."

At the hospital emergency room, a hand specialist told me the dog's fang had penetrated the periosteum, the protective membrane around the bone. The infection was spreading down into my hand bones and, without treatment, threatened to cause the loss of my hand and possibly more.

I was immediately wheeled in for emergency surgery, and emerged with both arms immobilized by needles, tubes, and IV's. My bitten hand was suspended above me with tubes for draining the infection. My other hand was receiving intravenous antibiotics. I could do nothing but lie in my hospital bed.

I had to stay in the hospital four days. I found myself in a room by myself feeling totally helpless. Barry walked in, and I cried, "I need you so much." It was reminiscent of the time in New York City when I was in the hospital, close to death, and my mother walked into the room.

Of course, I needed Barry deeply, but I had been hiding that need from both him and me.

"I'm here for you," he smiled confidently. My expression of needing him helped to open his heart, and the wounding of the past several months seemed to melt away as he held me close. Because of the betrayal and my leaving, Barry had realized his need for my love for the first time in our relationship. Now, it was my turn to let myself once again feel my need for his love.

Barry was asked to leave the room by a hospital official who needed forms signed. Minutes after Barry left, a man walked into my hospital room. He said he was a chaplain, but he had no religious collar or identifying badge. I had not signed a religious preference form and had only been in the hospital for several hours. How did he even know I was there?

With piercing blue eyes, he looked at me and said, "This accident can be the beginning of a whole new life for you."

I just stared at the man. I felt very peaceful in his presence. He then asked permission to say a prayer for me. Bow-ing his head, he asked for help for not only me but my marriage as well. Then he was gone as quickly as he came.

I lay there a long time wondering who that man was. How did he know my marriage needed help?

Barry returned and I told him what had happened. "Maybe that was your guardian angel," he half-jokingly suggested. I smiled through my pain and said, "I think you're right."

I found out later that the hospital never sends a chaplain to a patient unless it is requested, and even then, it can take many hours or even days as there were so few chaplains for the number of patients. I now believe it was an angel and certainly the brightness of his eyes suggested that. So many angels helping us just when we needed the help.

Barry came to my room every morning, during his half hour for lunch, and at the end of his day of work as a medical student. He tenderly fed me, washed my face, brushed my hair and supported me in every possible way. Without the use of my hands, I felt completely helpless.

We quietly talked about his betrayal. I shared my hurt and he shared his pain. He said he never imagined his actions would hurt me so much, and again, his vulnerability touched me deeply. I finally believed him.

Day by day, as my wounded hand was healing, we were also healing the wound between us. When the nurses, doctors, and assistants saw us in the room together, they left us alone. There was sacred healing happening on many levels, and everyone seemed to respect our privacy.

On the fourth day, the doctor removed my bandages, drainage tubes, and IV's. I had my hands and arms back and, more importantly, I had my beloved back. We still had more healing to do, but we were communicating again and had rediscovered how important our relationship was to us. We walked out of the hospital holding each other tightly. We vowed to do what it took to get our relationship on a loving and healthy track.

Chapter 14: Be Here Now

Joyce: When I was fully recovered, Barry got some days off from school and we took a little backpacking trip in the mountains north of Los Angeles.

We hiked down into Devils Canyon, near Mount Wilson. Sitting by a quiet flowing stream, we gently held each other and savored our time alone. We both knew we had almost lost each other, so to have found our way back was all the more precious.

We read from a book that had just come out, *Be Here Now*, by Ram Dass, and our hearts were opened to our next step. We realized we needed to find God together, to find the highest truth that would be common to both of us. We needed to find the spiritual cord that threaded itself through all religions, to make our spirituality the rock upon which we would build a new relationship.

We also knew we could no longer continue drinking, smoking pot, or taking psychedelics. We needed to find a new way to get "high" together, a way that would deepen, rather than erode, our relationship. We also saw that we needed to return to the sacred place of monogamy in our relationship to truly build our trust.

Sitting by the stream in the peace of the woods, we began our spiritual journey together. We did not know how we were going to do this. We only knew that our spiritual life together now had to be our priority. I thought about the mysterious visit from the "chaplain" in the hospital, the possibility that he was an angel in disguise, who had come to help open my eyes and heart. I especially remembered how he prayed for me—and us. So, for the first time in our relationship, we held hands, closed our eyes and asked for help. We committed ourselves to growing spiritually as a couple and asked for guidance and direction. That simple act has been the most significant step we have ever made.

Our request opened the door, and we were led to beautiful, heart-centered teachers and events in the ensuing years. Our newly-joined spirituality became the most solid, important part of our lives, helping and sustaining our relationship.

Barry: A few weeks after our backpacking trip, we heard about a weekend Gestalt Therapy workshop. This form of therapy was big in those days, created by Fritz Perls, a German-born psychiatrist. I was enthralled with this technique, and attended trainings in Los Angeles. Joyce and I knew we needed help. Even with our recent insights, there was still so much residual pain from my act of betrayal. We signed up for the weekend, not knowing what we had really signed up for.

During the weekend, despite the attempts of the leader to stop it, participants started judging Joyce and taking my side. "Why can't you share Barry with other women? I think you're being selfish," said one woman. A man said, "Barry is just exploring his sexuality. Don't take it so personally."

Even though people were taking my side, I felt worse and worse. I didn't want people to take my side. I didn't want people to take Joyce's side. I wanted people to take OUR side.

We left the workshop at the end of the first day, Saturday, and decided not to return the next day. We both felt devastated. Now, we not only carried the pain of my betrayal, but we also carried a new betrayal from the workshop. We felt misunderstood and judged.

We held each other in the parking lot outside the building. We remembered holding each other in another parking lot, outside my childhood temple, after feeling betrayed by my rabbi.

I said to Joyce, "Wouldn't it be great if, someday, we could provide a space for individuals and couples without judgment, where each person could be supported and no one would take sides, and each person could feel totally safe to share their feelings?"

Little did we know how prophetic that wish was, that just a few years later, we would indeed start to create that kind of supportive environment for people – and it would become our lifetime work.

Joyce: I'll never forget the evening I came home from a truly joyful day at work at Hathaway Ranch. Barry greeted me with a big smile and said, "I've been accepted for my residency in psychiatry at the University of Oregon Medical Center in Portland. We'll need to move in two months."

Of course, I was happy for Barry's acceptance, but there was something about the way he announced "our" move to Portland. There was no asking, or other consideration of my feelings. It felt in a way like he was choosing the next step in his career over me and our relationship.

My heart sank. I didn't want to leave. For the first time in my life, I was truly happy in my work. I felt needed, important and loved. I couldn't bear to leave my job. I knew this residency offer was important to Barry, but I was tired of following him around the country, tired of making all the sacrifices for his education. I left my family and my first nursing job in Buffalo, New York, to move to Nashville, Tennessee for Barry to start medical school. Two years later, I left my public health job in Nashville to move with him to Los Angeles to finish medical school. That particular move was also for me. But I felt I had sacrificed enough for Barry!

I blurted out, "I'm not going with you!"

I was actually surprised at the bold stand I was taking.

Barry looked at me for a moment in confusion, but then his face softened. He said, "I understand. You're really happy here. Why would I expect you to leave something so good?"

Part of me felt selfish, but a bigger part felt like I needed to stand up for myself. I reached out to hold his hands, and said, "Listen, we'll make it work. We'll see each other as often as we can. When you're finished with your residency in three years, and if I'm still fulfilled here in LA, maybe you'll move back."

This felt like the best solution, but there was an undeniable sadness in both of us.

Two weeks later, I returned home from work to find Barry waiting for me. He seemed peaceful and resolved when he spoke, "I decided to give up my residency program. It's more important for me to stay here with you. You're more important than my career. I can't bear the thought of living without you. I'll find a job here in LA, then reapply next year for a local residency."

I was in awe at the choice Barry had just made for our relationship – for me! He and I both knew that without an internship his medical education was practically worthless. His choice of job might include working as a laboratory assistant. He was willing to give up at least a year of his life just to be with me! I could tell this choice had come from a place deep inside of him. He was at peace, and I felt profound respect for him.

One week later, my own decision came from a similar inner place of peace. I gave notice at my job and prepared to move almost a thousand miles north to Portland, Oregon.

Barry actually tried to stop me from doing this. "Joyce," he pleaded, "you've always chosen me first. Give me this chance to choose you, to show you that you're most important in my life."

I smiled, "Right now, I feel completely chosen by you. You made your decision to choose me. That's all I needed and wanted. Please let me now choose you over my own career."

I often reflect on that time in our marriage. Without a willingness on both our parts to choose our relationship over our careers, our marriage might not have survived. Our careers were already trying to take priority over our marriage. Now a new precedent was set. Our marriage and family would remain our first choice for the rest of our lives.

Barry: Leo also had a profound influence on me at this time of accelerated growth. One night, I had a powerful dream. I was standing in a dark room, aware of many others in the room but couldn't see anyone. Leo was in the middle of the room, standing at some kind of altar. He seemed to be focused on trying to do something. Finally, a small, pleasingly warm, glowing light appeared on the altar. It was slowly growing in intensity, and then suddenly exploded into a blinding white light. It was terrifying! I let out a loud scream and jumped up in bed, waking and scaring Joyce in the process.

It was my first dream of the power of the light ... the "Great White Light" spoken about in many spiritual traditions ... and I wasn't spiritually ready for the experience, so it overwhelmed me.

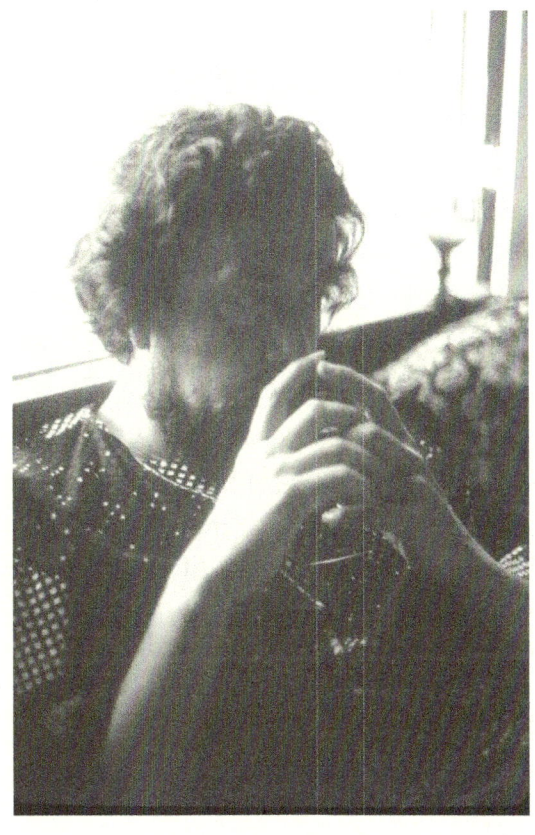

Several days later, Leo visited us at our apartment. I told him about the dream. He suddenly sat upright, eyes open wide. He excitedly spoke, "This is incredible! This has never happened to me before. Three nights in a row, I dreamed that I was standing at the same altar, in the same dark room, kindling a small light. I was feeling somewhat sad that no one seemed to be able to see it."

We quickly pieced it together. The third and final night of his dream was the night I had mine. Now, he knew his work had not been in vain.

The three of us sat there entranced with one another, letting the meaning of the dream sink in. We were deeply moved by the profound connection we had. We felt the sacred privilege that was ours in sharing this Light.

Chapter 15: Portland 1972

Barry: Joyce and I moved to Portland, Oregon in the summer of 1972, where I started my internship combined with a psychiatry residency at the University of Oregon Medical Center. I often worked seventy-hour weeks. I must admit, I was so deeply absorbed in taking care of seriously disturbed mental patients, that I wasn't taking enough care of my own soul. And I certainly wasn't taking care of my relationship with Joyce. I remember many days coming home late, feeling so burned out that I could manage only a brief hug. I headed for the hills to walk among the stately Douglas fir trees that seemed to absorb my stresses. To this day, often, when I walk by a Douglas fir tree, I still pick a small clump of needles, crush them, and smell the sappy fragrance that always reminds me of those walks in the forested hills northwest of Portland.

Even with the powerful lessons learned in Los Angeles, I still wasn't very good at asking for the love I needed from Joyce. I wasn't very good at even feeling my need for it. If I would have let her, she could have soothed me far more than the trees could have. Instead, I took her and the relationship for granted. We were drifting apart, our love getting buried once again.

It took Joyce's leaving me in LA to teach me about the little boy inside of me who needed love, the very human part of me I had been trying so hard to bury in the darkness of my soul. I learned that it was indeed okay to give this inner child permission to need love and to ask for it in healthy ways, to recognize my need for human love as just another manifestation of my need for spiritual sustenance. It was a time of major awakening for me, and I felt that, from then on, I would be free of the stubborn false sense of independence that burdened my soul, and led me to betray Joyce in the first place.

But this awakening needed time for integration, to fully become a part of my life. Instead, I was losing myself while taking care of so many others' serious needs. My inner child was steadily slipping back into hiding.

I particularly remember a hospitalized borderline patient named Joan, who was the same age as me. Borderline Personality Disorder can be a serious mental illness. Joan had a very fragile ego, was prone to "cutting" herself with a razor, and became totally dependent on me, not just as a psychiatry resident, but as a person ... and a man. She was perhaps my most difficult patient. She kept wanting more and more from me and, when I said no, she couldn't accept it. I felt exhausted every time I was with her. Joan, and other patients like her, seemed to suck most of the lifeforce out of me, leaving very little for Joyce.

One Saturday morning that I happened to be home, I had an experience that evaporated the distance between Joyce and me. We had hardly connected that morning. Joyce was up long before me. By the time I got up and dragged my exhausted body from the bed, she had meditated, eaten breakfast, and was preparing to leave to do some errands in Portland. All I could manage was a feeble, "Good morning," as she headed for the door.

Suddenly, Joyce stopped, turned around and came back to me. She threw her arms around my neck and pressed her body close to mine. She seemed to be holding on to me in a way that she hadn't in a while. It felt good. I felt how much I was missing our closeness. She pulled away slightly so she could look into my eyes.

"Barry," she said with that unmistakable tone of the little girl who was needing love and, unlike me, was willing to ask for and receive it, "I need you so much. Can we be together this afternoon?"

"Sure," I said, feeling slightly more alive in my still tired body.

Joyce smiled. I've always loved her smile. It seemed to light up my day more than the sun, which was seldom seen in these gray Pacific Northwest days.

Then she was gone out the door. "Drive carefully," I called after her. That was silly. She always drives carefully. I hadn't said that in a long time. Oh well, I thought, it's always good advice.

I made myself a cup of tea and went into the spare bedroom we had made into a sanctuary. There were flowers on the little table. Joyce has always loved flowers. I sat on my favorite cushion and closed my eyes. Meditation seemed to come so naturally to Joyce. For me, it was a different matter. While Joyce was attracted to a devotional approach, often feeling God as a loving Mother or Father, I preferred aiming for stillness, following my breathing as a way of quieting my mind. God, to me, was that rare and somewhat elusive feeling of deep peace.

This morning, my mind seemed to be on a racetrack. My thoughts were chaotic, not making sense at all. I remember thinking that perhaps I was spending too much time with psychotic patients, and their minds were having an effect upon me.

I brought myself back to my breathing, trying yet once more to quiet my mind. Abruptly, I had the image of Joyce in a head-on car collision. It was an awful sight, with twisted metal and blood.

Now, I'm really crazy, I thought, and tried to get the image out of my head. But it wouldn't leave. I tried focusing more intently on my breathing, in a desperate attempt to erase the vision, but without success. I said to myself, in a rare moment of surrender to what is happening, okay, Barry, just flow with it. Don't fight it. I gave in to the images...

Joyce: When I left home that morning, I wondered why Barry had said, "Drive safely." I hoped it wasn't some kind of premonition. I was driving through the hills on small two-lane country roads, while listening to my favorite music cassette on the stereo. At the same time, I was trying to decide how I wanted to spend the rest of the day with Barry. As I rounded a corner in the road, and started along a straight stretch, I saw a car speeding toward me in the distance. As it came into clearer view, I saw to my horror that the car was in my lane. It was heading right for me ... and coming fast!

Barry: I don't know that I ever made a decision like this before, to simply let such a disturbing image run its course through my meditation, rather than resist or simply change it. I surrendered to each scene in my mind and felt my feelings throughout.

An ambulance arrived onto the scene of the crash. Paramedics struggled to extract Joyce's limp body from the wreckage. I knew she was dead even before they did, even though I hoped beyond hope that her lifeless body would somehow gasp for breath. But it didn't. She was gone.

In the next scene, I was called by the police and informed of the news. The whole thing seemed so real, not just the rantings of a crazed mind. Too real! There were real tears in my eyes. How could this have happened to us? We had so much living to do, so much we still wanted to do together, so much love to be experienced. I felt robbed.

I saw myself calling family and friends, telling them the horrible news. With each person, I found myself reliving the awful feelings of shock and sadness. Our parents, our siblings, our best friends, each responding first with disbelief, then sometimes wild expressions of grief. It was, in fact, my worst nightmare coming into full view.

Joyce: I realized the car was heading straight for me. As my foot hit the brakes, I knew it was too late. There was no way I could stop before the oncoming car hit. Besides, even if I stopped, the other car seemed to actually be accelerating. In the split second before impact, I thought of turning off the road but saw the road drop off down the hill. I held tightly onto the steering wheel, pressed hard on the brakes, and braced myself for the crash…

Barry: My next image was a memorial service. While each person spoke their love for Joyce, I sat growing in loneliness. What was I going to do without my beloved Joyce? My psychiatry training seemed to have so little meaning for me. Living out here in the country was something we wanted to do together. Our plans of travel were dashed to pieces. I was deeply missing holding Joyce in my arms. I was aching to gaze into her smiling face just one more time.

Soon, everyone was gone. After all, they had their own lives to live. I was alone … utterly alone. More alone than I'd ever been before. The feeling was oppressive, stifling.

I was angry. Yes, I was angry with God for taking Joyce away from me, my beloved wife so young and vibrant with life. It seemed so unfair, so heartless and cruel.

The anger was short-lived. Underneath the anger was profound grief, and under the grief was fear for my own future. How could I go on without Joyce? Would I go on without her?

It was in the next moment that two very powerful things happened. First, I heard Joyce's voice. It seemed to be coming from a distant place but, as I listened, it came closer. *"Barry,"* the voice said, *"Where could I have gone? I haven't once left your side. I'm now more a part of you than ever. In love, we're eternally joined."*

Of course, I thought, feeling myself waking up as from a bad dream. Joyce has always been such a deep part of me, and is now even more so. It felt like a shaft of light penetrated the blackness of my loneliness. I need never feel alone again. It was a moment of clear spiritual truth.

A second thing happened. I remembered that all this was just happening in my mind, that I was sitting on my meditation cushion in our spare bedroom. The images were so real they had swept me away into another reality.

Waking up more fully, I felt a burst of joy that Joyce was still alive. We still had our lives to live together, a whole world of experiences and adventures that would deepen our love. How could I ever take this woman and this love for granted again? I resolved inside myself to remember this experience so I would never make anything else more important than love. I would always remember that Joyce and I are united in our hearts. And I knew without a doubt that it was safe for the little boy inside me to ask for and receive love from her, from the infinite source of that love, and from everyone.

When I opened my eyes, the flowers on the altar were once again a display of Joyce's living presence in my life.

Joyce: In the moment before impact, I could now see a group of wild teenage boys in the car ahead. In the last possible moment, the driver swerved and narrowly missed hitting me. They were playing a dangerous game of "chicken," seeing how close they could come without hitting me. They were seeking thrills.

I came to a complete stop, leaned on the steering wheel and burst into tears. I felt badly shaken. It was perhaps twenty or thirty minutes before I felt capable of driving again. Even though my body was trembling out of control, I managed to turn the car around and slowly drive home.

Barry: When I heard the car pull into our driveway, I felt elated. I ran out to greet a still-shaken Joyce. She ran to greet me. We held each other a long time. Through her tears, she told me what had happened and how scared she felt. I looked deeply into her eyes and said, "Joyce, our love is the most important thing in the whole world to me. I hope I never again take this love for granted. Please know that I always need your love."

Her smile said more than any words could have in that moment.

That Saturday morning's experience changed everything. Even being with my patient, Joan, Monday morning felt different. Joining deeply with Joyce had made me stronger. I was able to set loving but firm boundaries with Joan and all my patients.

Hiding Our Closeness

Also, during that year in Portland, Joyce and I were getting more and more negative feedback about our closeness. It seemed like everyone, family, friends, and colleagues, thought they were helping us by criticizing our bond. Some viewed our closeness as codependence. Others were offended by how affectionate we were with each other. Typical comments were:

"You're smothering each other."

"You both need to spend more time apart."

Or the metaphor:

"You're like two trees trying to grow in each other's shade."

One friend of Joyce's blurted out, "You're giving too much to Barry. It's like you're putting all your eggs in one basket. Someday he's going to die and then you'll lose everything!"

This last angry comment hurt Joyce the most. It also ended her friendship with this woman.

And the result of all this criticism? We started to hide our closeness from others. We'd arrive for work together some days at the medical center. Joyce had a job training pediatric residents to interview children. From the car to the elevator, we didn't even hold hands. We'd stand together waiting for the elevator, but not too close to one another. The elevator doors would open, and we'd walk in. If we were alone, a slight smile would barely be noticeable on our faces as the doors closed.

As if the doors touching one another gave us permission to do likewise, we'd fall into an intimate embrace, kissing and touching, until the bell rang at our destination. That was our warning that the doors were about to open. Quickly, we'd separate, straighten our clothes if we needed to, and when the doors opened, we'd look like two "proper professionals," even though there might be somewhat of a bulge in my pants.

However, despite our passionate attraction, we could not help the doubt that was creeping in to our minds as the months passed. What if everyone was right, and our closeness was keeping us from growing? What if we were unaware of the possible damage we were causing one another?

In the beginning of that first year of my psychiatry residency, there were many humanistic elements. This is what initially attracted me to this program. My fellow residents and their spouses participated in psychodrama groups, doing deep personal growth work. We all had the opportunity to share our deepest vulnerability. One resident told the group about coming home from school as a child, walking into the garage, and seeing his father hanging by a rope from a rafter. While he convulsed with sobs, we all held him in our love.

Soon it was my turn. I was truly vulnerability-challenged. I showed no vulnerability, no fear, no pain. Instead, I presented myself with a smile on my face and peace in my life. Some of the residents were gentle and compassionate in their probing for my depth. Yet my smiling mask never faltered. Looking back at my level of emotional immaturity, it's embarrassing to me now.

In that workshop, one by one, all the residents came around me and began confronting me. Each, in their own way, asked me to be more genuine and honest with all my feelings.

One resident asked, "How can I feel close to you if you're pretending to be happy all the time?"

Another said, "It looks like you're hiding behind a mask."

And yet another blurted out angrily, "It's pissing me off how phony you're being right now!"

Remember, this was 1972, and Encounter Groups could be brutal.

This last comment reminded me of what Leo Buscaglia had said to me. I had obviously backslid from my growth in Los Angeles. I had not learned the lesson of vulnerability fully enough.

Still, I remained frozen in my phony happiness. I just was not able to access my vulnerable feelings.

So the confrontation escalated. Some of the residents were angry at my apparent resistance. I was sitting on the floor while all ten residents stood above me. I felt real compassion coming from some of them, impatience and outright anger from others.

Finally, something broke inside me. I just wasn't strong enough to withstand the mixed barrage of love and anger. I started crying ... then sobbing. I had flashes of being a little boy and not wanting my tormentors in the tough neighborhood in Brooklyn to know that I was scared and hurt. I learned that, if I showed my sensitivity and fear, I'd get attacked. I learned to show the world how strong I was. I learned that my vulnerability couldn't be trusted with anyone else. It was me against the world.

In that moment of the workshop, I felt completely vulnerable with ten psychiatry residents. Now they could pounce on me and finish me off. I was defenseless.

A COUPLE OF MIRACLES

That didn't happen. When I opened my eyes, I saw the gentlest, most caring faces looking down at me. I saw loving fathers, mothers, siblings and friends. I heard gentle compassion in their words. I felt accepted ... and acceptable. It was a moment of "coming-out" as a sensitive, vulnerable human being.

It was also a turning point in my life. From that moment on, I knew my spiritual and human growth depended on my opening to all my feelings. I have accepted this work as essential. I'm far from perfect at identifying my feelings. It's hard work. Sometimes, when I need Joyce's love, I push her away instead. It's such an old habit. Sometimes, when I feel hurt, I still rationalize and talk myself out of the feeling. I do recognize that, because I am committed to feeling all my feelings, I am becoming a better counselor, teacher, husband, father ... and person.

About halfway through that first year, a new head of psychiatry came aboard, and completely changed the direction of the department. In one fell swoop, all the humanistic programs were thrown out. Instead, the focus became physical and medical. Drugs replaced psychotherapy and group therapy.

ECT (Electroconvulsive Therapy) became popular. Basically, it involved "shocking" the patient's body with an electric current to produce a Grand Mal epileptic seizure. After the seizure, the patient experienced memory loss and tranquility. However, the benefits were always temporary. To me, it felt like a medieval torture. Each time I performed this "therapy" on patients, and watched as the patient's body, even though strapped down, still bounced around on the table, I felt heartbroken.

I was becoming seriously disillusioned with my psychiatry training. I grew increasingly unhappy. I knew more and more that this was not the work I was meant to do in this life.

Sometimes in life, guidance appears in the most unusual forms. But when it does come, and you are open to it, it can dramatically change the course of your life. In my case, at that unhappy time in my life and career, divine guidance arrived in the form of a movie.

One evening, hoping to cheer me up, Joyce looked in the newspaper and found a movie that looked interesting, *Brother Sun, Sister Moon*. The movie was about the early life of Saint Francis of Assisi, made by the famous director, Franco Zeffirelli, with original songs by Donovan.

Neither one of us anticipated that a single movie would shatter especially my whole world. Never before or since have I been so affected by a movie. Looking back, I now realize I received in that movie a profound blessing from Saint Francis.

I walked, or rather, staggered (I felt almost drunk with the spirit of Saint Francis) out of the theater. I took Joyce's hands and pronounced with utmost sincerity, "Let's live just like St. Francis. Let's give away everything we own. Let's go begging house to house. I'm done with psychiatry!"

Joyce was also deeply inspired by the movie, but was a bit more practical than I was. She said, "Barry, if you leave now, you wouldn't be able to get your medical license. You've worked too hard all these years to just throw it away right now. At least finish the year, only a few more months. Then you'll complete the requirement for your license and be able to practice medicine or psychiatry just the way you want."

Her words sobered me, and I realized she was right. I needed to be a bit more practical and finish out the year. But the spirit of Saint Francis has stayed with me all these years, so much so that we started bringing groups to Assisi, Italy, each fall. And each time, we again immerse ourselves in Francis's life and teachings, especially the spirit of simplicity and joy.

We also discovered Sufi Dancing, which put sacred phrases from all religions to music and added simple movements. Originally founded by Murshid Samuel Lewis in San Francisco at the height of the hippie era, he got many young people off drugs by getting them high naturally. Now called Dances of Universal Peace, it was like singing mantras while you ceremonially progressed from person to person around a circle. There was often a guitarist and drummer in the center of the circle, enhancing the trance-like effect.

It was my weekly saving grace, an evening in the middle of a very stressful week that became a sort of spiritual infusion. Typically, the next day back at the medical center, my fellow residents and even the instructors would ask me why I seemed so happy (and this time, they trusted my happiness!). I told them about Sufi Dancing.

The next week, Joyce and I would show up to the dance meeting and find a few of my colleagues or instructors there. At the end of the meeting, they would come up to me and say, "I don't get it. I don't feel any different than when I got here." As if Sufi Dancing were some kind of pill that would make you feel better or different. My colleagues didn't understand the state of receptivity that was required for a truly spiritual experience.

Joyce: Barry did make the radical decision to quit his residency after the first year. No one did this!! Doctors usually opted for more training, but never quit after one year. He was strongly advised not to do this, but he was determined. Completing the first year would, however, count as an internship and would allow Barry to take the National Board Exam and get his license as a medical doctor. I also was hesitant about Barry's decision, but he was so strong in his determination that I supported him completely, even though I had difficulty understanding why he couldn't finish the final two years. As it turned out, Barry was absolutely right in his decision and neither one of us have ever regretted it.

So he left The University of Oregon Medical Center in July, 1973, and we moved to Rhododendron, Oregon, a town with a single general store, on the western slopes of Mt. Hood. Our stay there was idyllic in a beautiful wooden cabin right on a raging Zigzag Creek, carrying snowmelt down from the glaciers on the mountain. The tiny bedroom of the cabin had a window facing the creek, so we slept to the heavenly sound of cascading water.

Barry: We heard about an upcoming ten-day Vipassana (Buddhist meditation) retreat outside of Portland. We signed up immediately, not knowing a thing about it. We had been practicing Transcendental Meditation for twenty minutes twice daily, since being initiated the year before in Los Angeles. We were simply not prepared for the extremity of this course, where we alternately sat for one hour, then practiced a walking meditation, all day long except for short breaks for meals, and the whole time in complete silence.

The first seven days were torture. It seemed like every part of my body and mind took turns aching. I often asked myself why I was there. Each evening, back in our VW van, Joyce and I broke the rule of silence, and shared our misery with one another. Okay, we also broke another rule, we were physically intimate, which we desperately needed. It was the only pleasure in our bodies during that first week.

Now, these Vipassana retreats are gentler. Teachers have realized that the same or even better results can be achieved without such strict austerity. The course we attended was one of the first courses taught in America. They hadn't yet learned how to adapt to American students.

By the eighth day, everything changed. Perhaps I let go of what I thought should be happening. I stopped resisting. I felt joy. I felt peace. The meditation became almost effortless, each hour passing as if it was minutes. I was able to sit still without pain. Now, I didn't want the retreat to end.

Chapter 16: Mexico 1973

Joyce: November came and it rained steadily for the entire month. It seemed we were constantly wet and cold. We ran out of firewood, and the cabin began to smell moldy.

We decided it was time to leave Oregon and our wet, moldy, cold cabin, and head south in our blue VW hippie van. We put all our belongings in storage and packed very little into the van. Our first dog, Bokie, of course would come with us. Barry was excited and happy, as he has always loved adventures. My mood shifted to concern. Would I really like being away from an actual physical home for several months (which turned into a year)?

The day before we were to move out of our little mountain cabin, we went for one last walk on the slopes of Mt. Hood. I felt an ache in my heart, as I am a Taurus homebody and really enjoy a physical home.

When we returned to the cabin, we noticed someone had placed a small unusual photo of Paramahansa Yogananda on the door. Who could have put that photo on our door? We lived so isolated from all our friends in Portland. And which of our friends even knew who Yogananda was? We had heard the name, and someone had long ago given us a copy of his book, *The Autobiography of a Yogi*.

When I took the photo off our door, the ache that had been in my heart suddenly went away. Holding the photo, I told Barry that I felt better. He ran in the house and located Yogananda's book. We both decided that the book must come with us, even though we had both decided to bring very few books. For some reason, I felt guided to bring my childhood

bible. Barry had installed a set of drawers in our van, and I placed the bible in the top drawer, with all our cash hidden inside. Out of curiosity, I sat down later with The Autobiography of a Yogi, and carefully looked for the photo that was given to us. There were many other photos of Yogananda in the book, but not this one. "How odd," I thought.

Barry: While traveling south through Mexico, Joyce and I stopped at an outdoor market in a little village and bumped into William, a man we had previously met in Portland. William came across as an authority on everything, something that should have been a red flag to us. Standing there in the market, he told us the best places to travel in Mexico, the best foods to find, and finally, he reached into his pack and showed us the "best LSD you could ever get." We weren't sure we could trust William, but when he offered it to us as a gift, we let go of our suspicions and accepted the drug from him. Then we parted ways.

We had only taken LSD a few times before, given to us by people we completely trusted, faculty at my medical school and my residency training. Each time, it was research-grade LSD made by Sandoz Pharmaceuticals. Hey, it was the seventies, a time of exploration into the nature of consciousness.

Meanwhile, in this marketplace, William raved about a certain home-made cheese, which he pointed out to us. We bought some and ate it.

Sure enough, the next day we got sick with Dysentery. Frantic for a place to stay that wasn't camping, we found a small hotel. We asked for their quietest room, and were given a room that opened onto a courtyard. Minutes after we moved in, a band set up right outside our door, and began playing loud Mexican music.

By the time the music began, we were both too sick to even notice. Our temperatures skyrocketed, and the diarrhea was worse than we have ever had. At one point, I became delirious, and Joyce dragged me along the floor into the bathroom, then into the shower, and turned on the cold water to revive me. Thankfully, we had brought some Tetracycline with us on the trip, which eventually brought us back to the land of the living. I can't even begin to describe the mess we left behind in that hotel room.

Weeks later, we were staying in a little village on the Pacific coast north of Puerto Vallarta named, of all things, San Francisco. Most of the village had poverty conditions, with families living in tiny huts with dirt floors. (We have since learned that this is now a very expensive area because of its beauty.) In stark contrast to the poverty of the village, on the end of a peninsula on a hill, there was a wealthy estate. We found a place to camp right on the ocean just north of the village on a primitive dirt track, and we stayed surrounded by incredible beauty.

The children from the village were attracted to us whenever we were on the beach. More than us, they were attracted to Bokie. They had perhaps seen other gringos like us, but they had never seen a dog like Bokie. The dogs of the village were scrawny and small, always underfed, and had to rely on scavenging whatever scraps of food they could find. Bokie, on the other hand, was a large, beautiful golden retriever. It wasn't just his looks that attracted the children. It was his very unusual passion for rocks that had them all wide-eyed. He'd find a rock, place it on the sand, and begin digging in front of it. As he dug, the rock fell into the hole, and he'd dig some more. The process would continue until Bokie was actually out of sight, in a crater bigger than him, while the children roared with laughter all around the cavernous crater.

One day, while walking on the beach, we met a slightly older man who spoke flawless English. We got to talking and, when he found out I was a medical doctor, he invited us to his house, the wealthy estate on the hill. He wanted us to meet his friend, who was also a medical doctor. Our acquaintance turned out to be the son-in-law of the president of Mexico, and an important person himself.

We spent the afternoon visiting with him and his doctor friend in his extravagant home. We walked along the beach where he brought us to his secluded "bungalow" and, when he saw our delighted response (it was magnificent!), he invited us to stay there a few days. It was quite an upgrade from our VW van!

While there, we remembered the LSD and decided to try it, but we needed someplace much more secluded than the bungalow or the village of San Francisco. We hiked on a primitive trail through the jungle, north along the coast and finally found a tiny beach where we could be alone. It was not easy to get down to the beach. There was no trail, just a steep hillside covered with thick vegetation. Once we got down to the beach, we were totally alone.

We stripped off our clothes in the warm sunshine.

We sat on the sand listening to the sounds of the ocean.

We took the LSD.

About an hour later, the drug started to take effect. It seemed to be many times stronger than anything I had ever taken before. I felt like I was being catapulted into vast realms of light and, looking around, saw the divine essence within everything my eyes touched. The word "high" took on a whole new level of meaning. I gasped at the splendor of the universe!

I looked at Joyce, and it felt like she took off a mask she had been wearing all the years I knew her. Behind that mask was the most gorgeous being I could ever imagine. Light infused every part of her face and body. She was still Joyce, but just a thousand percent more. I felt myself looking into the eyes of a heavenly goddess.

Everything started going much too fast! I wanted to savor each miraculous moment but, instead, I felt like an out-of-control truck, careening down a hill without brakes! It didn't feel like the pure LSD I had taken before. I felt the presence of some other substance added to the LSD.

It seemed that at the apex of my euphoria, something started to shift in my mind. It was like I had touched the highest heaven, but hadn't earned the right to be there. I was now being thrown out of the "wedding feast." It started with the thought, "What if this was not LSD? What if this was some kind of poison instead?"

I thought about the person who had given us this LSD, William. We certainly couldn't trust him, especially after recommending the local cheese that got us so sick.

I turned to Joyce, who was obviously deep in her own trip, and felt I needed to warn her. "Joyce, I think we just took poison!"

She had trouble shifting gears from her state of reality to mine. She wasn't comprehending what was the beginning of my descent into a "bad trip."

I looked at our full water bottle and took another step into paranoia. I blurted out, "It's possible our water may have been poisoned, too."

Before Joyce could respond, I opened the bottle and dumped it onto the ground.

"Barry, what are you doing? That's our only water!"

But I was already on to the next thing. I picked up an orange, the only item of food we had packed for the day. I started studying it for needle holes, suspecting someone may have injected our orange with more poison. It was obvious that I was going off the deep end.

Again, without notice, I threw the orange far into the ocean waves.

Now Joyce was starting to worry, but she was also tripping and was having a hard time focusing on my sad state of affairs.

I was getting desperate. Now I felt convinced that I had been poisoned. Actually, you could say that I was, but it was a psychedelic, not a physical, poisoning. In my altered state, I couldn't make that distinction.

I spoke with urgency, "I need to swim for help." I thought perhaps I could swim out into the ocean and stop a ship for help. I didn't seem to care about the immense size of the waves crashing onto the beach. And I didn't seem to understand that it would be a suicide mission. There was no way I could survive for long out in the ocean, let alone be seen by an ocean-going vessel.

Hearing my crazy plan immediately mobilized Joyce into action. With superhuman effort, she somehow threw off the effects of the LSD, and whatever else was combined with it, in her own system. I don't know how she did it, but she shut down her own trip. Perhaps it was the energy of the mother within her because, in that instant, she focused one hundred percent on me.

As I stood up to head for the waves, she grabbed me and said firmly, "I won't let you risk your life like that! Please stay here with me. We've not been poisoned."

I looked into the eyes of my beloved, eyes that had always been a refuge for me. And suddenly I lost my trust for Joyce. In my deepening paranoia, I felt that Joyce did not understand the gravity of the situation.

I broke away from her, a new plan in mind. I started scrambling up the steep cliff that had taken us forever to get down. As I climbed, I shouted out, "I'm going for help in the village."

There were a few problems with this plan. First of all, both of us were completely naked. And second, a crazy naked man running into a Mexican village screaming for help would probably not get the kind of attention he wanted. He would instead most likely get arrested.

The owner of the apartment we rented when we lived in Los Angeles, a police chief, told us the story of his son, who had been arrested in Mexico while tripping on some psychedelic drug. Even as a police chief, it took him six months, and a whole lot of money, to get his son out of the Mexican jail.

Joyce, who was now on hyper-alert, took off after me up the cliff, with our golden retriever, Bokie, close behind. I got to the top of the cliff and launched myself into the jungle. I also launched myself into the middle of a bush with one-inch thorns. I was pierced in multiple places and trapped completely. Bleeding, feeling no pain, and unable to move, Joyce caught up with me and carefully, branch by branch, freed me from my trap.

In a moment of submission, I let her lead me back down the cliff to the beach. I hadn't yet formulated my next brilliant plan. Before I could, however, Joyce gently took my hands in hers and spoke with compassion, "Barry, remember your patient, Allen, during your residency?"

I nodded that I did.

"Remember that he took a psychedelic drug and it messed up his mind for weeks?"

Allen was eighteen years old, a very sweet kid, but trapped in a complete psychotic nightmare. I developed a deep bond with him, and helped him out of his psychotic state.

"Barry, please think about it. Couldn't the same thing be happening to you?"

I thought about it, and it was just like a switch suddenly turned on. One moment, I was psychotic and paranoid, and the next, I felt clear as a bell.

I looked at Joyce and saw her awareness and compassion. She was instantly transformed back into my beloved wife once more.

"You're right, Joyce. I'm so sorry. I'm back now."

And I collapsed in her arms. My ordeal was over. Just like that!

These psychedelic-induced psychoses don't always end well. One week before writing this, a gentle and well-loved teen a few miles from where we live, took LSD that was evidently mixed with some other drugs. He flipped out and stabbed his father and uncle, but not fatally. A family member called 911. The police arrived and ordered him to drop the knife. He refused, so they tasered him, but still couldn't get the knife away. They even released a trained police dog that grabbed the boy's knife-holding hand. Even that failed, so they ended up shooting and killing him. It was a real tragedy, as well as a horrible police failure.

Now, looking back on my own psychedelic-induced psychosis, I realize that this experience has given me so much more compassion and understanding for mental illness. I received a rare inside view of the fragility of the human mind. Not that I would wish this upon them, but if more mental health professionals had the kind of direct experience that I had, there would be a whole lot more compassion and empathy in the field.

That was the last time either one of us has used psychedelic drugs. We vastly prefer feeling love and gratitude in our natural state. We're very happy and at peace without the added rocket fuel.

Joyce: Even though this area on the Mexican coast was beautiful, we did not feel safe. We heard many stories. One person told us about a couple who were sleeping in a truck camper while a burglar broke into their truck, hot-wired the engine to start it, and drove off while the frantic couple in the camper on the truck scrambled out of their bed to find out what was happening.

Since we didn't own a credit card at the time, we had brought cash with us that we kept in a bible in the top drawer of a dresser that we installed in the van.

One day, we went for a long walk and returned to find our front windshield broken. A log, the obvious tool of entry, was still hanging halfway out, making our van look a little like a monstrous unicorn. The thief had tried to open the top drawer of the dresser, but the hardbound cover of the bible got wedged and prevented the drawer from opening. Finding nothing of value elsewhere in our bus, the thief left.

Barry quickly figured out a way to open the drawer, and there was my childhood bible, still holding all of our cash, along with our passports and other important documents.

This message of the bible saving our valuables was not lost on us. We went into the nearest city, Tepic, to get the windshield fixed. While driving there, we decided to spend the rest of our time in Mexico in a deeply spiritual way. And thus, we began not only reading the bible but also *The Autobiography of a Yogi*.

Once we started reading Yogananda's classic book, we could not put it down. We read it out loud to each other, and would only allow ourselves to read just a few chapters a day. Throughout the day, we talked about the chapters we had read that morning. And at night, we read them again. We became filled with the desire to receive the Kriya Yoga meditation technique that was described in the book. It was sad for us to finally finish the book. I think I have never enjoyed a book more in my life than that one.

As much as we were enjoying the sublime beauty of the ocean, waterfalls and lush tropical jungle, and reading about Yogananda, we were also at times afraid. Someone, perhaps the same thief that had broken our windshield, was stalking us. We could feel it every single night. Our golden retriever, Bokie, also seemed to be on edge. We wanted to go back to the United States, even though we had planned to stay much longer. We left Mexico, after six weeks, with a grateful heart and also the deepest desire to receive the Kriya Yoga initiation.

Chapter 17: Kern River Miracle

B**arry:** As soon as we entered California, Joyce and I drove right to Encinitas, the home of The Self Realization Fellowship that was founded by Yogananda, and now houses the members who carry on his teachings and give initiations. We spoke with a woman who was very kind, but she told us it would take us at least two years to receive the initiation, and maybe longer as we needed to take lessons and even pass examinations. We were also told that we needed a permanent address as the lessons were mailed each week for a fee. We were heartbroken as we left.

We headed north from Encinitas. We spent a week visiting relatives and friends in Los Angeles, where we were hit with the inevitable, "Where are you going to live?" Their well-meaning question triggered a place of deep sadness, especially in Joyce. Although my Gemini nature allowed me to feel more content on the road, Joyce's Taurus nature longed for a physical home, a place to put roots down.

We continued north. Once on the road, I glanced over at Joyce in the passenger seat. She was quietly crying.

I probed gently, "What's going on, Sweetie?"

She took a minute, then said, "I'm so tired of all the traveling. It's been eight months. I'm not like you. I need a home."

"I understand," I said, "How about we head up into the Sierras for the night and talk about where we want to go?"

I thought gaining altitude might offer us a better perspective for the next step of our journey.

Joyce managed a feeble "Okay."

I saw a sign announcing the Kern River Highway, and exited. Soon we were winding up the foothills, closely following the river. I glanced over and saw that Joyce was crying harder now, and I felt it was time to stop. I turned into a picnic area and parked the van.

I leaned over and held Joyce, and tried to comfort her as she sobbed the words, "I feel so far away from home. Please, Barry, I just want a home."

We sat there a long time in the lengthening afternoon shadows, Joyce alternating between crying and praying for guidance. I felt helpless in my attempts to reassure her that it would all work out somehow, but I kept trying.

Finally, she said, "Please, Barry, stop trying to fix me. Just be with me and hold me.

That I could do, even though I am a man.

After a while, I insisted we go for a walk. We left the van and proceeded down a path to the river. Joyce found a rock she could sit on right at the river's edge, where she could be alone with her feelings. Sitting by a river, watching the sunlight sparkle on the moving water, is one of her favorite things to do.

I wandered upstream a few hundred feet along a path through the sycamore trees. Walking in the woods has always helped me. I must have been looking at the ground, avoiding roots and rocks, for I didn't notice it until I was within a few feet. There, directly in front of me, carved on a sycamore at about eye level, in big bold letters enclosed within a heart, were the words, **"JOYCE, HOME IS JUST A FEELING."**

At first, I couldn't believe my eyes. In a trance, I walked over to the tree to touch the carving, to make sure it was actually there. No, it wasn't a hallucination. My fingers traced the carved letters.

I looked around in amazement. My mind was racing. Could this be some strange practical joke? Could one of our friends from LA have raced up here ahead of us, anticipate the picnic area we would stop at, then dash into the trees to madly carve the message? They would have had to use power tools to carve it so quickly. And psychic tools to know which picnic area and which tree I would see.

Come on, Barry, you're getting a bit paranoid. I turned around in a complete circle, waiting for someone to jump out of the trees and yell, "Surprise!" But there was not a soul around.

I looked again at the strange carving. It would have been much easier for me if the carver had omitted the name Joyce. The generic message, "home is just a feeling," would have been enough. But no, the impact had to be very personal!

My legs felt strangely wobbly, and I really don't remember if I was laughing or crying as I ran to get Joyce. By the time I reached her, she had settled into a peaceful meditation, and seemed at first a bit annoyed at my excited intrusion. She got scared. "Barry, you look like you've just seen a ghost. What happened?"

I could barely speak as I reached out, took her hands, and helped her stand up. "Joyce, you won't believe this. Come with me."

As I guided her along the trail, she kept asking, "What is it? What's going on, Barry?"

"Just wait."

Along the way, my mind started questioning everything. What if we get back to the tree and nothing's there? What if I dreamed this whole thing? Or what if the carving was made by non-human hands, meant only for me to see one time, then it would disappear? In Mexico, we had entered the world of Yogananda where the miraculous was commonplace.

All these thoughts simply evaporated as we approached the tree and I saw that the carving was indeed still there.

It took Joyce a moment to register the carving but, when she did, she became transfixed. We stood there a long time, glancing at the tree, then one another, then back to the tree. We thanked God for this obvious, and miraculous, message just for my beloved wife.

Had not Joyce seen the carving as well, I could've had trouble trusting my senses. I've hardly ever seen carvings on a tree much different than "John loves Mary" or "Frank was here." This message was so intimately personal and relevant. I had my camera in the van, but it almost seemed sacrilegious to record this miracle on film. Our hearts had been permanently imprinted with the truth of this divine message. It really didn't matter whether the carving was done by human hands or was materialized just for us. It mattered only that a Higher Power led us to this tree, and is leading us still.

Since that moment on the Kern River, we have been in the process of looking within for the feeling of home. We would, of course, find a series of physical homes leading up to where we now live, but where we physically live is becoming less and less important. How wonderful to remember that divine signpost, arriving just when we needed it, that our true home, our spiritual home, is a feeling available to us at any time and place.

Chapter 18: Initiated by John Lawrence

Joyce: After reading the *Autobiography of a Yogi,* our desire to receive the Kriya Initiation was so strong we could hardly think of anything else. We drove north to San Francisco and, while we were in a natural food market, we got talking to a man about our time in Mexico and how we had read *The Autobiography of a Yogi.* The man said to us, "I know the Reverend John Lawrence. He is a direct disciple of Yogananda and he gives the Kriya initiation." And right there in the market as we were buying lettuce, this man handed us John's phone number.

We ran to a pay phone (remember, no cell phones yet) and called Rev. Lawrence who answered on the first ring. We explained our desire to receive the initiation for the Kriya meditation described in the book.

"Come right over. Maybe I can help you," he lovingly responded. It all seemed so quick. We arrived at the address, walked up a flight of stairs to the front door, and knocked.

A round little man, perhaps in his sixties, dressed all in black with dyed black hair and a merry face, answered the door. The way he looked, we assumed he was the butler.

"Excuse us, but is the Reverend John Lawrence here?"

This man replied, "Yes, you're in luck. He is here, and I am he."

So much for appearances.

We thought of all the various teachers we had met. Most were good and helpful to our spiritual growth. A few were not. If someone knew of a spiritual teacher, we just went, no questions asked. There was no Google to research that particular teacher.

Once, while we were in Boston, someone told us about an "enlightened master" named Karmu. Evidently, he was a car mechanic who someone proclaimed to be a guru. We went and found an elderly dark-skinned man, dressed in a mechanic's coveralls, surrounded by a group of young hippies, singing kirtan (sacred chants). We actually don't remember a word of what he said. While the singing went on, and it was lovely, Karmu appeared to be sleeping. We left unimpressed.

We couldn't help but wonder if this Reverend John Lawrence would also not quite make the cut.

He ushered us into his living room, and there on his wall in a very prominent place was a large photo of Yogananda, the very same photo that was on our front door when we left Rhododendron, Oregon, months earlier.

We stood there transfixed with our mouths open.

Reverend Lawrence saw us staring at the photo and said, "That is a very rare photo of Yogananda. Not many people have it or have ever seen it before. It is my favorite."

We knew that we were in the right place. John, as he asked us to call him, was absolutely delightful and carried the presence of Yogananda, whom he loved so much. He had had the great blessing of being able to be with Yogananda in person. According to him, Yogananda gave him permission to give the initiation of Kriya if he felt a student was sincerely ready.

He asked us a few questions, closed his eyes a moment, and said, "Master feels you are ready." He gave us the Kriya initiation that we desired so much.

When we later settled in Santa Cruz, California, we were able to travel the two hours by car to visit John. Whenever we were with him, all we wanted to hear were stories of his times with Yogananda. John would start to speak about his beloved guru, and tears would come into his eyes and he would go into a silent rapture for a period of time.

He would feel very embarrassed that he had kept us waiting, and explain, "Whenever I talk about my guru, I am overcome by his presence!" We loved that about John.

The Kriya Yoga meditation that we learned from John brought such a deepening to my meditation and spiritual life. I began having extraordinary experiences in my meditations and became completely devoted to my practice. I was able to continue my meditation practice through having two daughters, but with the birth of our son, and with the advent of the earthquake and needing to live elsewhere, I could no longer continue. I was stressed to the max, and finding a full hour to meditate deeply without any interruptions was a luxury I just could no longer have. Instead, I learned to meditate in action: while walking, cooking, even cleaning; and that has served me very well.

What I learned from those fifteen years of disciplined Kriya meditation has stayed with me until today, and I am forever grateful for what I received from Yogananda through John Lawrence.

Chapter 19: Pir Vilayat Khan

Barry: We were eager for more spiritual exploration. Another friend told us about a six-week retreat in the French Alps led by the Sufi teacher, Pir Vilayat Khan, the son of Hazrat Inayat Khan, who is generally credited with bringing Sufism to the western world. Similar to our extreme jump from Transcendental Meditation to ten days of Vipassana, we prepared to jump from attending an evening of Sufi Dancing once a week to a six-week immersion into Sufism.

First, we drove our VW van across the country to spend some time with Joyce's family in Buffalo, NY, and then my family in Elmsford, an hour north of New York City. Along with the usual criticism about our closeness, one relative, after hearing about all we were learning, said, "You two are like the Dead Sea. Rivers flow into it but nothing flows out of it. You need to start giving back instead of just accumulating knowledge."

This comment didn't hurt as much as the criticisms about our closeness. Perhaps this relative was right about us, but we just weren't ready to go back to work. Our desire for learning and growth was more important to us.

We had left our golden retriever, Bokie, with a friend in Portland. Free of responsibilities, we flew to Europe with just our backpacks, and hitchhiked our way toward Chamonix, France. One late afternoon, in the foothills of the Alps, we hiked up a trail past some kind of conference center. We found a place to set up our tent, and settled in for the night. It started raining, then became a deluge, most of the night. Early in the morning, we woke up wet and cold. Everything in the tent was soaked.

We packed up in the pouring rain and hiked back down the trail. We were not happy campers! Passing the conference center, some people saw us, must have taken pity on us, and invited us inside to dry out. Their generosity was nearly overwhelming. They dried our clothes and gear, served us warm food, and insisted we spend the night in a real bed, which we did. These people were like angels to us. And not one negative comment about our closeness as a couple!

The next day we finished our journey to Chamonix, then rode up a cable car to an alpine meadow high above the valley with gorgeous views of Mount Blanc. This was to be our home for the rest of the summer. The actual retreat would not be starting for a few days. We were there with a core group of Sufis from all over Europe and America to help set up for the retreat.

We thought, finally we're with Sufis, who surely will accept our closeness. After all, Sufis are all about the heart, all about love and connection.

How wrong we were! Once again, the negative comments about our relationship started. One man said, "I don't even like to look at you because your closeness makes me feel so uncomfortable." A woman, and one of the teachers at the camp, launched into a popular quote from *The Prophet* by Kahlil Gibran:

"Let there be spaces in your togetherness, and let the winds of the heavens dance between you. Love one another but make not a bond of love: Let it rather be a moving sea between the shores of your souls. Fill each other's cup but drink not from one cup. Give one another of your bread but eat not from the same loaf. Sing and dance together and be joyous, but let each one of you be alone, even as the strings of a lute are alone though they quiver with the same

music. Give your hearts, but not into each other's keeping. For only the hand of Life can contain your hearts. And stand together, yet not too near together: For the pillars of the temple stand apart, and the oak tree and the cypress grow not in each other's shadow."

A lovely quote, but she spoke it more as a subtle condemnation rather than the inspired verse that it was meant to be.

We started to feel more and more unwelcome. We thought this camp was the wrong place for us. We were seriously thinking of leaving, but we decided to stay a few more days to at least meet Pir Vilayat.

Finally, the day came when the camp's beloved teacher was to arrive. Everyone was excited. We were not. While we were working, someone yelled, "Here comes Pir Vilayat!"

We peered down the mountainside meadow and saw a small man in a brown robe with white hair and beard briskly walking up the hill, followed by a few students who seemed to tower over him. People started running down to greet him. Joyce and I stayed in camp, preparing ourselves for the possibility of yet another criticism of our closeness – this time from an important teacher.

We watched Pir Vilayat greet each of his students warmly. Then he noticed us standing off to the side. He appeared to be studying us for a moment. Then, to our complete surprise, he walked swiftly over to us and, while we cringed, he threw his arms around us, and starting saying the Arabic words, "Ishq Allah Mabud Li'Allah" (meaning "God is the highest love and God is also the beloved") He enthusiastically said, "You two are one! You should always be together! Never hide your closeness!" Then he left.

The students near us were dumbstruck. Joyce and I were dumbstruck. This amazing acknowledgment was the last thing we expected, but the thing we most desperately needed. Someone not only approved of our closeness, but actually celebrated it.

From that point on, we never again hid how close we were and how much we loved each other. If someone took issue with our closeness, we considered it their problem. And so far, our closeness has been a great asset, not only giving other couples permission to be close, but also giving singles hope.

There have been times when our profound closeness has caused problems. A number of years ago at one of our Hawaii couples' retreats, Joyce broke tooth number thirteen at breakfast. At lunch the same day, I broke tooth number thirteen. There happened to be a dentist in our group at the retreat. When he heard what had happened, he said, "I knew you were soulmates, but toothmates …?!"

Some years ago, Joyce went to see an orthopedic surgeon for pain in her left knee. The next week, I went to see the same surgeon with pain in my right knee. We both ended up having arthroscopic meniscus repair. At one of my post-op visits, the surgeon commented, "Barry, I've been a surgeon for over twenty years, and I've never seen anything like the two of you. I suppose with love anything is possible!"

We will always be grateful for Pir Vilayat's acknowledgement of our love and closeness. But that wasn't all he did. Later that evening, Pir Vilayat summoned us to visit him in a little cave further up the mountain where he preferred to stay. When we arrived, he asked us to sit on some rocks … the cave was fairly rustic. He said, "I'd like you both to teach a class on relationships here at the camp. What do you think of that idea?"

I said, "We've never done that before. We don't have experience. We also don't know enough about Sufism."

Joyce said, "Maybe someone else is better qualified."

"Nonsense," he said, "You're more qualified than anyone here. It's your closeness and obvious connection that qualifies you. I spotted it when I first saw you. My students need to learn the very thing you already have. There's just too much suffering when it comes to relationships. I'll help you every step of the way. We'll meet here in my cave before each class and I'll coach you as best I can."

And with those final words, our future service and work in the world started in a little cave in the French Alps. Starting the next day, we taught the relationship class to about a hundred people. Although we didn't really know what we were doing, we spoke from our heart in English, while interpreters translated our words into French, Italian and German. Our classes were loved by everyone who attended.

The other teachers at the camp, however, were not so accepting of us and of what we were teaching. Even with Pir Vilayat's endorsement, we were still the "co-dependent couple who were trying to grow in each other's shade." It would be years before other spiritual teachers would accept our model of relationship as an integral part of the spiritual path. It wasn't until 1984 that we finally presented our ideas to the world in the form of our first book, *The Shared Heart: Relationship Initiations and Celebrations*, officially launching our career on the world's stage. At the time, there was precious little written about this subject. The common view held that relationship was separate from spirituality, or even that relationship actually took you away from spirituality. Pir Vilayat gave us the following endorsement, *"First the One became the many. Now the many are uniting back into the One by the miracle of love. Joyce and Barry, in The Shared Heart, show how the human relationship is the first step."*

Joyce: For me, the experience of being with Pir Vilayat was extraordinary. He was significantly older than we were, and I thought he was almost like a God. In truth, he was very much a human man with weaknesses and strengths. But his strengths were amazing. Through his talks and leading us through practices, he was able to open our hearts to the presence of God. He was a little man, but he had great power of the heart to love and serve. Even when he just looked at me, I felt the stirrings of my own desire to be of service to God in this life.

And Pir Vilayat taught us practical life lessons as well. He wanted us to be able to understand the importance of saying "no." He emphasized that saying "no" is a vitally important part of the spiritual path. He taught us that until we can say "no," our "yes" will not be very strong.

In the camp, we learned a very important Sufi practice called Zikr. We repeated the sacred phrase, "La illaha il Allahu," with specific head movements. The first word, "La," means "No." The literal translation of the phrase is "There is no God but God." The deeper meaning involves saying no to the unreal, to illusion, to the material world, before you can say yes to the real and divine. Zikr was an important part of each day at the camp.

Chamonix is such a beautiful place in the French Alps. The Sufi camp was spread out on a mountain meadow, high above the town in the valley below. A cable car ran from the town to the bottom of the meadow. So there were tourists who would come past the camp and wonder what we were doing.

One day, a large and burly French man, who was quite drunk, staggered into our camp. He took one look at us hippie flower children and started yelling curses at us in French. A group of us made a circle around him, held hands, and started singing a Sufi song to sweetly soothe the anger out of him. It didn't work. He got more agitated.

We thought we would just sit in silence around the man and send him love. This got him even more agitated and it seemed that he might become violent.

Someone ran up the mountain to Pir Vilayat's cave to get him. Pir Vilayat quickly came down the mountain with his white robes and white beard flying in the wind as he walked. We all wondered what he would do. Would he put his hand on this man's heart and quiet the yelling and bring him into a beautiful place of love? The man was big and growing more violent with each minute. Pir Vilayat was a short, very thin man but, to our amazement, he briskly marched right up to the man, grabbed him by the arm and, with a fierce expression on his face, loudly spoke one word in French, "Non" (no). He then roughly marched him to the beginning of the trail that would take him back down to the cable car.

The sight was shocking to all of us. The Frenchman towered over Pir Vilayat, and yet became meek as a lamb, putting up no resistance, all the way down the hill. All we could do was watch in utter amazement.

Pir Vilayat briskly walked back up the hill to our little group. Eyes blazing, he spoke in a voice that carried his frustration with us, "When will you learn to say NO?!"

He left us as quickly as he had come. We looked at each other in silence, sure that none of us would ever forget that lesson. It was, for all of us, a lesson on practical spirituality. You could call it "tough love." We had been practicing the Zikr for weeks, but had failed to actually put it into use.

I especially enjoyed the times with Pir Vilayat when he would sit privately with us and have us explain what we wanted to do in the next relationship class. In the privacy of his cave, he was relaxed and reflected deeply on what we wanted to do. Besides being a spiritual teacher, he knew a lot about psychology as well and blended the two beautifully.

From these meetings in his cave, Pir Vilayat knew without a doubt that both Barry and I taught these classes together every few days during the summer. However, the evening after our last class, he announced to the whole camp, "I wish to thank Barry for giving these wonderful classes throughout the summer. Barry, please stand up."

Barry stood up and everyone applauded. I was shocked. First of all, how could Barry just stand there and take the credit for something that we had completely done together. But also, I was hurt by Pir Vilayat for leaving me out.

I sulked the rest of the evening's gathering. When we were excused and were finally alone, my anger exploded out of me toward Barry. He listened, and apologized for not correcting Pir Vilayat. He said, "I admit I could have handled it much better when I stood up. I wish I would have spoken up on your behalf. But your anger is really at Pir Vilayat. He totally left you out."

I had to admit that Barry was right. What do I do with anger that is at someone so holy and spiritual? I was ready to let the whole thing go when Barry said, "You need to confront Pir Vilayat. You have to tell him how much his action hurt you, and that it wasn't fair."

I looked down and said, "I just can't. Who am I to correct such a powerful teacher?"

Barry only looked at me, and I knew he would not let me get away with this. I decided that the following morning I would speak to him.

I hardly slept all that night. The fear of confronting a man I so deeply admired was frightening to me. What if he brushed aside my feelings as nothing, as my parents used to do? I just didn't think I could cope with that outcome.

Sunday morning dawned bright, with a chill in the air that matched the chill in my heart. Barry insisted we get out of our sleeping bag, leave our tiny A-frame hut, and wait for

Pir Vilayat to come down the mountain. He was taking some of our group to perform in a church in the town of Chamonix in the valley below. I hid behind a large rock and watched up the trail as Pir Vilayat walked majestically down the mountain. He had on his finest white long robes and truly looked the part of a very holy man.

I was shaking. As he approached the rock I was hiding behind, Barry gave me a gentle push out into his path.

"Oh, good morning, Joyce. Isn't it just a gorgeous day! I'm so excited to have our choir sing for this church this morning!"

I decided it is now or never, so I timidly spoke, "I don't feel it's fair that you gave Barry all the credit for the classes that we both gave all summer."

There was a moment of silence as he took in what I said, and the smile faded from his face.

I panicked and thought, what if he totally rejects my feelings? What if he says no to me like he did to the drunken French man?

A pained look came onto his face, and he said, "Oh, Joyce, I did it again. You see, I'm from India and there the men are most important. It's such an old habit of mine to give the men all of the credit. I have been criticized before about this. I am so sorry. Come with me."

He took my hand and together we marched down the mountain with Barry trailing behind. Once at the breakfast line, he gathered everyone together and made an announcement. "I need to make a public apology. I am so sorry that I neglected to include Joyce in the appreciation for the classes that she and Barry have given. I was wrong as she fully participated with Barry. Right now, I want everyone to give her a full round of applause."

And everyone cheered and clapped.

He took me aside and said, "I have so much trouble with this. From now on, if you are in the audience, can I look at you during my talks and will you please let me know if I am giving the men more credit?"

And true to his word, for the rest of that summer and later, when we would attend his seminars in San Francisco and Marin, he always looked at me from time to time, wondering how he was doing. If he saw me smiling, he knew he was treating the genders equally. He sincerely wanted to change and honor women, and was so grateful to me for helping him change this outdated behavior.

At the end of the retreat that summer, we had our goodbye meeting with Pir Vilayat in his little cave. We started telling him about our plans to go to India to meet Ram Dass's guru, Neem Karoli Baba (Maharaji).

He interrupted us waving his hands from side to side, "You don't need to go to India. You're needed too much in America. Go home. Start helping people heal their hearts and their relationships."

So much for our plans for continued pilgrimage, of learning just for ourselves. Just like that, our plans changed and we journeyed back to America. It seemed our "Dead Sea" days were over.

Chapter 20: Hari Das Baba 1974

It was autumn, 1974, and Joyce and I were driving to the West from the East Coast once again struggling with the decision of where to live. We had visited a spiritual community in Northern California which we were hopeful would be the perfect place for us to settle, but upon meeting with the spiritual leader of the ashram, we both felt a very strong NO. Now we were on the road again with no idea where to go. It seemed a common theme in our lives, despite the miraculous message carved in a heart on that tree next to the Kern River, "Joyce, home is just a feeling."

One morning, I unfolded a map of California and started studying it. I have always loved maps. Joyce sat next to me, finishing her breakfast.

"Look on this map, Joyce. There's a whole wild area, the Mendocino National Forest, just north of San Francisco. Let's go."

And just like that, we took off in our VW van. I have always appreciated Joyce's great love of the outdoors, and her adventurous (most of the time) spirit. Given what was to happen, I am surprised she still goes on adventures with me!

We didn't know just how primitive the roads were, how undeveloped it was. We just drove. Or rather, I just drove. Joyce was too scared to drive on bumpy dirt roads that hugged the sides of mountains ... with no guide rails and a sheer drop off.

We had recently had our first rain of the year, after months of no rain. Being new to California, we didn't realize what that first rain did to dirt roads in the mountains. Conditions were muddy, slippery, and treacherous.

After a few close calls ... we almost slipped off the cliff in a few places ... I realized that we had no business being here without four-wheel-drive. But how to turn around? There didn't appear to be any places wide enough. We had to keep driving up the mountain. To make matters worse, it was beginning to grow dark.

Finally, I spotted a turnout ... sort of. It would have to do. I slowly and carefully negotiated a turn, but started to slip sideways toward the edge of the drop-off. With every move I made, our van slipped a little more toward the edge. Forward gear, a gentle push on the gas pedal, and slipping to the side rather than forward. Reverse, and the same thing...

The situation looked grim. I got out and surveyed the scene. This was long before cell phones, so there was no calling AAA or any other form of help. Instead, realizing we needed divine help, we prayed a very sincere prayer.

We decided there was nothing more to do until morning. We camped that night in the severely slanted van. For most of the night, Joyce was pressed against me and I was pressed against the wall of the van. It was not our best night's sleep. Okay, Joyce pressed against me had its perks.

The next morning, I walked over to examine the drop-off. It wasn't as bad as I thought the night before. It didn't go straight down. Instead, it sloped steeply for about thirty or so feet, then it leveled out on a fairly level spur road that rejoined our road a little way down the mountain.

I told Joyce to get out of the van, just in case. She was worried. "Barry, what are you going to do?"

"I think I'll try one more time."

I didn't sound convincing. She didn't even try to hide her worried expression.

I got into the driver's seat, put the van in gear, and slowly let out the clutch. The rear wheels turned, but again we did not go forward. Instead, we slipped to the right, both right wheels dropped over the edge of the turn-out. The van leaned precariously over the edge, and seemed to be on the verge of rolling over.

I acted quickly. I opened the driver's door fully, jumped out of the van, hanging onto the open door as a sort of lever to try to keep the van from toppling. Now I was in a desperate situation! If the van started to go over the edge sideways, I would have to let go of the door, and just let it go. As long as I kept my full weight on the end of the door, the van stayed put.

Now what? I knew I couldn't stay there forever. Without help, we were really in a bind. We hadn't seen one other car since we had been on this dirt road.

My mind flashed on the worst outcome. If the van rolled onto its side, it probably would either slide or continue rolling down the bank. We stood a chance of losing the van and all our belongings.

Just when I didn't think I could hold on to that door any longer, we heard voices. A few minutes after that, out of the woods above us came three big young men wearing backpacks. They lost no time in jumping into rescue mode. One of them had a climbing rope, which he quickly secured to the roof-rack on our van. All three of them, with Joyce and my help, tried to get the van back up top, but without success.

I made a decision. I announced, "Okay guys, this is what I'm gonna do. You hold onto that rope to keep the van from toppling over, and I'm gonna turn the van down the bank and drive straight down to the road below us."

Joyce said, "Barry, that sounds crazy!"

I answered her, "Yeah, maybe, but I really think I can make it. And it looks like it's our only hope."

The three men looked grim, but nodded their consent to me.

One man spoke, "Go ahead. We'll do our best to keep the van on its wheels."

Sometimes there are just no guarantees in life....

I got in the driver's seat once more, this time turning the steering wheel to the right, down the bank, shifted into first gear, and let out the clutch. The van started to slip sideways, going into an even more precarious tilt. Without those three strong men holding the rope, I would have surely rolled over.

Then another miracle happened. The rear wheels grabbed enough of the hillside to propel the van forward just enough to begin the turn down the steep bank. The next second, I was part rolling, part slipping, accelerating straight down the bank, hit the bottom with a loud clunk, and then bounced onto the road. We had made it! Without any damage to our van!

I heard a whooping cheer erupt from above me as Joyce and the men crept and slid down the bank toward me. There was hugging and congratulations.

Joyce said to them, "We want you all to know that you are the answer to our prayers. We couldn't have gotten out without your help."

One of the men said, "I hurt my ankle last night, and the three of us decided to abort our trip. We knew we had a thirty-mile hike out, but we had two choices. One way was by trail all the way down the mountain. The other way was a trail the opposite way to a dirt road we saw on our map. It was significantly longer to walk to our car via this second route, but we chose it. We didn't know why. It just felt right.

Little did we know we would come out onto the dirt road right here and be able to help you."

We offered the men a ride back to their car, for which they were grateful. At their car, we said our good-byes, and again commented on the amazing synchronicity of events. It was yet another miracle in a long string of miracles called life.

From their car, we started on a different road going down the mountain. This was before the days of the GPS and, without the help of road signs, we became utterly lost. We had absolutely no idea where we were. But, I reasoned, as long as I kept mostly heading downhill, we should come out into some kind of civilization.

And finally we did. There in front of us was the vast open stretch of the Pacific Ocean. We came to a stop sign at Highway One. Across the highway, another sign announced "Sea Ranch." Something about that name was familiar to me, and I reached for my little blue address book. There I found a list of names and addresses given to us by Ram Dass. One of the names was Hari Dass Baba, and the only address Ram Dass had for him was Sea Ranch, CA.

In Ram Dass's book, *Be Here Now*, we had read about Hari Dass, who had taken a vow of silence many years previous. He was well-known for the tiny chalkboard hanging from his neck, on which he could write a few words that could zero in on your deepest issues. (Picture texting but only on a black board the same size as a cell phone)

Joyce and I felt this was no coincidence. We must have had a divine appointment to see Hari Dass Baba. We would simply drop in on him. In our innocence, we did not realize the immensity of the task that was ahead of us.

We followed signs to Sea Ranch Administrative Office, where we announced our intention to visit Hari Dass Baba.

The woman at the reception desk seemed to be studying our dirty and disheveled camping clothes and curtly asked, "Do you have an appointment?"

We said no, but told her the story of how we ended up there.

Slightly softened, she said, "I'm sorry, I'm not allowed to let you see him without an appointment."

We would not be turned away. "Could you please just call the house and let him know that Ram Dass sent us?"

She excused herself after telling us to have a seat in some chairs, and disappeared into a back room. Ten minutes later, she reappeared and announced, "I'm so sorry, but he is apparently in seclusion and not seeing visitors. Perhaps you could call and make an appointment."

This just plain felt wrong to us. After all, we had a divine appointment. We had driven many miles over treacherous mountain roads, had almost lost our van, and then miraculously ended up at Sea Ranch.

We stood up but didn't leave.

I said, "Perhaps we'll just wait."

The woman said, "That won't do any good."

There was a tense silence between us, a little longer than was comfortable, when her phone rang. It was Ma Renu, who owned the house where Babaji was staying. She said Babaji would see us.

So off we went, slightly dazed and not a little apprehensive about what we were getting into. We approached the house, which commanded a beautiful view of the ocean, perched on the top of a bluff. We were greeted at the door warmly by Ma Renu, but told we should not stay long. We were shown into a bedroom where Hari Dass was sitting on his bed writing a letter. He motioned us to sit on the bed with him.

Almost as soon as we entered his room we felt at ease as he had such a warm and loving presence. Before there was a chance for any pleasantries, or even any introductions, he looked at Joyce's finger, with her wedding band on it. He looked at both of my hands, and saw there was no wedding band.

Immediately his chalk produced the following on his slate, which he held up facing me:

"Where's your ring?"

"Oh, packed away somewhere, I think."

"Why aren't you wearing it?" next appeared on the slate.

"I've never been able to wear rings. It's uncomfortable. It gets caught on things."

The reasons even sounded lame to me. They certainly didn't appear to convince him. I started to feel uncomfortable and defensive. I glanced over at Joyce, who was smiling at me but obviously in agreement with this stranger.

Feeling cornered, I made a final, and somewhat desperate, attempt to explain.

"I really tried wearing it for quite a while. But one day, while meditating in a darkened room with a stick of incense burning near me, I reached for something and caught the burning tip of the incense under my ring."

I became dramatic, waving my hands and looking panicked.

"I felt my finger burning, but I couldn't dislodge the burning ember. That did it. From then on I stopped wearing my ring."

There followed a long moment of silence. Then Babaji smiled, looked at me with immense warmth, and wrote on the chalkboard:

"You need her more than she needs you. Wear your ring. It will help you."

I felt like a balloon with a critical air leak. My defensiveness melted away. I felt exposed, but it felt good. I felt seen, so I no longer needed to hide.

I remembered our Los Angeles experience, my affair with Joyce's best friend, and my revelation about the little boy inside me who needed Joyce's love. It all came back up to the surface.

I looked over at Joyce. She was thrilled by what he had written.

Hari Das Baba (Babaji)

Joyce: The next question he asked us was, "Where do you live?" This was exactly the biggest question and hardest to answer because we had no idea where we wanted to live.

I said, "We have no idea."

He immediately wrote on his chalkboard, "I am moving to Santa Cruz tomorrow."

We took that as a sign and I simply said "I guess we'll move there as well." Barry looked a little confused.

At the time we had no idea of where Santa Cruz was, nor did we know anything about it. This nice man was moving there, so at least we would know one person.

The next day, just like Babaji, we traveled to Santa Cruz. I remember so clearly driving down Highway 1 from San Francisco toward Santa Cruz and enjoying the views of the Pacific Ocean. Highway 1 turned into Mission Boulevard and there was a big sign, "Welcome to Santa Cruz," and for the first time we realized that Santa Cruz was a town right on the ocean, with redwood-covered hills on the other side. It was just gorgeous. We both felt that we had finally found a place where we could live peacefully and with purpose.

We were driving down Freedom Blvd as someone had told us about a place in Watsonville, the next town to the south. All of a sudden, Barry made a quick right turn up a small private road called Redwood Heights Road.

"Why did you turn here?" I asked.

"I don't know. Something about it just felt right," was Barry's reply.

There were no houses to rent on this little private road, so we headed back down again. We both commented though, "It sure seems like a nice place to live." Two years later and pregnant with our first child, we ended up living on Redwood Heights Road. And now, all these years later, we are still here and absolutely love it and know it is our right place to be.

Chapter 21: The Cosmic Mass

Joyce and I were staying at a Buddhist center in Felton, a little town nestled in the redwoods north of Santa Cruz. We were having doubts about living in the Santa Cruz area. We were thinking about moving back up to Oregon. We found out that Pir Vilayat was leading a weekend retreat in San Francisco, an hour and a half north, and therefore on our way to Oregon.

We left in our VW bus to attend the retreat, always happy to spend time with this Sufi master. As we expected, Pir Vilayat had us sit near the front of the room, and periodically glanced over at Joyce to make sure he had no male-dominated slips. I thought it precious how much he respected her opinion.

At the end of the retreat, Pir Vilayat shared his vision of the "Cosmic Mass," a celebration of the unity of the world's major religions. His creation would involve a theater in the round, with five stages simultaneously portraying some of the major events in five of the world's major religions. In the center would be a seven-level stage, corresponding to the seven levels of heaven as described in many different religions. The famous Sufi Choir and Orchestra would perform all the music. It was to be a spectacular pageant, at a major theater in the Bay Area – in three months!

Joyce and I looked at one another sadly. We were leaving to head north the following morning. Our plans were set.

Pir Vilayat asked for all the men in the audience who wanted a role in the Cosmic Mass to come up onto the stage. Without thinking, I stood up and started walking toward the stage. I vaguely remember Joyce whispering loudly, "Barry, what are you doing? We're leaving tomorrow morning!"

I couldn't explain the pull to walk up on that stage. It was simply an irresistible prompting. However, when I got there, I started to feel foolish. My mind kicked in, and I thought, "What am I doing!"

There were probably a hundred men crowded on the stage, with Pir Vilayat sitting on his stool on the edge of the stage, eyes closed and face tilted upward, perhaps meditating on the different roles he envisioned. I quickly hid behind all the men, embarrassed, hoping he wouldn't see me.

A long time passed by in complete silence ... an agonizingly long time. Finally, I couldn't take it any longer. I peeked out from behind some heads until I could see Pir Vilayat. And wouldn't you know it, at that very instant he opened his eyes and looked directly at me. His hand came up with his finger pointing at me, and he pronounced, "Jesus!"

I looked around, somewhat confused. Was he pointing at me, or someone near me? It was me. I had just been cast in one of the major roles of the Cosmic Mass. No audition, no nothing. Pir Vilayat was a director being directed from inside.

Talk about a change of plans!

After Pir Vilayat finished casting the men, I went back to my seat next to Joyce. She had every right to be annoyed at me. After all, I didn't consult with her first before casting our plans to the wind and going up to the stage. She didn't know what happened on the stage. She had a curious, but bewildered expression.

I sat down next to her and said, "Joyce, you'll never believe what just happened. Pir Vilayat chose me to be Jesus!"

At first, Joyce looked incredulous, but then she smiled at me warmly. She didn't have time to say anything. The next moment, Pir Vilayat called up all the women who wanted parts, and Joyce stood up. She hesitated for a moment, and I gave her a gentle push. That was enough to send her down the aisle toward the stage.

Pir Vilayat chose Joyce to be the Mother of the World, to sit on the highest level of the stage and, veiled together with the Father of the World, meditate and send out waves of peace from the highest heaven. What a role!

We returned to Santa Cruz and to the same Buddhist center. The folks there were understandably a bit confused. We moved out on Friday, and were moving back in Sunday evening.

We needed to find a more permanent home in the Santa Cruz area. We didn't want to live too close to San Francisco. It was too big a city for our liking. The Cosmic Mass would require us to travel up to the city several times a week, but that was doable from Santa Cruz.

We had trouble finding a house to rent. In desperation, we called John Lawrence, and he told us to come up and see him in San Francisco. When we got there, we sadly commented, "We've looked in the paper every day and have found nothing."

He calmly explained, "You have not given God a chance to work a miracle. When you go back home, place an ad in the paper saying who you are. That ad will be the physical anchor that will allow God to bring the people to you."

We were doubtful, as we had been trying for weeks. He took our hands and said a prayer with us for the right house to be found.

We went back to Santa Cruz as instructed and placed a very nice ad in the paper with our qualifications and stating that we take very good care of a house and that we love the country.

The very next day, three people called with available houses for us. One man said, "I wasn't even going to rent this house because it is not quite finished on the inside, but I saw your ad, and something told me I just had to call you right away."

This house was perfect for us. It had 360-degree views of the mountains and ocean, and miles and miles of trails to walk on. Yes, it wasn't quite finished, but we didn't mind, as the setting was so beautiful and the rent was only $100/month.

John was right. God had a chance to work a miracle.

It was the rehearsing for the Cosmic Mass that really changed both of our lives. There was the outer rehearsing, practicing for the actual performance. Then there was the inner rehearsing. Pir Vilayat was very clear with Joyce and me. "Your full-time job," he said to me, "is to fully immerse yourself in the life and being of Jesus. You are to become Jesus, feel what he feels, do what he does." And to Joyce, "You are to become the Mother of the World, the female aspect of God. Let every meditation be an act of compassion for the world."

A tall order? Yes, indeed. Those three months launched Joyce and me into a profound spiritual practice. Being raised Jewish, there was much I needed to learn about Jesus. I read everything I could find, from the Bible to The Aquarian Gospel. Learning about and being Jesus became my full-time job for three months. It's not that I became a Christian. My current spirituality embraces practices from many different traditions. But, for three months, I became Jesus, trying to think like him, feel what he felt, and walk how I imagined he walked. This became a life-changing practice, so much more than a rehearsal.

Then came the evening of the performances, three of them in one evening, with massive crowds, including the governor of California at the time, Jerry Brown, Sr.

As long as I live, I will never forget that evening. The first and second performance, although beautiful, I was still aware of playing the part of Jesus. Then came the third performance. I was no longer aware of playing a part. The energy of Jesus came through me. It was truly sublime! In the final scene, my ascension, I climbed up the seven-level stage in the center and approached Joyce. But it wasn't Joyce. Instead, through the thin veil, I beheld Divine Mother, the highest aspect of the feminine. And in one glorious moment, I was united with Joyce, not as man and woman, but as divine beings, the highest moment of our lives thus far. And all this in front of thousands of people in the audience!

Chapter 22: Rami 1976

When Barry and I first moved to Santa Cruz, and before we had children, we used to visit Baba Hari Dass every week at the home where he was staying. Babaji, as he was called, came from India to this country and founded the Mt. Madonna Center, which is the largest yoga center in the country, as well as a school for preschool through 12th grade.

One day he asked us, via his little chalkboard, "When will you have children?"

We politely told him, "Babaji, we have no plans to have children." We had been together for ten years at that point and were very close. "We don't want our lives to change."

Babaji wrote "Life is about change. Your lives will change anyway."

From then on, whenever we visited him each week, he asked the same question. We stopped answering the question and instead just shrugged our shoulders. And he would smile and write "Change is a good thing." I can see now that Babaji was very subtly working on us to open up to the change to becoming parents.

One beautiful summer afternoon, we decided to try having sex without protection for the first time ever. I don't remember whose idea this was. Perhaps we simply decided to trust in a higher plan.

We visited Babaji several days later and, this time, he did not ask us the question, instead he kept looking at the top of my head and smiling. He was seeing something I was unaware of.

Several weeks later, our pregnancy was confirmed and we were thrilled. We rushed to tell Babaji. He smiled and said he already knew. He then wrote on his chalkboard with conviction, "The baby will be born on my birthday, March 26."

We said, "No, Babaji, the baby is due two weeks later in April." We had carefully calculated the dates.

He patiently wrote, "No, the baby will come on my birthday, March 26."

Every time we saw Babaji after that, he wrote on his board, with a clearly mischievous look on his dark face, "March 26."

Soon everyone knew, but we did not believe what he said. We are trained medically and trusted the medical calculations, and our baby was clearly due two weeks later in April.

On March 6, we walked into a satsang (gathering). Or more accurately, I waddled with my swollen belly. Babaji saw us enter, smiled, and wrote something on his chalkboard. He held it up for all to see. It said simply, "20 more days." Everyone laughed.

Many people said that they were sure we were having a boy as the energy of the baby was so strong. People came up to me and put their hands on my belly, and said they are never wrong, the baby was a boy.

At four o'clock Thursday morning, March 25, 1976, Barry suddenly awoke and felt my huge belly. It was hard as a rock. Wondering why he was suddenly awake, he listened to my breathing and heard a slight change.

Several minutes later, the same thing happened. He leaned over, kissed me, and announced when he saw my eyes open, "Joyce, you're in labor now!"

I thought he was kidding and laughed at him, thinking he was just overly excited.

"Really, Sweetie, a powerful energy woke me up just now. You are definitely in labor."

I looked at my dear husband incredulously, and stood up to go to the bathroom.

GUSH!! The waters broke all over the bedroom rug. Barry was right. I was in labor.

After going to the bathroom, cleaning myself off, and Barry putting a towel on the wet spot on the rug, we got back in bed. We lay there, much too excited to sleep.

I said, "I guess Babaji was almost right. We're one day earlier than he said."

We both were quiet for a few minutes, trying to grasp the enormity of this event. I felt a strong presence of the Mother God filling me with tremendous peace and love. I reflected on how the greatest lesson of this pregnancy had been about forgiveness. When I was two months pregnant, in a moment of inspiration, I asked God to remove from me all negative feelings for others. That this baby might be nurtured without my petty negativity toward other human beings. Though a tall order, the actual asking had seemed so simple. The experiences that followed were not! I had allowed myself to become hurt by thoughtless, unkind words from two people concerning my pregnancy. I had found it impossible to forgive them.

Now I lay in bed, feeling waves of compassion for these two people. With each contraction, I continued to feel the presence of God, showing me that people only act unkind out of a need to feel this same divine presence that I was feeling. I squeezed Barry's hand, as I felt released from this negativity.

There would be no more sleep that night. Barry finally rose at sunrise and stood naked in front of the open window as the first rays of sunlight lit up his body. To me, he was the most beautiful sight in the world. My heart felt bursting with love for him.

When I hauled my huge body out of bed and stood naked with him, Barry kneeled down and kissed my belly. He stood up, stepped back a little, and said, "You could never look more beautiful than you do at this moment!" Even though I couldn't quite agree, it felt so good to take in his love and adoration.

We had decided to do the labor and delivery entirely by ourselves, depending only upon God's help. Most people discouraged this plan, saying that surely, we would need extra hands to help. One friend told us that, with an experienced midwife present, it would free us to be more available to each other.

Of course, that made sense, but we didn't waver from our decision to be alone. It felt like there was a bigger reason, something we would receive from being just the two of us.

Later that morning, we took a delightful walk into the woods on one of the many trails that Barry had built on the property next door. It was, of course, a slow walk, with mild contractions coming all the while. We returned home to meditate. I remember those morning hours as such a blissful experience.

Like most women laboring for the first time, I did everything I could to ease off the heavier contractions. I sat very still, moved cautiously and, as I later realized, slowed labor down, all the while priding myself on how well I was doing.

Twelve hours after my bag of waters broke, Barry finally looked at me and said, "All right, we've had enough of this.

It's time to get this labor going and have our baby. I'm going to give you an enema!"

I looked at him communicating both my pain and my trust. I happen to be one of those people who hate enemas.

"Do I really have to do this?"

Barry didn't answer. He just turned on the hot water faucet and waited for the right temperature.

The enema was an ordeal! But it did bring me right into heavy labor. Strong contractions came, and I needed Barry's total attention in order to cope.

When I was finally getting used to that degree of intensity, Barry looked at me with the kind of love that pushes the beloved into harder things, and said, "Now, let's go for another walk in the woods."

My eyes pleaded, but his eyes were steady and confident, so off we went for another walk as the sunset lit up the sky. The contractions would stop me in my tracks, and all I could do was lean my body on Barry's. He became my strength, and we became as one.

When we returned from the walk, it was dark and cold. Barry started a fire in our living room fireplace, and I sat in front of it, working alone with the still intense contractions, while he ran into the kitchen to light another fire in our wood-burning stove. It was really getting cold.

He also needed to prepare things for the delivery. He had previously sterilized instruments so they would be ready for the birth. Although Barry was a medical doctor, he had minimal training in labor and delivery. So yes, we were taking a risk on a home-birth with just the two of us, but it still felt right.

During the pregnancy, we had found an extraordinary couple from Germany. He was an obstetrician and she was a midwife, but neither one was licensed to practice in this country. They became our backup, as well as our coaches throughout the pregnancy. They would be on-call in case of problems. So, really, we were not completely alone.

It was very difficult being alone in front of the fireplace, even though I was warm enough. I needed to call on all the inner strength I possessed.

Barry finally returned and we settled into a nice rhythm. The contractions came with immense force. He sat behind me applying pressure to my back and, for the resting phase, he held me and supported me with his love. We felt what it must have been like for a young pioneering couple, giving birth alone in the wilderness.

Around nine that evening, it became clear that I was entering transition, the part of labor after the cervix is dilated and before the actual delivery. Barry made this entry in my journal afterwards, "I started to feel very high, that wonderful feeling of God-Presence. I was filled with assurance that all events were being guided. I definitely knew for the first time that everything would go well. The last remnants of doubt burned away in that moment. Joyce picked up on my feelings and we felt very close ... and felt our gratitude to God."

I had read that transition can be the hardest and shortest part of labor, so I gave it my all. Wave after wave of intense contractions came, and we worked as a team, even though Barry, in between contractions, would dash off to put more wood on the two fires, to keep the house warm enough. Even with these interruptions, I felt united with Barry.

An average transition is usually well under an hour. After two hours had gone by, we wondered if something was wrong. Barry examined me and said, "It feels like a lip of the cervix might be holding up the progress. Let me try to massage it..." So that's what he did.

We went back to our spot in front of the fireplace and worked more as a team. But the contractions diminished in intensity. Barry tried a second exam and cervical massage, but nothing happened. My womb came to a standstill.

At this point, I looked into Barry's eyes for reassurance, but that strength and confidence were gone. He looked pale when he spoke, "Come, we have to go to the hospital now."

As a nurse who has seen many drug-induced hospital births, my fear was the opposite of that of most women.

"Barry, please, no, I don't want to go to the hospital."

Until that point, Barry had been the strong one taking care of me. From then on, that strength would have to alternate between us. Right now, it was my turn.

"Barry, we can do it. Let's pray and ask for help, and surrender this birth to God."

We prayed and that seemed to help us both, but my uterus still didn't respond. We both felt like innocent and helpless children, waiting for our Divine Mommy to come and take care of us. Gone was the pride in doing this birth by ourselves. We knew we were totally dependent upon a higher power, a feeling that would continue throughout the rest of the labor.

We tried walking again. It was freezing outside, and I felt so weak that I could barely walk. Still, labor didn't pick up. It was as if the baby was waiting for something, before he would begin to leave his secure home in the womb.

Barry looked at me in the most tender way and asked, "Joyce, what is it? You know in your heart what is stopping labor."

Although his face was pale and worn, in that moment his voice was used by a greater voice. Something broke within me, and I burst into tears. A flow of unconscious fears surfaced. Barry and I had spoken about these fears intellectually, but they had never been cleared in my feelings.

Through my tears, I blurted out, "I don't know if I really want this baby. What if it changes the love and closeness between us? You told me that your father was often jealous of the attention your mother gave to you. What if that happens to us? Oh, Barry, I love you so much. I can't bear thinking that another will come and take our closeness away."

During my pregnancy, I had always been excited and enthusiastic about having a baby. These fears would come up every once in a while, but I would push them aside as silly. Now they were in full view, and our baby wasn't about to come until I dealt with them on the spot.

It was at this point that we had one of the peak experiences of our life. There was my beloved husband, weary from helping me through twenty hours of labor. Yet, when he next spoke, it was the voice of a master speaking through him, and divine wisdom poured out...

"It is a great blessing to be chosen as care-takers of a conscious, aware soul, a being coming to help bring in an age of enduring peace. Just being in the presence of such a one, will tremendously speed our own spiritual journey. Contrary to our fears, this child's arrival into our lives will increase, not decrease, our closeness, and bring us closer to God. There would be no jealousy, since our selfishness would be replaced by true giving, and in this giving, we would receive more than we could ever dream."

When the words stopped, we both felt elated, raised up to a higher consciousness. We both felt that we had been gloriously blessed by an angel, or some other being of immense love. And the air had been cleared of all doubt and fear.

Ever so gently at first, then powerfully, my womb began to contract, and Rami started her descent down the birth canal. It was as if she had heard, and was satisfied that we understood.

Still, the "pushing" stage of labor was quite an ordeal, because my cervix had apparently become swollen and sore. We worked together for three more hours. During that time, we took turns feeling too exhausted to go on, while the other was able to be strong and help.

Finally, Rami's head emerged, and Barry whispered, "He's born." That's how certain we were about having a boy.

He later wrote, "The moment her head was born was one of those magical moments that can never be adequately described in words. I gently turned her head and found myself looking directly into the eyes of an old and very wise being, as well as a new-born baby. The predominant feeling was one of mutual recognition ... not only me recognizing her, but she also acknowledging our eternal connection. I was awed by her awakeness."

One more push and the baby was out, twenty-five hours after the waters broke. Barry informed me, "We have a baby girl!"

I will never forget the thrill of divine joy that passed through my body. I had wanted a girl so much that I hadn't even dared hope for one.

He gently placed her upon me, and we both experienced the greatest joy we have ever known. Her look was so intent, so steady, so filled with love for us both. She never cried! The only sound in our bedroom was a faraway sweet melody of angel's singing. That moment more than made up for any pain experienced. Now we were a family! Welcome beloved baby! We love you so much!

I had never felt so much love in my entire life. I looked at Barry, and he was no longer a being outside of me. He was within me, and the love we felt for each other touched the depths of the universe.

When labor started in the early hours of March 25, we naturally thought Babaji was wrong in his prediction of March 26. But twenty-five hours of labor allowed him to be right after all.

Ah, such bliss! But our ecstasy was short-lived. My placenta was not coming out, and I had a steady flow of bleeding.

My mother had experienced the same difficulty delivering me. Reluctantly, we put our precious bundle down near me on the bed, and worked to remove the placenta for several more hours. Barry was again at the point of exhaustion, and his fear made his thinking process cloudy. We both knew I was slipping into shock from loss of blood. I began to feel that I could easily drift off and leave my body. The presence of angels was so strong, it would have been so easy to join them in the spirit world. Just as I felt myself beginning to slip away, a strong voice resounded within me, "Stop! Call the German couple!"

That same voice that commanded me to alertness then commanded Barry into action. He called Helmut, the German doctor. Thankfully, because it was so early in the morning, he answered his phone, got the update from Barry, and headed right over to our house. When Helmut arrived, he told us that he had been praying the entire time, since this situation can be quite dangerous. He had us pray together.

After he put on surgical gloves, he told me what he was about to do would be painful, but for only a short time. With one hand, he pulled on the umbilical cord, and with his other hand, he made a fist and pushed down on my lower belly putting pressure on my uterus. It was so painful that I almost passed out. I was close to passing out anyway because of all the blood loss.

Out popped the placenta, which he examined to make sure it was whole. Helmut and Barry breathed a sigh of relief. The bleeding soon stopped. As a tender good shepherd, he took care of everything for us, and sweetly bid us all sleep for a while. Before he left, he said a prayer of blessing for Rami. In our altered state, this German doctor seemed more like an angel than a human being.

After he left, the three of us lay in bed and slept for hours. When I awoke, Barry and Rami were still sleeping. How heavenly to watch them both. I got out of bed, still feeling weak, drank a huge amount of water, and lay down on a blanket in the afternoon sun. I couldn't help feeling a little sad. Somehow, I equated the difficulty of the labor with failure of some kind. I asked God why it had been so hard for me. Perhaps because I was so vulnerable and open, the reply came immediately:

"God provides the greatest opportunities for growth to those who deeply ask."

I felt how I needed it all to make me stronger, to bring Barry and me to a point of complete dependence upon God, and to bring us closer to one another. The sadness was replaced by extreme gratefulness and, to this day, I feel thankful for every precious and difficult minute of that labor experience.

Rami has grown up to be a very strong and caring woman. Besides getting her PhD in psychology, she also trained among 28 men and became a firefighter. Strength is not about maleness.

We originally gave Rami the name "Jemila," which means "beautiful" in Arabic. When we brought her to be blessed by Babaji, he wrote down on his little chalkboard, "Rami," named after the powerful prophet and warrior, Ram. At first, we disagreed with Babaji but, in the end, we saw that he was once again right. Yes, Rami was beautiful, but her strength and power were even more striking.

When Rami was one week old, I was sitting outside holding her. In the old ranch house, the heavy steel frame windows cranked outward, and the corners of the window frames were wickedly sharp. Barry once mentioned how dangerous it could be to inadvertently walk into one of them.

The phone suddenly started to ring. This was before cell phones and even before answering machines, so if the phone rang, a person usually picked it up. We received very few calls, and I was expecting and wanting to receive a call from my mother. Holding Rami's head very tenderly in front of me, I walked quickly forward up our back stairs toward the back door. I was looking down at Rami the whole time. Just as Rami's tiny head was about to be pierced by the corner of that open window, I distinctly felt being firmly pushed to one side, and narrowly missed that sharp corner.

No one else was around. I am convinced that Rami's guardian angel was watching over her and protected her from what could have been serious injury. This experience has strengthened my faith that angels indeed exist and are there to help us when we need them.

The bliss of Rami's birth faded slowly after about one month, and I was faced with the day-to-day care of a baby. I worked full-time seeing psychotherapy clients right up to six hours before labor started, and I tried to go back to work two weeks later. I tried taking Rami with me into counseling sessions, but it didn't work. She was very sensitive toward others. She immediately cried if someone expressed the slightest negativity. Rami would sense the energy of each client, start screaming, and be unable to nurse. I realized that I needed to stop working and devote myself completely to surrounding Rami with a peaceful, loving environment.

At first, my ego screamed in protest. There was no recognition from others. Just the simple day-to-day tasks of caring for an infant. In my heart, I knew I was doing what God wanted of me. Yet the voice of my heart was still quiet compared with the screams of my mind. It gradually changed. Caring for Rami was teaching me the way of love. I was learning to truly give, without ego gratification.

One morning, when Rami was six months old, I awakened with a sense of complete fulfillment and joy. The day that stretched before me was the same as any other day ... love and care for my child. Barry was scheduled to see six clients that day, all of whom were my favorites when we were counseling together. As I gazed at the schedule, I waited for that usual pang of jealousy of feeling that Barry would be doing more important work than me. Instead, I felt grateful to simply be a mother.

As I was nursing Rami later that day, and my heart felt overwhelmed with love, I felt a presence and soft light fill the room. I heard the words,

"There is no greater service, or work in the world, than loving and raising a holy child."

In affirmation of these words, I heard a faint but distinct sound of angelic singing. I had heard this same sound only once before, when Rami was born. No amount of career importance or worldly recognition could be better than the fulfillment and joy I felt from doing God's will.

We loved being parents to Rami and felt that one child was enough for us. We took her camping and had all kinds of fun adventures out of doors. We were in the house sometimes, but mostly outside. If we were inside the house, Rami sometimes sneaked outside as a very little girl of maybe just two years old and walked down the country road to our neighbors Norris and Marie. We were very careful in watching Rami, but she was also very skilled about slipping away, opening doors and leaving. It was not unusual to get a call from Norris in his Texas accent, "Barra, the baby's down here again and she's got no clothes on." The fact that she did not have any clothes on was more upsetting to them than the fact that she had walked barefoot all the way down the country road by herself. We quickly ran down and retrieved her. Adventure could have been Rami's first name as that is what she is all about.

When Rami was almost three, I wanted to somehow convey that God is not some distant being, but very close and within her. So, each night before she fell asleep, I would lovingly rub her heart, sing a little song, and then gently say, "God is in your heart, dear Rami."

We never know how things will be received by our children. We can only try, wait, and then make adjustments when necessary. By the end of several weeks of this approach, I could tell something was beginning to stir and awaken.

One night, while I was rubbing her heart and repeating about God being in her heart, she looked up at me with pensive eyes and softly asked, "Doesn't God want to get out and play sometimes?"

Looking into her bright blue eyes, I vividly saw my own seriousness about spirituality, my wanting to confine God into a package. The door of my own heart opened, and out came God ... playful as could be, dancing, loving, smiling, eyes twinkling and full of humor.

Together, we tweaked the concept a little. God is in our hearts and also all around us. Rami was pleased, and I learned a valuable lesson.

An amazing miracle occurred when Rami was six years old. She wrote the following in her book, *Rami's Book*, when she was eleven:

"We went on a camping trip to our favorite lake. We were totally alone. My sister, Mira, was just a new baby and needed lots of care and attention. My mother and father were very busy with Mira, so I often played alone with our dog, Kriya. One day, while Mira was crying and my parents were changing her diaper, I decided to get some peace and quiet. I called Kriya to come for a walk. We went through the meadow and crossed a little stream. I played at the stream for a while and then continued up the meadow. I picked wild flowers as I went. Soon I came to a woods and kept walking. Kriya followed and I felt very happy. I even skipped a little.

After a while, I felt I should go back to our camp spot. I looked around and discovered I was lost. I had no idea which way to go. Everything looked the same.

I asked Kriya how we should go back. She lay down and just looked up at me. She wanted more of an adventure. I knew she wouldn't help me get back home.

I sat down on a rock and started to cry. Kriya came very close to comfort me. After a while, I realized crying wouldn't help, so I started screaming as loud as I could. The screaming didn't help either because my parents couldn't hear me.

I remembered what my parents had said about my Heavenly Mother. I thought I would try asking for her help. I closed my eyes and tried to imagine what a Heavenly Mother would look like. I asked if she would please help me to get back to my parents.

I sat with my eyes closed for a short time trying to hear her talk to me. I couldn't hear anything except the singing of birds and Kriya's breathing. When I opened my eyes, I could hardly believe what I saw. There was a light golden mist hardly touching the ground. It led in one direction and I knew I must follow it. It disappeared behind me as I walked. I felt so light and happy as I walked along. I followed the golden mist all the way back to our camp. When I looked back, there was nothing but the meadow.

I ran to my mother and hugged her tight. Mira had cried a long time and had just fallen asleep. My parents had just started looking for me.

Now I know that I do have a wonderful Heavenly Mother."

Chapter 23: Pearl Dorris

Barry and I were forever curious and hungry for as much spiritual knowledge as we could receive. One day, a man at a spiritual gathering told us that he had heard of a woman named Pearl Dorris who could see your entire life and could help you attain full enlightenment in a short period of time. This turned out not to be true, but at the time it sounded like something we should investigate. He gave us only her address in Mt. Shasta. Her phone number was unlisted.

I was six months pregnant at the time, and it was one week before Christmas. We decided that we would travel the seven hours by car up to her house. We had never been to Mt. Shasta and did not know anyone there. We found the address and a very sweet, plain-looking older woman answered the door.

"Are you Pearl Dorris?" we timidly asked. "Yes, I am," she answered with a lisp. We felt rather foolish. We had driven seven hours and now stood in the snow by her front door. This woman could have been anyone's grandma, but not someone who could give you enlightenment in a short period of time.

We told her we were sorry for bothering her, and told her someone must have given us incorrect information. Pearl invited us into her living room, and wanted to know what was said about her. Feeling embarrassed for bothering this dear, apparently simple, woman who had curly gray hair, we told her.

She had a big laugh and said the stories sure get blown up. Then she seriously looked at us and said, "I help people hear their own inner voice and promptings. I help people know what is most important in life."

As she spoke, we both saw a subtle golden light around her. We settled into our chairs and thus began a very interesting adventure with our next teacher, Pearl Dorris.

On that first visit, we stayed for two days, and met with Pearl each of those days. And from then on, we traveled up north whenever we could and, when our daughter Rami was just one year old, we rented a house in Mt. Shasta so that we could see Pearl every day.

Pearl was not an easy teacher. Sometimes she was very loving, and other times she would reprimand us. Sometimes she spoke with pure wisdom, and other times not. It was difficult to know the difference, but after a while we understood when we were with the very advanced part of Pearl and when we were not. Our other major teachers, Leo Buscaglia, Ram Dass, Pir Vilayat, and Baba Hari Dass, were more fun and predictable. But as hard as it was sometimes, the lessons from Pearl were perhaps the most valuable. For Pearl taught us to listen within and constantly check what we do by our inner guidance.

Barry had left his psychiatric residency just two years previously. Though he was away from medicine and was now meditating each day, he still very much thought like a doctor, especially a trained psychiatrist. To a lesser degree, the same was true of me. Pearl repeatedly told us, "Until you experience people as the divine being that they are, rather than judging and making a diagnosis, you will never really help them. As long as a person feels judged, they will not fully trust you."

Barry's psychiatric training taught him to make a diagnosis and proceed from there. Since I worked also with psychiatric patients, I had the same difficulty.

It was not possible to make an appointment with Pearl. She allowed people to just come whenever they wanted. You might be having a very private conversation with her and six others might show up and also sit in the living room with her. At first, we both found this annoying and, rather than going with her flow, we would judge whoever it was that had "interrupted" us.

When the people would leave, at least early on in our training, she would yell at us, "I saw you judging those people. You were not seeing their divine nature." And pointing a finger usually at Barry, she raised her voice even a bit louder and said, "I saw you even giving that one man a diagnosis. Yes, he has a hard time in this life as he is so sensitive. But he is a child of God just like you are. No different. You will never be able to really serve God in this life as long as you judge and see imperfection in others."

This went on time after time, and sometimes I wondered why we drove seven hours to Mt. Shasta just to be yelled at.

The deeper part of us knew that she was right. Finally, she gave us this beautiful meditation to follow that has helped even to this day.

> *Close your eyes and imagine you are in a cluttered office: papers everywhere, piles of things to do, and an uncomfortable pressure to do them.*
> *Now turn around and notice a door in the back of the office.*
> *Go ahead, approach it and open it.*
> *There is a staircase behind the door leading downward.*
> *Walk down the stairs.*
> *At the bottom of the stairs there is another door.*
> *Open it.*
> *Walk into a vast, light-filled room that is neither indoors nor outdoors.*
> *This is an expansive, sacred space like a beautiful temple or cathedral.*
> *It is filled with light and warmth, balance of color, uncluttered simplicity, and great beauty.*
> *You have just travelled from your mind to your heart.*
> *Feast your senses upon all that is here... the wisdom, strength and inspiration found in your heart.*

The summer that we lived in Mt. Shasta, I felt that we progressed in our learning from her more than any other time. Now, rather than every few months, it was almost every day. One of us watched one-year-old Rami while the other spent the day on the slopes of Mt. Shasta and the evening with Pearl. The next day it was reversed.

Barry: At the time, we were enamored with mystical teachings and paranormal phenomena. We were spending as much time with Pearl as we could, and reading the *I Am* books. Pearl often spoke about the hidden realms inside the sacred mountain. We heard stories of dedicated and devoted seekers gaining admission to these secret places, and being initiated into the higher mysteries of life. Could this possibly happen to us!

Our plan was to take turns each day, one of us seeking "enlightenment" on the slopes of the fabled mountain, while the other took on the "worldly, non-spiritual task" of caring for our toddler. Of course, now we realize our folly, and relish any opportunity to spend time with a baby or child as one of the highest paths to the divine.

It was my turn on this particular day to be the "spiritual seeker," and to go forth seeking enlightenment upon the sacred mountain. Kissing my family goodbye, I ventured high up the alpine terrain and finally found my "power spot" on a ledge with a magnificent view of the mountains on the western side of the valley. There I sat seeking otherworldly experiences for several hours to no avail. I did not gain access into the mountain. I did, however, become more peaceful, something that today I would consider a huge success. I finally gave in to fatigue and took a nap in the warm sunshine.

By late afternoon, it was time to leave my ledge. I sadly considered my time on the mountain a failure. I picked my way down the steep slope to Panther Meadow, with its little stream gurgling down the center. As I descended along the trail, I noticed a man lying on the grass close to the stream. I was passing him perhaps thirty feet to the side, and had a peculiar feeling something was wrong. I paused for a moment to make sure he was breathing, which he was, then continued walking but was stopped again by a strange impulse to go over to him. Immediately, my mind judged this as foolish. The man was probably taking a nap, probably seeking solitude, maybe even on the mountain for the same reason I was there, seeking spiritual growth.

I started to pass him when I again felt stopped by a stronger prompting to sit next to him. Again, my mind kicked in with all the reasons I shouldn't do this. He'll probably think you're some kind of weirdo, or picking up on him, and he'll ask you to leave him alone. I wouldn't blame him. If I was meditating or relaxing beside a stream in the wilderness and someone sat down right next to me, I probably would be upset too.

The sensible thing to do was to leave him alone, but I just couldn't ignore the urge I was feeling. Perhaps it was all the meditation on the mountain that enhanced my sensitivity to this seemingly inappropriate prompting, but I hesitated no longer. I turned, took a deep breath, walked up to this man, and sat one foot away from his head. I felt like a complete idiot, and braced myself for his likely negative reaction.

The man opened his eyes and looked at me with an expression that registered no surprise whatsoever. I had the eerie sensation that he seemed to be expecting me. He sat up and, without small talk or any form of greeting, proceeded to speak, "I've been lying here planning my suicide, but prayed one last time in desperation, 'If there is a God, please send someone to help me.' A few minutes later, you sat down beside me."

I spent perhaps thirty minutes speaking with this man, and listened to his sad story. In that time, it became crystal clear to both of us that there indeed was a higher power in the Universe, and this power sent me to him in his time of deepest need. He looked directly into my eyes and proclaimed, "Now I don't need to kill myself. I have proof of God's existence. How can I ever thank you?"

I said, "You've already thanked me. I needed the same divine proof you did. You've probably helped me just as much as I've helped you."

And I meant that. I felt so light that I almost felt as if I could float away.

We stood up together and hugged, then he gave his farewell and started walking down the path. He stopped after about fifty feet, turned and waved, and I saw a radiant smile light up his face. Then he turned away and was gone. I never saw him again.

I continued to sit in that holy spot, mesmerized by what had just happened. I didn't even know his name, but I did know that I was used as an instrument of love. I also knew without a doubt that this fellow would never kill himself. And it wasn't my psychiatric training and experience that convinced me of this. It was a deeper knowing that comes from true spiritual realization.

That afternoon on Mt. Shasta changed the course of my spiritual quest. Previously, spirituality was something to acquire, something just for me. Now, spirituality was more than just for me. I realized that the highest mystical experience was the joy and fulfillment of truly helping another. I realized that immature spirituality is selfish. It's about acquiring more power, happiness, or peace. Mature spirituality is not selfish. It's about helping and sharing, creating a larger good than self.

Since that day on the mountain, I try to listen more carefully to that sometimes-irrational intuition. I really want to be of service here on earth, and I can't do the highest job by just listening to my mind. I need to listen to that deeper prompting, the voice of my heart, which may seem completely irrational, and then I know I am really helping.

That day on the mountain, I was looking for the divine masters outside of myself. I ended up finding the divine master that lives inside me ... as me!

Sometime later, on my day to explore on my own, I drove into the mountains above Lake Siskiyou, on a road following the upper stretches of the Sacramento River. I had heard about a magical lake that was only accessible by four-wheel drive vehicles. Since our VW van was only two-wheel drive, I drove to the end of the paved road, parked, then walked several miles on the rough road to a truly gorgeous small lake set in a glacial bowl. There was granite everywhere, with a gem of a lake set in the middle like a sparkling diamond in a granite setting.

I spent the day meditating and frolicking in the lake. I had it all too myself. And I knew I had to bring Joyce and Rami here to experience this wonderland. Because I had walked the road to the lake, I had the chance to really evaluate the possibility of getting there in our van. I decided it was doable.

That night, I told Joyce about the lake, amply describing its glories. I was not prepared for her reaction. She said, "Barry, I have a bad feeling about going there."

Deflated, I still rallied, "But why? It's gorgeous! And I checked the road out carefully. We can make it in our van."

Joyce has often had a hard time opposing my desires. Still, she said, "I can't explain my feeling. The more you go on about this place, the worse I feel."

I wouldn't give up. I promised her a great time, and finally she relented. We went the next morning, despite her misgivings.

We left the paved road and ventured onto the four-wheel-drive road. I have to acknowledge, it was not easy going, but slowly, carefully, we bumped along for several miles.

We were just about to the lake, when I started to press down on the clutch and the pedal fell to the floor. I immediately knew that the clutch cable had just snapped.

I looked over at Joyce, who had been tense the whole trip. She saw a strange expression on my face, and asked with concern, "Barry, what's wrong?"

I said, "The clutch cable just broke."

Now she was worried, and asked, "What does that mean?"

I'm not exactly a car mechanic, but I did know a thing or two. I did my own tune-ups and minor repairs, closely following a book called, *How to Keep Your Volkswagen Alive: A Manual of Step-by-Step Procedures for the Complete Idiot.*

"It means changing gears won't be easy, but it can be done without a clutch. The lake should be just up ahead. Do you want me to keep going? We could still have a good time there."

"Absolutely not," was her vehement reply. "Please get us turned around and let's get home."

And thus began a very difficult journey, first getting our van turned around, and then creeping along in first gear for several hours, dodging boulders and holes. All in all, it was a long and miserable trip back to our house in Mt. Shasta. Rami cried pretty much the whole time. Joyce appeared to be praying at times, deeply worried at other times. Even when we reached the main road, it required the utmost finesse to time gear changes to exactly match our speed, otherwise there would be a loud grinding of gears.

That night, after we put Rami to bed, Joyce sat with me to "talk." She began, "Barry, I'm really angry at you for pressuring me to go on this trip. You know I have a hard time saying no to you, especially when you're so enthusiastic. But I'm angrier at myself. I didn't have a good feeling from the very first time you brought it up, but I didn't fight for my feelings. I didn't listen to my intuition. I gave up on myself. From now on, I'm giving you notice, if I don't have a good feeling about something, I'm not going to let you change my mind!"

After that day's experience, what could I say? And to this day, I have gradually learned to listen to Joyce's feelings. Sometimes I don't like them, because they go against my desires. Of course, I also listen to my own intuition, deeper than my desires. And if my intuition differs from Joyce's intuition, we each have to listen very carefully to the other side. We try to find a compromise, a very important art for couples.

Not long ago, I wanted to raft the Owyhee River in very remote Southeast Oregon. The window for doing this had just opened and was very short. In other words, the river levels were dropping fast. I proposed the trip to Joyce. I always prefer that she come with me. I love her company. But she had a strong reaction, a bad feeling, which actually was rare for her. Joyce tries her very best to honor my need for the wilderness, even though she worries about my safety. On some of my trips, I can go for days without seeing another soul.

I felt disappointed by her reaction, but something in me (perhaps my own intuition) listened and stayed home. What would have been in the middle of my trip, our beloved nine-year-old golden retriever, Rosie, went rapidly downhill. She had been treated for cancer and seemed to be thriving. She died, and I was there to comfort her and Joyce.

How glad I was to honor Joyce's premonition and put my desires aside.

Joyce: Because we had a baby, we could never go to see Pearl together. Our friend, Steve, agreed to watch Rami while she slept one evening, and we went together to see Pearl. That evening, it was just the two of us for several hours with her. Barry reached out and took my hand. I smiled at him in return.

Pearl looked for a moment at our joined hands, then spoke up in a sharp voice, "You two are too close. You will never find your way to God as you are too busy loving each other. You need to lead separate lives."

Oh no, not this again, remembering our experience in Chamonix in which Pir Vilayat gave us permission to be together always and love each other as much as we could. I thought Barry would sense that this was not true for us, but he was taking it in a hundred percent.

Driving back that night, he announced that we should sleep in separate bedrooms and be totally separate for the rest of the summer. I honored Barry's decision, but I was miserable. We led separate lives, talking only to exchange information about Rami. Everything about this felt wrong to me.

A week later, it was my turn to be alone on the mountain. I prayed so deeply for help as I was so unhappy. I wanted to honor Barry, and I wanted to believe Pearl, but it all felt wrong.

Then it was Barry's turn. He took off for the mountain bright and early. Rami and I both had a difficult day. She was teething and in pain, and I was feeling overwhelmed with loneliness. I had spoken to no one in the past four days except Rami, whose vocabulary mainly consisted of "mama, daddy, and dolly." She cried a lot over her teeth, while I was assailed by doubts. "What a stupid thing to be doing. It's not right that you don't talk with Barry, or sleep with him. This is getting you nowhere..."

Rami finally settled down for the night and I went to my lonely room downstairs, where I felt lonelier than I had in a long time. At that moment, I heard the familiar sound of our VW van, and ran to the window. I watched Barry get out of the van. He seemed to be shining like the sun, and I could tell he had a good day by the way he walked. I longingly watched him as he skipped up the outside stairs to his private bedroom. My mind and body were aching to be with him. He had been my best friend for thirteen years, and I knew just being with him for a few minutes would erase the dreadful loneliness I felt. I was ready to run to meet him, but something stopped me. My heart clearly said, "No, don't go, continue to be alone."

Sad and resigned, I went out for a walk in the evening air. The darkness seemed blacker than usual and even the presence of our beloved golden retriever, Bokie, didn't cheer me up. Tears flowed as I cried out to God for understanding.

Suddenly, I was filled with the feeling of being with my very best friend. It was as if that friend surrounded me as I walked, loving me completely. Yet I was alone. How could that be?

I got it. My best friend can never be someone outside myself. My truest friend is within. When I look only to Barry for that friendship ... or to Rami ... or to any other human being, I will never be totally satisfied. It is the friend within our own heart, the divine presence inside us that fills the loneliness and gives us the feeling of being totally loved.

I began to dance with joy.

The next evening, I went to Pearl's home and found her sitting quietly with Steve and another man, two of her closest students. I sat quietly with them. After about a half hour, Pearl opened her eyes and said, "I have a message for one of you. Do not worship the messenger. Seek your own message inside."

I knew that message was for Barry and me. Pearl was just a messenger, and sometimes not a perfect one at that. I needed to trust my own message, just like I needed to trust my feelings about not going to the lake that Barry was so excited about.

I drove immediately home and told Barry what I had just experienced. His eyes softened and he said, "I've been so miserable trying to do what Pearl suggested. Let's sleep together and be close."

Later that night, after making unbelievably sweet and passionate love, as we lay close in each other's arms, we realized we had been given another lesson in learning to trust our own inner voice and never again give our power away to someone else.

Very soon, we would be tested again. Still thirsty for spiritual training and a deeper understanding, we found out about a visiting Sufi teacher from England, who was living in Santa Cruz.

This man was very charismatic and had many students who would do anything for him. I also could not help but notice that he drank quite a bit of hard liquor. This man loved us both very much and kept urging his other students to notice how much we loved each other. He was amazed that a man could look at his wife of many years with as much love as Barry looked at me.

One evening he said, "I can bring you closer to God, but you must come to me and allow me to give you direction, even if you do not like the direction. It is in following that you will grow closer to God."

So, easily forgetting my past lesson from Pearl, I humbly went forward with others and knelt before this man. He touched our heads and gave us what he said was an initiation. I thought I would feel something wonderful, but instead I felt strange and ungrounded. Barry, for whatever reason, did not go with me to bow at his feet.

The next day, I felt even worse and this feeling grew over the week. I could not meditate and could barely properly take care of our then two-year-old Rami. Barry made a decision on his own and announced, "I'm taking you to be with Pearl. I'll watch Rami and you sit with Pearl." I went along with what he said, and we left for Mt. Shasta.

While Rami slept in her car seat in the room, Barry and I both were able to sit with Pearl. Pearl took one look at me and said, "Oh my, what happened to you? You are not doing well at all. It's like just a part of you is here."

Barry and I explained. Pearl spoke with such tenderness and love, "You have given your power over to this man, and he is not a clear channel. He drinks too much and that is interfering in his work. I will help you to come back."

For over an hour she sat with me and helped me to come back into my body and into my power. When I felt fully back, she very gently said, "Don't ever let this happen to you again. Don't give your power over to someone else. The voice in your own heart is the most important. That is all the direction that you need. You can get encouragement and inspiration from others, but the direction for your life will always come from your own heart."

I am so grateful to Pearl for many things, but the very most important thing she gave me is this lesson of fully honoring the voice within your own heart. I was thirty-one then and, now in my seventies, that lesson is still such an important one. I have never made that mistake again. It may take longer to hear the message when you listen inside, but it will be the right answer if you take long enough. Going to a psychic can be quick, but it can never be as pure a message as what comes from your own heart.

Pearl's words continue to live in my mind, even though it has been perhaps thirty years since she passed from this world. "Lead a simple, humble life. Always know that your strength and power come from God. Don't pretend to be anything other than a simple, ordinary person. Focus your energies on loving each person who comes to you for help. Constantly tune into your heart for direction and guidance. Remember how much you are loved and cared for. Knowing this is the greatest healer of all."

Such a blessing and a miracle to receive such wisdom from a simple ordinary housewife with a lisp.

Chapter 24: Ram Dass

Barry and my introduction to Ram Dass began in 1971 when we read his first book, *Be Here Now*. We were absolutely transfixed as it answered so many of our questions. Sitting in our backpacking spot in the mountains above Los Angeles, we felt that it would be so wonderful if some day we could meet him.

Ram Dass was a Harvard professor of psychology who traveled to India, found a guru, Neem Karoli Baba (Maharaji), and then brought back the lessons of his guru to our country. He became an instant hit in America. Our country was deeply involved in Viet Nam, Nixon and civil rights. There were big marches in Washington DC. Young people were upset and some of them were dealing with being upset by getting involved in drugs. Ram Dass's message was perfect for the times and the hippie culture. It brought in a sense of grounded energy and spirituality that was needed. Although we felt a strong affinity to the hippie culture, Barry was in medical school and I had a full-time job. But we were needing Ram Dass's message of spirituality.

Ram Dass sold a box of records called "Love, Serve, Remember". (yes, this was a box of LP's, no tapes or CD's back then) This boxed set held perhaps five records and he sold it for five dollars, probably just what he paid to have it made. The records contained talks and singing. We listened to them over and over until we knew them by heart, and then still we listened some more. Every word, every song, seemed to resonate with something from deep within us both.

After medical school was over, we moved to Portland, Oregon for Barry's residency. We brought our box of records of course. One day, we noticed that Ram Dass was actually coming to Oregon, speaking at a small town south of Portland. Barry and I got the day off from school and work and traveled there. The group gathered there was small, so we got to sit up close. We could simply not believe our good fortune to actually be sitting in the same room as Ram Dass. He was very intelligent, handsome, funny and charismatic. He was always making jokes about his own shortcomings as well as showing vulnerability. We loved him even more in person. After the talk, he said he needed to go into Portland to speak on an all-night radio show, but his car had broken down.

Could anyone drive him? Our hands shot into the air before he even finished the question. It was decided. We would drive him and someone else would get his car fixed and bring it to Portland so that he could have it after the radio show.

Ram Dass was actually in our car!!! I had to keep pinching myself to believe it was really true. After almost two years of listening to his voice on the records, he was sitting in our car. The interesting thing is that he seemed just like an ordinary man with a Boston accent. And yet it was his ordinariness that made us love him all the more.

We stayed for as much of the all-night show as we could, given that we had school and work the next day. We sat in a little room adjoining the studio with a large window in-between. As usual, we soaked up every word he spoke. And periodically, he looked at us with a face beaming with love.

Before we left, he gave us his address in Massachusetts at his father's summerhouse, and welcomed us to visit him if we were in the area.

One year later, we did visit him there. He sat with us for a while and gave us addresses of people we should meet. It was a simple very short meeting. At the end of the meeting, he looked at me with his piercing blue eyes and said, "It's difficult being with you because you see me as someone more special than you. I am not. I want you to know that."

It was hard for me to take in his words, for I had him on such a high pedestal but, over time in the next years, I saw his wisdom and understood why he said what he did – and why he didn't spend much time with us.

We did not see Ram Dass again for three years. By this time, our little girl was two years old. We heard that he had moved to Soquel of all places, a little town just ten minutes from our home in Aptos. We found out his phone number and called him. He reluctantly agreed to let us come over.

Barry and I had changed since our last visit with him in Massachusetts. Now we no longer had him on a high pedestal. Instead, we actually felt that we had a lot to teach him. We had spent much time with Pearl and felt somehow above Ram Dass. It is embarrassing even to admit this.

Anyway, he ushered us into his backyard and invited us to sit on one side of a picnic table. He took a seat on the other side of the table and started eating an apple. We tried to explain to him all the ways in which we now felt very holy. After all, we were dressed in white clothes with beads. At least we looked the part. He sat there eating his apple and listened to us for a while, those piercing blue eyes moving back and forth between us.

Finally, he said, "Stop! You both are giving me a giant headache. You really need help!"

Stunned, I looked at Barry, who also seemed to be in shock.

Ram Dass continued, "I'll agree to help you get back on the true path, not this "phony holy" path you are now on, but only if you come one at a time. I cannot be with you both together, or you'll probably continue to give me headaches."

Talk about a humbling experience, but we needed it.

Ram Dass normally lived in Marin County north of San Francisco. He was writing a book about his guru, Neem Karoli Baba, called *Miracle of Love,* and wanted to live in a different place away from all that was familiar. He shared later that he had no idea why, but he just chose Soquel. He decided ahead of time to work with four people, so that it could help ground him as he spent all of his time writing. Barry and I became two of those people. Thus began an in-depth and very humbling experience of sitting and being counseled by Ram Dass, a very wise psychologist and spiritual teacher. He saw us for free, sometimes every week, sometimes every month for two years.

Our experiences with Ram Dass were amazing, funny and difficult at the same time. He gave so much of himself and we were eager students. And he helped us to sort through all that was not working in our lives, including all that was not working in our relationship with each other.

Barry: Although we had learned a powerful lesson from Pearl, to listen to our own intuition, we again lapsed back into the idea that celibacy was a faster spiritual path. That having sex might somehow cause us to lose our connection with our divine Source. We stopped having sex, this time for six months. We were actually proud of this accomplishment!

During this time, we began to have headaches, and our full counseling practice dwindled down to only a few clients. It was like our juiciness was drying up.

Ram Dass was not impressed by our sexual abstinence. He said we were trying to be spiritual from our neck up. That our sexuality needed to be included in our spirituality.

We finally got the message, and began an important journey of integrating sexuality with spirituality, of actually allowing our sexuality to be a form of meditation and prayer. It was liberating. Miraculously, our headaches disappeared and our counseling practice filled back up.

One of my visits happened to coincide with Halloween, which triggered some old memories from my childhood. I told Ram Dass about my childhood obsession with monsters. I had watched every horror movie that came out, read monster stories, played monster games at night with my friends in the neighborhood, delighting in scaring them with my various expert monster sounds. One night while my parents were next door at the Cooper's house, they heard a loud roar and scream coming from outside. Upset, the Coopers asked what had happened. My mom casually remarked, "Oh that's just Barry playing his monster games."

Yes, part of all this was perhaps innocent, but there was another part that was shameful to me, that I hid and didn't tell anyone but Joyce. It was my cruelty, the ways I took out my anger that hurt others, that was particularly shameful. In a way, the monster part of myself represented this aspect of cruelty.

Ram Dass listened compassionately as I bared my soul to him. He asked me to close my eyes and feel this shameful part of myself as deeply as I could. While I did so, he secretly reached down beside his chair into a bag and quietly pulled out a mask that he planned to wear that evening for Halloween. By "coincidence" it just happened to be a full-head, very realistic, cruel-looking monster mask. He slipped it on and asked me to open my eyes.

I was in a very vulnerable state when I opened my eyes and, unlike a traditional therapist, Ram Dass was sitting with his face perhaps two feet from mine. The scene was surreal. I felt like I was in the Twilight Zone. There was this hideous life-like face immediately in front of me, my complete projection of the cruel monster inside of me, scary beyond belief. And then I noticed the eyes through the mask. There was no cruelty there, only compassion and love pouring out to me. The combination was so incongruous that I felt a shift occur inside of me, an acceptance of the monster part of me, and especially the pain and anger that was behind it.

I started laughing. Ram Dass looked kind of cute with the mask but, more importantly, I felt the cuteness of my own inner monster persona. Not that my cruelty was cute, but that *I* was cute, and thus could more deeply forgive myself for the actions that hurt others.

I was touching upon the heart of self-acceptance. Behind my shame was my pain, and behind my pain is the precious, innocent child that deserves love.

Joyce: When his book was done, Ram Dass moved back to Marin. Before he did, he counseled us to write a book about relationships, "You have much to teach, as you are the closest couple I have ever met. The world needs what you have to say and there is no book out there that is really honest about relationships. Your book will be a pioneer in the field of relationships. I'll edit your words and give you all of my contacts to find a publisher. Do it!"

Obviously, we no longer gave him headaches!

Chapter 25: The Bokie Test

To gain further inspiration for this book, Barry and I decided to go on a camping trip to our favorite place, Mount Shasta. Our first day there was a glorious, cool and colorful early November day. Some friends who lived there were watching four-year-old Rami for a night and a day, a very rare treat. It gave us time to be just the two of us. We visited our beloved Pearl. We hiked the slopes of the mountain, stopping often to kiss and feel how much we loved each other.

We camped for the night at Panther Meadows at 7500 feet elevation. It was gorgeous, with scattered patches of snow, a little stream bubbling icy water from a magical spring at the top of the meadow. The glistening snow-covered mountain majestically towered above us. The air seemed charged with electricity and I felt as though I could fly.

Instead, I danced throughout the lush, green grasses of the meadow. Barry laughed and caught me in his arms. There was so much love and attraction, our bodies begged to be closer, so we retreated to our VW van, pulled my hand-made tie-dyed curtains closed, threw off our clothes, and merged physically, emotionally, and spiritually. During the height of our ecstasy, we both felt the nearness of a third being, a great and majestic presence, pouring forth love and blessing us.

Back in our home in Santa Cruz three days later, while I was lying down to take a nap, something within me felt different. I intuitively felt that an egg and sperm had united inside me. I was pregnant.

Tears of gratitude filled me, and I rose to give thanks. For the next ten days, I felt a beautiful soul so close to me that I could almost reach out and touch this being of light. With each new day, I grew more in love with this wondrous being. I was thrilled that this soul was coming to us. My hopes and dreams took off like a skyrocket.

Soon after, Barry took Rami for a little overnight camping trip. I was happy to be alone ... to love and dream of my new baby. I sat outside in our garden. It couldn't have been a more beautiful day.

Suddenly I began to bleed and bleed. My baby was leaving me. I was devastated! I had heard about the loneliness and despair that women experience when they lose a baby through miscarriage. I never really understood it until it happened to me. It felt like a great treasure was suddenly taken away from me, even after only ten days. It didn't matter, so deeply bonded I was to this baby. Why couldn't I keep you? Did you find me unworthy to be your mother? The painful questions kept coming like a storm. I couldn't help blaming myself. I prayed for an answer.

And then the answer came. I felt an inner reassurance that this child would, indeed, come to us. It was just not the right time. And we were not ready yet. There would be certain tests that would prepare and ready us. We needed to be thankful when the tests came, and remember their purpose.

One week later, my most beloved friend in the animal kingdom, Bokie, who was now ten years old, died quite suddenly. How deeply I adored that boy! He wasn't merely a dog to me. He was my special friend, my first child, a comforter, a teacher, and yes, even a mother at times. Whenever I felt sad and could not be with Barry or Rami, I'd turn to Bokie and put my arms around his body. I could feel his unconditional love and compassion take my pain away. It seemed his greatest pleasure came from just being near us and pouring love from his huge liquid brown eyes.

His health seemed to begin to fail right after the miscarriage. He grew worse and worse, and died within a week. What a hard test! Barry and I had never before felt the pangs of death so deeply. Our grief was profound!

Barry, especially, blamed himself as a medical doctor for not realizing the seriousness of his downward decline. He found Bokie in the morning. He had fallen in a small gap between our cement back porch and a playhouse my dad had built for Rami. It was very hard for Barry to find him wedged into that gap, to imagine that he might have suffered and died alone in that confined space.

In the end, we needed to realize that death comes when it comes, and it may not be pretty. We needed to trust that it was Bokie's time. It took me a long time to stop missing his lovable body, and begin to concentrate on his essence ... to know he would always be with us.

Chapter 26: Mira 1982

Sometime later, Barry and I took off on another camping trip, this time with Rami. From our 6,000-foot-high perch in the mountains, sitting with Barry watching Rami pick wild flowers, life seemed absolutely perfect. We were coming to peace over the loss of Bokie. Barry and I had the secret wish that nothing would change, that life would stay as simple and sweet as it seemed in that moment.

I closed my eyes to enjoy that peaceful moment and immediately felt the presence of another being. I started and quickly opened my eyes wondering who had come, only to discover Barry sitting next to me, and Rami still picking flowers. There was no one else there.

I closed my eyes again. Someone was there. I felt another presence even stronger than before. It felt like a very dear and special friend. I heard the words deep within my heart:

"You are ready now. I am coming to you and Barry. My presence in your lives will bring more depth to your relationship, as well as more balance and harmony into the family. I would like to be conceived soon."

I felt myself being surrounded by a peaceful warmth. I let myself bask in the joy of that experience.

I opened my eyes. I felt like I was bursting with joy and the desire to conceive and bring this special soul to earth through my body. I had to share this great news with Barry.

"Barry," I said, hardly containing myself. "We are going to have another child. I was just visited by the most amazing soul. Isn't that incredible?"

I was totally unprepared for the pained expression that came over his face, as well as his words, "I really don't want any more children right now. Can we just enjoy Rami?"

I felt almost jolted back to earth. I understood. I was the one who had this mystical experience, not Barry. And I believe our recent miscarriage had especially shaken him. I dropped the subject.

Several weeks later, this soul again visited me. I was meditating at home one morning. It's hard to describe how uplifted I felt after this visit. I knew without a doubt that it was time to conceive.

A little more cautiously, I shared my experience with Barry. I could see he was trying to catch my vision, but he just couldn't. His face finally settled on the same familiar pained expression. He started to open his mouth to speak, but decided against it. No more was said.

One month later, again during my morning meditation, the being again visited me. Again, I felt a profound peace and inspiration. This time, I simply addressed this radiant being the way someone would talk to a dear friend on the phone.

"Please, you must know I am open to having another child. I welcome you with open arms. You also must know that Barry is feeling quite resistant. I've done my best to get him on board. It hasn't worked. If you want to come to earth, you'll have to somehow visit Barry."

I had to smile to myself, it seemed like such a clever plan.

Three weeks later, Barry woke up one morning so filled with the desire for another child, he could hardly talk about anything else. For several nights in a row, he had vivid dreams of holding an infant girl after seeing her being born.

Several days later, I heard her voice again and this time she said,

"Now you are both ready, I want you to travel to Mt. Shasta and conceive me on the mountain on New Year's Day. There is a power on that day and in that place that I need."

We traveled with Rami to Mt. Shasta and while it was snowing in the evening, after Rami was sound asleep, we conceived Mira in our little camper on the slopes of Mt. Shasta. Mira brings such a blessed sweetness, joy and love to our lives and to Rami. I marvel at her ability to express her wants and needs even before birth so powerfully and indeed she is a powerful being.

Rami's birth lasted twenty-eight hours. Mira's birth came so fast that we barely could ready ourselves. Her birth was on the hottest day of the year, over a hundred degrees in the back bedroom of our house, the coolest room. To make matters worse for Barry and our two women friends who were there to help, I somehow couldn't get warm enough, and needed an extra electric heater to make the room warmer. Barry, dripping with sweat, said it was just like a sauna.

One push and Mira popped out. Barry brought her up to my left breast to nurse but, instead of nursing, she faced away from me to the left. I turned her head around to face me and my breast, but she quickly turned away from me. I had the momentary thought that she was rejecting me, but Barry assessed that her neck was stiff from the birth process. Smiling, I brought her around to my right side, and she eagerly latched on to my breast.

Rami holding Mira

One week after Mira was born, I felt strong enough to go for my first walk. It was the night of the full moon, and everything seemed magical outside. After Mira was asleep, I asked Barry to come with me, but he felt we shouldn't leave such a new baby alone, and urged me to go by myself.

I was out the door, across our little dirt road, and facing the dark woods, when an old fear hit me. Having been raised in a metropolitan area, I was also brought up with the fears of what could happen to a woman walking alone at night. As a child, there was a period of time when a rapist prowled our neighborhood in Buffalo, and I was not allowed to go outside by myself. And as a nursing student in New York City, besides my harrowing adventure on the subway, I had a few more times of being followed by men when I was out walking alone at night. The other nursing students thought I was crazy, but I had a thing for being out in the fresh (at least sometimes) air of the city. They said, "Why don't you just open a window if you want fresh air." That was not the same thing as actually being out there.

Standing there facing that large expanse of woods that felt so welcome in the daytime, I tried to talk myself into walking since the night was so special. I ventured somewhat fearfully onto the trail and into the darkness, where the large oaks and Monterey Pines blocked the full moonlight. I heard a small animal rustling along on the leafy floor, and my mind transformed it into the footsteps of a sinister prowler.

I was just about to turn around and get back home, when I felt a distinct rubbing sensation on my leg. I knew that sensation. It was, without a doubt, the spirit of Bokie. He was letting me know he was there, and would protect me every step of my walk. What a splendid walk it was!

Chapter 27: The Shared Heart Miracle

With the advent of our second pregnancy with our daughter Mira, Barry and I also started writing our first book, *The Shared Heart*. True to his word, with each chapter we wrote, Ram Dass edited and sent back his comments. Finally, we were done and we contacted his agent and publisher with a letter from him. The book was rejected. Pir Vilayat also gave us his publisher and agent, and again the book was rejected. As a matter of fact we were rejected thirty-five times by publishers. We were all ready to give up when Ram Dass called and I spoke to him.

"How is the book going?" he asked.

I replied, "We are thinking of giving up the project as thirty-five publishers have rejected us."

He said words that changed everything.

"If you are thinking of giving up just because you have been rejected by thirty-five publishers, then you are not the people I thought you were. I was rejected even more than that with my first book, *Be Here Now*.

Barry bought a book about self-publishing and, after many edits and proofreading parties with friends, we were ready to self-publish *The Shared Heart*. I remember that we were on a camping trip and, while our two little girls slept, we had a long and serious talk. We both realized that there was a part of us that was scared of publishing the book as it might change our lives. We led such a simple, humble life with our two little girls living in the woods. Publishing a book might bring us more into the public eye. What if we lost our quest for humility and developed a big ego, which was our biggest fear? What if it took us off the spiritual path that we were so dedicated to? There were many fears.

Finally, we prayed that if the book took us away from our spiritual path and we began to get lost in our egos, then we asked that we would become disconnected with each other and the pain would bring us back to what is most important, our hearts.

Later, deeply inspired by our talk, Barry took off into the woods and wrote the final chapter for our new book, a fictitious story about a couple's initiation. When he came home, he told me the story literally wrote itself. He felt lifted to a higher realm while writing.

Barry: The cover of the first edition of *The Shared Heart* was done by a woman named Nivedita Phoenix, a true hippie. It was hard for people to believe that an MD and an RN had actually written it. But it was an instant success. We were so excited when the books first arrived into our empty garage, a little like giving birth to a new baby. Both Ram Dass and Pir Vilayat gave us their mailing lists, totaling twelve thousand names. We printed twelve thousand flyers with information about the book, great testimonials, and detailed ordering information. Joyce and I managed to put address labels on about six thousand flyers, and took them to the post office.

That evening, we hosted a Thanksgiving service in our home for about twenty people. Each one of us shared the most difficult challenge in our life, and tried to give thanks in advance for the resolution that we couldn't see at the time.

After the service, we were so excited to show everyone the flyers. Our friend Nancy looked at one of the flyers curiously. We saw her turn the flyer over and over, a serious expression on her face. She looked at us and said, "I don't see the price of the book on the flyer."

I smiled confidently and took the flyer. "Of course, the price is on the flyer. How else can people order the book?"

I was wrong. I studied the whole flyer. Nowhere was there a price for the book.

With a sinking feeling, I realized six thousand flyers were on their way to six thousand homes where people would be unable to order our new book.

Swallowing hard, we realized that we needed to give thanks for this costly error. To ease our situation somewhat, the twenty people in our home that evening sat right down with pens and handwrote the price in the remaining six thousand flyers.

We made an expensive decision to send out a postcard to the original six thousand. On this card, we wrote, "In our eagerness to announce our new book, we neglected to put the cost of the book in the flyer you recently received. We discovered this the night before Thanksgiving, and realized that we needed to give thanks for this mistake." And yes, we included the cost of the book.

Before people could get the second flyer, I can't tell you how many people contacted us about our "priceless" flyer, some joking, some serious. So many people were touched by the lack of a price for the book, feeling our sincerity to share our new book, instead of just selling it.

The postcard did the trick. We couldn't have planned it better, the first flyer adding the mystery, and the postcard solving it.

We sold several thousand books just within the first week, sending them out from our home. Our daughters helped as well, little two-year-old Mira so excited to see a photo of mama and dada on each book.

Nervously, we waited for peoples' reactions. First to arrive was a small package. Inside was a cassette tape, nothing else. We rushed to find our boom box, stuck it in, and pushed play. After a pause, a man's voice said, "I just finished reading your book, and I want to tell you…" Then there was a long pause. Joyce and I looked at one another. Perhaps the tape malfunctioned. But no, we started hearing what sounded like crying, then full-on sobbing, for what seemed like several minutes. What on earth was going on?

Finally, the man seemed to have composed himself enough to speak, still full of emotion, "Your book has changed my life, and the way I now see relationships."

Then there was more crying.

It was the first reaction to our new book and, to this day, probably the one that has meant the most to us.

Joyce: We sold eighty thousand copies of *The Shared Heart* within just a few years. People liked our honesty and willingness to share difficult topics, like Barry's affair. *The Shared Heart* opened the door for our work in the world. It paved the way for our other books as well as the formation of the Shared Heart Foundation.

So much more than how many copies of our first book we sold, we have been deeply touched by the most amazing miracle stories. Here is one of them:

We once received an email from a woman who said the following, "I was on my way to take my life. I prayed to see even one thing that could give me hope. As I was walking toward the place where I would take my life, I passed a dumpster. Carefully resting up against the dumpster was a copy of your book, *The Shared Heart*. I stopped right there by the dumpster and began reading it. Your words gave me hope and the desire to go on. I have since gotten the help that I needed and I have a fulfilling life. Thank you for your book."

We feel the first miracle is the person who carefully placed the book by the dumpster. This person was probably going to throw it out, but instead decided to place it so someone might see it. It probably took ten seconds to do this thoughtful act, and yet those ten seconds saved a person's life. This person was a miracle for her life.

I often think about Ram Dass's decision to move just ten minutes from our home. He didn't really know us or even knew that we lived there. It just felt right to him. Because we had our little baby, we could not have traveled very easily to Marin to see him, nor would he have welcomed us there. Our time with him was meant to be in the quietness of Soquel. Those several years with him certainly shaped how we do our work. We never would have considered writing a book subtitled *Relationship Initiations and Celebrations*, as both of us are medically trained. I had one writing course in English in high school and Barry did not have any. And yet, with Ram Dass's encouragement and support, we wrote our first of ten books. Those years we spent with him, and the encouragement he gave us, all make up a beautiful miracle, and I feel so deeply grateful.

Chapter 28: The "California" Book

Barry and I sent my parents a copy of *The Shared Heart* as soon as the first shipment came. Coincidentally, the same week, my only sibling, my older brother, Bruce, sent my parents his first published book about power systems engineering. My brother is a genius in math and science, and I'm sure his book was excellent, if a person could understand what he was writing about. His book was professionally published, leather bound in dark brown with gold letters, and it was probably three inches thick. Our book was a self-published paperback, was light blue with the previous-mentioned hippy-like drawing on the cover, and was a little more than a half-inch thick.

Several months later, Barry and I and our two little girls made a trip to Buffalo, New York to see my parents. My parents have always kept their house very neat and so it was not hard to notice my brother's book resting all by itself on the coffee table as I entered the living room. I quietly looked around for our book but did not see it.

It was the next day that I began a serious search and found it in a back room, way up high on a book shelf mostly hidden from view. Hurt stabbed at my heart. All my life I have thought that my parents thought of my brother as more important than me. I got good grades in school, but my brother got perfect grades. Teachers knew me as Bruce Wollenberg's sister. I was shy. My brother was outgoing and very funny and could keep a room going with his humor for a long time. And then there was the embarrassment of my sensitivity and feeling nature.

The hiding of our book was too much for me to bear. I asked my mother why she placed our book so out of the way when my brother's book was in plain view. She hesitantly replied that she thought it should remain a "California" book and shouldn't be in other states. A huge rush of angry and hurt feelings came to the surface. I wanted to scream at my mother. Just as I was about to, a quiet voice inside of me said, "Go for a walk instead." I excused myself, hurried out of the house as fast as I could, and walked the streets of their neighborhood for over an hour.

My mother's parents immigrated from Sweden right before the first baby came. They were very poor with eight children all very close in age. My mother was the seventh. My grandfather had to work as a coal miner in Pennsylvania, which was not only very difficult and dangerous but, as we now know, a huge health risk of dying early from lung disease. My mother's mother died in childbirth when my mother was six years old. The premature baby lived, and the rest of the siblings had to somehow take care of the baby while their father worked. My mother grew up very poor and in survival mode. There was a lot of love in her family, but there was no room for arguing, no room for raised voices, no room for having a disagreement with one another. They all were forced to band together to help each other grow up. My mother's father died when she was sixteen of lung disease from working the mines. They had moved to Buffalo, New York shortly before he died.

My mother loved God, and she loved other people. She was probably the friendliest person I have ever met. She was also a great baker and cook, and could make great meals with very little money. My mother excelled in these qualities, but she did not know how to work through conflict, and anger absolutely scared her as she had never heard it growing up. In my own growing up, I learned that there was also no room for my anger and upset feelings with my mother. I learned to internalize my feelings and work with them myself and continue to love her. As an adult living far away from my parents since I was eighteen, I learned to express my anger and I learned to work through conflict with other people. When I was upset with Barry, I could express it right away and, eventually, he did the same with me.

Now, here I was, perhaps more upset and angrier with my mother than I had ever been in my life. As I walked the streets of their neighborhood, I kicked stones, I cried, I yelled out my anger within my head. Perhaps after forty-five minutes, I began to settle down and open my heart to my mother. She was a simple woman, and the openness with which Barry and I wrote about our relationship was obviously very embarrassing to her. Especially because Barry had talked about his affair and the healing that we went through thirteen years before the book was published. I had never told my parents about that. I began to understand why she didn't want any of her friends to see our book or even to have it leave the boundaries of California. I saw that I could never change my mother, nor did I need to try. She was a simple woman who concentrated on loving people and loving God.

I returned to my parents' house and peeked in the window of the kitchen. There was my mother teaching our little daughters how to make cookies. She was being very patient with them, and they loved this time with their grandma. My mother also taught me how to bake and every Saturday we had baking day, making delicious things for the whole week. My brother was never included in these times. It was something very special that just my mother and I shared. My brother was not even allowed in the kitchen but had to do chores with my dad which he did not enjoy.

I walked into the house and our girls ran to greet me. My mother walked over and gave me a hug and invited me to sample the cookies. She had no idea how to work through the feelings that had caused me to leave so abruptly one hour before. She was offering me her love in the way that she knew how.

My mother left this world in 2007, but to this day, I am grateful for the miracle of the inner voice that lovingly spoke to me and encouraged me to take a walk rather than blast my mother with my anger. The anger might have caused a wound that would have been difficult to heal. Instead, we had twenty-three more wonderful years together, the last fifteen she was right next door to us. And right up until six months before she died, she still made cookies for us.

Barry and I went on to write nine more books. My mother, after several years, became a strong supporter, giving out books to her friends and family. *The Shared Heart* became a best seller (we later got a more universal cover) and not only left California, but was translated into seven other languages and became a best seller in Germany. It even made its way into my mother's home country, Sweden. My brother's engineering book, though very impressive on the outside, and I am sure was excellent on the inside, had limited sales to mainly graduate students.

Barry: Most people's garages have space for cars. Not ours. Our garage is filled with boxes of books. In the old days, we used to print 5000 and even sometimes 10,000 copies of a title at a time. That's a lot of boxes of books! These boxes essentially fill up the whole 2-car garage with just an aisle to be able to walk around them.

Not long after our fourth book, *Light in the Mirror*, arrived from our printer and all the boxes were stacked on wooden pallets in the garage, a skunk decided this would be the perfect place to set up house. There was just enough room under the pallets to make a cozy, dry den.

This, however, was unacceptable to me. It was also unacceptable to our golden retriever, Charlie. He ran around the stack of books, barking at the skunk and, for all his efforts, he'd get sprayed from under all those boxes. Then we had the pleasure of Charlie's odorous company.

I called Animal Control and was told it was probably a pregnant female skunk looking for a safe place to give birth. I was also told that skunks are very stubborn and hard to get rid of. Then I was advised to put a radio in the garage, loudly broadcasting a talk show station day and night. This turned out to be worse for us than having the skunk living there. Some people enjoy talk shows. Not us. And I swear, I think the skunk actually enjoyed the talk shows. Since she didn't get out much because of Charlie, she probably wanted to keep herself informed as to current events in the world. She stayed.

Not knowing what else to do, I came up with an extreme plan. I had to. Not just Charlie, but the whole garage was starting to smell really bad. I dragged a garden hose into the garage. My plan was to spray a stream of water under the pallets, then run away as fast as I could to hopefully avoid any spray counterattack from under all the books. The plan seemed solid. I only hoped all our books could somehow stay dry.

All was quiet in the garage. Charlie was confined to the house. I tip-toed stealthily into the garage armed with the hose. My movements were slow and deliberate so as not to alarm the skunk. I got into position with the hose nozzle aimed under the books, but with me ready to sprint out the garage door. I let loose a burst of water, dropped the hose and ran. Even as I ran, I could hear the skunk retaliate, spraying the spot I had just left.

But instead of retreating, she held her ground. I waited maybe fifteen minutes for the "smoke" to clear, then cautiously re-entered the garage. I sprayed again, then ran. She sprayed back. It was beginning to feel like a battlefield, with two enemies trading cannon fire.

Again, she did not leave.

I thought to myself, just one more try. The third time has got to be the charm. If it doesn't work, I'll have to come up with some other idea.

I sprayed a third time. The return fire was rather weak, as I assumed she was running low on ammunition.

I waited a few minutes, then walked around the garage to the front, the main entry door for "cars." And there I saw them, wet skunk tracks coming out from under the books, crossing our driveway, and entering the woods. She had left! I had finally won! And she never came back. I wished her well, and hoped she found a suitable den to have her babies.

Meanwhile, we had work to do. Reviewers needed to get copies of *Light in the Mirror*. We sent them out. Weeks passed. Still the skunk stayed away.

Finally, reviews came, and one in particular stood out. It said, *"Dear Barry and Joyce. I've read your book. It stinks! But besides that, it was also one of the best books I've ever read on relationship!"*

Starting that day, we placed a small piece of incense into the package with every book we sent out.

Chapter 29: The Shy Public Speaker

I used to have nightmares when I was a young woman, and woke up sweating and tense. The repeated nightmares consisted of me standing in front of a group of people with a microphone in my hand giving a talk. That image was terrifying to me. I have always been a quiet person, reluctant to talk in front of any size group.

Attending the Columbia Nursing School was a major challenge for me. The other students were all very competitive, super smart, and spoke up very quickly whenever a teacher asked a question. They often interrupted each other to answer the question. I also knew the answer but hated to compete and interrupt someone else.

One day, one of my teachers took me aside and said, "You never answer a question when I ask the class!" I told her how difficult it is for me to speak up in a competitive way. She looked at me sternly and said, "I will not pass you unless you assert yourself more and answer some of my questions. If you fail my class, you will have to drop out of nursing school even though this is your senior year and you are almost ready for graduation."

I started interrupting others just so I could pass the class. I did it, but everything about this felt wrong.

When I graduated, I moved away from New York City and became my usual very quiet and reserved self. In my public health job in Nashville, Tennessee, I had individual clients, not groups I needed to speak to. After completing graduate school at USC in Los Angeles, I needed to find a full-time job. A nursing school needed an instructor and I applied for the job. Halfway into my interview, the woman interviewing me said, "You are definitely the most qualified person who has applied for this job. And yet you are so quiet. You are not teacher material and we cannot consider you for this job."

I walked out very sad and humbled with the firm conclusion that I could never become a teacher of anything. I found the amazing job at Hathaway Home for boys with emotional challenges. It was a low-key job that allowed me to be outside most of the time. I never had to talk in front of a group of adults; just be with the boys and my low-key staff.

When we moved to Portland for Barry's residency, I once again had to find a job. With great references from the last job, I applied for a position as a psychiatric nurse for adolescents at a residential treatment center. The psychiatrist who interviewed me was so intense in his questioning that I felt unsafe and froze up. There was nothing warm about him. Halfway through the interview he said, "You have an excellent education and fantastic references from your last job, but I do not see what the other job saw in you. You are too quiet and lack strength. Frankly, I am disappointed in you, and I would never hire you. I actually do not know what kind of a job you would be good at."

I walked out feeling devastated. Now of course I see that it was how unsafe this man made me feel that caused me to feel so quiet and guarded. At the time, I just felt that probably it was better if I stuck with working with children.

I did find a good part-time job working on the same floor as Barry's psychiatry residency. This job only required that I interview children in a room with a two-way mirror so that the pediatric residents could watch me from the other side. The physician instructor who hired me did so because he was thoroughly impressed with my rapport with children. He wanted his residents to somehow learn what I intuitively knew.

After that job, we traveled for two years and eventually ended up in Santa Cruz, California. I soon became pregnant with our first daughter and then five years later with a second. I loved being a mother and being with my girls. I spent just about all of my time playing with them and, except for Barry and long visits with my parents, I was hardly ever with other adults.

If I had known that writing *The Shared Heart* would actually put me right in front of large audiences, I never would have written it with Barry. And yet, within one month of the book being printed and off into the hands of others, the invitations started coming. When the first invitation came by telephone (no emails at that point), I was horrified listening to the message. Not until that moment did I realize that writing a book meant that also I would need to speak in front of groups, even holding a microphone like in my nightmares.

I was very tempted to erase the message, but I did not. I left it for Barry to find. He was ecstatic and ran to tell me. I started to cry and told him I simply could not do something like that. Barry was very tender with me and held me and told me he would help me.

Our first talk was at Joe and Gwyn Miller's house in San Francisco. Joe and Gwyn were a darling senior couple, a legend and very influential in the Sufi movement in the West. They loved our book because we wrote about very real feelings in a relationship: vulnerabilities, anger, hurt, confusion, doubt and mostly love. It was not just a "high up in the air" book. Joe had been in Vaudeville, and his famous line that he said in a booming voice just about everywhere was, "You can get more stinkin' from thinkin' than you can from drinkin', but to feel is for real." They loved that we wrote honestly about feelings and wanted everyone they knew to buy it.

For our talk, they crammed their house with people and saved a space for us to sit. I was so totally scared that no one could hear me, even though they politely asked me several times to speak up.

Joe felt that they had given us the wrong place to sit in the house, so they had us come up one month later and placed the chairs all different so that people were closer and could easily hear us. The same big crowd of people came, with the same result. No one could hear me. Joe and Gwyn were very nice and understanding, but did not invite us back again. I thought that perhaps the issue of speaking in front of people would never come up again. That experience had proved that I just could not do it.

Then an invitation came from the Unity Church in Seattle. This was a big church and they assured us there would be a microphone, so that even if I whispered, people could hear me. I "generously" offered for Barry to go alone, but they insisted that they needed both of us. It was a very good offer with the chance to sell many books. Here was my nightmare finally coming true. Again, Barry was very supportive and sincerely believed that I could do this. He said, "When you look out into the audience, don't just see adults. Try to see each person as how they must have looked when they were a child. Imagine you're in front of a large kindergarten class. If you see innocent children rather than scary adults, you'll do just fine."

Honestly, there was not even one part of me that trusted I could. I did not sleep for nights leading up to the Seattle talk.

Somehow, I made it up to Seattle and got dressed for the evening of the talk. When I saw how many people were there, my whole body started to shake. Barry took me to a little chapel in the church and we prayed for help. After that prayer, I felt a drop better. But the moment Barry and I walked up to the stage, after a long, heartfelt introduction, I found myself shrinking behind Barry, as if he was somehow my shield. It must have looked a bit like a comedy routine, with Barry every now and then reaching behind him to grab my hand and gently pull me alongside him, like a magician pulling a rabbit out of his hat.

Somehow, I made it through the talk, and people commented later that my extreme vulnerability was actually inspiring. I had done it. I had begun my journey of walking through my fear, and started to understand that I helped people most by my vulnerability, much more than any wise words I could speak.

Our next talk was at our own Unity Church in Santa Cruz. The church was very large at that time and the minister, our beloved Emily Sanford, told everyone they should buy our book after our talk. There was a very long line of people waiting to buy the book and have us sign it. Many of these people I knew. But I was so embarrassed by people waiting for my signature, that I made an excuse to use the restroom and locked myself into a stall until Barry was done signing books. You are probably getting the idea of just how introverted I really was.

It took years before I felt comfortable giving a talk but, with Barry's support and love, I persisted. Currently, we have given over a thousand talks and presentations. Now they are second nature to me. Some of the talks have been for hundreds of people but most have been for smaller groups of maybe thirty.

I have learned that I can call upon divine help for each talk and the help will be there. I have learned to work with my vulnerability, just be myself and that is good enough. I am not a polished motivational speaker. I have never had training. I do not even seem gifted to be able to wear the right kind of clothes for a talk. I am just a simple woman seeking to humbly be of service.

The miracle is that a woman, me, so quiet, shy and reserved, could learn to overcome such large fears and actually be able to speak in front of groups and give her gift. Sometimes, even right in the middle of speaking to a group of people, I remember how I used to be and I am reminded that, with God, miracles indeed happen.

Chapter 30: Kriya and the Coyotes

Kriya, our second golden retriever, was eleven years old when Barry and I found out she had inoperable cancer. I lay on the floor petting and loving her. The news came as a shock to us, for Kriya had been so healthy all of her life. She was the children's dog, and we lovingly referred to her as our "nanny." When the girls went swimming in a lake with their floats, Kriya circled them, let them grab hold of her tail, and then pulled them around for a grand ride before heading to shore. She even tolerated being dressed up in fancy clothes and necklaces, or being hitched to a homemade wooden wagon Barry built, and pulling the girls along the dirt road outside our house. Her mission in life was to protect and watch over Rami and Mira, a job she did with great skill. Barry and I could totally trust Kriya.

Like any dog, she had her quirks. She had a shoe fetish. Not really. She had an amazing knack for finding abandoned shoes. Luckily, she left our good shoes alone. Even while hiking on a trail, she would disappear for a few minutes, only to show up with an old shoe in her mouth.

Often, on hikes, she lay in waiting ahead of us on the trail. Her preferred hiding place was on the downhill side of the trail, the steeper the better. We'd come around a corner, wondering where she was, and if we looked carefully, we'd see her snout sticking up from some gulley or hillside, often with a shoe in it. Our family nickname for her: Kriya of the Cliffside.

Now she lay on her favorite rug in our living room, unable to eat, and barely able to stand. Each day, her condition deteriorated rapidly. It caused me great sorrow to see our once lively dog, who one week ago was retrieving tennis balls from the ocean waves, as well as gifting us with old shoes, now almost too weak to lift her head. She was very conscious of my presence, however, and occasionally wagged her tail in appreciation of my attention.

In that moment, tears streamed down my face, and I felt like my heart was breaking. I wanted to leave the room to distract myself from the pain. I started to get up to busy myself in the kitchen, but a strong feeling rose within me, "Stay here and continue to be with Kriya until you can see death as beautiful. This is her final gift to you."

I stayed and focused on the beauty of Kriya's life. She had lived her life with pure dedication to serving us all. Now she was ready for a greater life, dwelling in her body of light to continue protecting children everywhere. Her compassionate brown eyes told me she was ready to leave her old, worn-out body.

Finally, the day arrived we were all dreading. She stopped drinking, and we knew her time had come. That evening, as we were getting ready for bed, Kriya suddenly got up and staggered to the back door. She wanted to go out.

We were in shock, since she had not moved for days. We opened the door and followed her onto the back porch, then down the steps into the back yard. Five years previously, we had buried our first golden, Bokie, in a special spot in our back yard. Now, miraculously, Kriya zeroed in on this very spot, and lay down. The message was crystal-clear: she wanted to join her old, dear friend.

Then, as if her mission was accomplished, she got back up and headed back into the house, where we directed her into our bedroom, and onto her special rug. Rami begged to sleep next to Kriya, so we made up a bed for her. She lay down, reached over to pet her, and said, "The fur on top of Kriya's head is as soft as a puppy!"

It took a while, but finally all of us were asleep.

Sometime in the middle of the night, she again got up and walked, first to my side of the bed to wake me, then to Barry's side to wake him. Rami was already awake. Then she lay back down. We all felt this was her moment. We lit candles and gathered around her on the floor. We sang a song for her and told her she could now go to her new home in the heaven world.

She lifted her head and looked up at us one last time, stretched her legs, then lay back down. Her breathing slowed … then one more breath … then stillness. All three of us felt her light-body rise out of her. It was magnificent!

At that very moment, the night outside came alive with the yips and howls of coyotes all around our house. They sang their tribute to a great dog. They all, amazingly, knew and respected Kriya. For years, she had let them know how close they could come to our house. She had created a clear boundary for her cousins, across which they were not allowed to cross.

In their canine sensitivity, the coyotes all knew the moment Kriya left her body. And we, her human companions, sat there on the floor in utter awe.

Chapter 31: Falling in Love with a New Man

In the spring, I elected to take a weekend course on healing to comply with the continuing education requirements for renewal of my nursing license. I wasn't particularly looking forward to this course, but I have to admit I was looking forward to a weekend away from Barry. Barry and I were in a bit of a slump in our relationship. He was gone a lot from home, either working at the hospital or counseling clients. I was home, taking care of Rami, but also writing and meditating. It seemed to me that he was losing his spirituality. When he was home, he seemed to be obsessing about doing his own repairs on our aging VW bus. I felt he was spending too much time under that vehicle and, when he was not there, he was reading his new favorite book, *How to Keep Your Volkswagen Alive: A Manual of Step by Step Procedures for the Complete Idiot.*

As my spiritual sensitivity grew day by day, his seemed to lessen each day. I hate to admit it, but I began to see Barry as materialistic and, worst of all, I began to feel spiritually superior.

My nursing course was to be held at Asilomar Conference Center, a beautiful location looking out on the Pacific Ocean near Monterey. As I was packing up, I was hit by the strangest feeling that I would meet and fall in love with a new man during the course of the weekend! This feeling disturbed me as I hadn't had the slightest interest in any other man since I had been with Barry. The feeling also intrigued and excited me, and this made me feel embarrassed. I tried to push away the feeling of anticipation over meeting this new man, but it would come back all the stronger.

The Friday afternoon of my departure came, and Barry and I spent a warm and loving time together before I left. I felt close to him, but it just wasn't the closeness that I knew we could feel. At several points, I wanted to tell him about my strange intuition, but I just couldn't. I imagined it would hurt him too much.

Barry and Rami had great plans for outdoor adventures for the weekend, and there were many hugs and kisses as I drove off. As I backed out of the driveway, I thought, "At least I have the van so Barry won't be tempted to work on it!"

As I caught one last look at my two beloveds, the feeling of meeting this new man pierced me like an arrow.

The nursing course was about mental and spiritual healing, and how the body continually gives us signals on how we should change our lives. As I nervously entered the conference room, I looked all around the room at the participants. Of the forty people present, I counted only seven men, and only three or four seemed age appropriate. Still, why was I so nervous?

The program began and the leader of the course started to take us through a series of meditative exercises. He asked us to pick out one area of our lives that needed healing. Most participants needed physical healing for all kinds of conditions. My choice was clear. I needed to heal my relationship with my husband. I wanted to stop seeing Barry as less spiritual than me. Most of all, I wanted to stop feeling superior.

As we were instructed during the exercises, I placed before my inner guide and healer my problem and asked for guidance. The answer repeatedly came to concentrate on Barry's goodness and beauty, to let go of what I judged as his weaker areas and instead focus on the deep spiritual nature that was already there.

We did this exercise five times as a group, each time going a little deeper. The first time was hard for me. I had to let go of the image of Barry under our VW bus, covered in grease, with the open "idiot manual" next to him. My spiritual husband the aspiring auto mechanic! It reminded me of our experience with Karmu the guru in Boston. It took deep concentration to remember and feel his spiritual side.

Then, as we progressed in the meditations, Barry's spirituality emerged more and more. I began to see him in ways I had rarely seen. I started seeing rays of spiritual light pouring from his heart, and I started to feel deep remorse for having felt spiritually superior. I felt our spiritual equality and, going beyond that, our oneness.

Barry once again became my beloved, my soulmate. I felt so much love and devotion for him, I could hardly contain myself. The love I felt for him spilled out into every area of my life. I couldn't wait to see him, so I called and invited him down to join us for the last morning. He agreed and I was thrilled!

Sunday morning, Barry arranged childcare for Rami, and hitchhiked to Monterey and Asilomar Conference Center. Meanwhile, I was tingling with eagerness to be reunited with my beloved. It had been less than forty-eight hours since I had said good-bye and here I was eager to see him again.

During the morning break, I sat outside hoping Barry would show up. Then there he was! His outer appearance hadn't changed a bit. Two days ago, I would have judged him as unspiritual. Now he was the most beautiful sight in the world to me because my perception of him had transformed on the inside.

I ran into his arms and we hugged and kissed. Even the smell of auto grease did not detract from his beauty. I was so proud to introduce him to the new friends I had met. One sweet, older woman approached us with a knowing look and said, "I know new love when I see it. This is your honeymoon, isn't it?"

I smiled at her and simply said, "Yes, you're absolutely right!"

Then I turned to Barry and said, "It does feel like a honeymoon." And I thought to myself, "This is the new man I was to meet, and once again fall in love with."

Chapter 32: A Heavenly Vision

When I was a little girl, I had several mystical experiences that involved Jesus. He became my best friend, my comforter, my guide and a source of steady love. My love for Jesus was simple, non-religious, non-judgmental, just the pure love of a child. When I became confirmed in our church and knelt before the altar, I felt a distinct presence of Jesus placing his hand upon my head. I felt safe in my devotions to Jesus.

When I grew into a young adult, I found myself in several churches where Jesus was portrayed as a scary judge who was watching out if I sinned and was grading my performance. Since none of us are perfect, I felt that most of the time I was probably failing. I also experienced people confronting me in a judgmental way and asking if I was "saved." If I tried to explain that I felt close to Jesus since childhood, they usually responded by saying it wasn't good enough and I wasn't actually saved. I had enough of these experiences to close my heart and mind, and I eventually put Jesus in a distant, hidden place within me. Sadly, I came to think that maybe those wonderful experiences of my childhood were just fantasy.

Years later, I was playing with three-year-old Rami in our living room. It was evening and we were having fun together. Barry was working at a hospital for a thirteen-hour shift as a general physician. While Rami and I were playing happily, a song came on from an old cassette I had forgotten about. Something about the words of the song brought me right back to the beautiful, uncomplicated feelings I had about Jesus as a child. I looked over at Rami and she was so sweet and innocent, just like I had been at the time of those mystical experiences. In that moment, I yearned with all my heart to experience Jesus again in such a pure and beautiful way. I wanted a vision of Him to help me to know that my childhood experiences were real. Tears came to my eyes.

Rami noticed my tears and asked what was wrong. I told her in simple language that she could understand. She took my hand and said, "Mama, let's ask God to send a vision of Jesus to you tonight." Then she bowed her head and prayed for that gift.

We continued our play until it was time for her to go to bed. As I settled into sleep, I remembered her simple prayer said with such faith. I closed my eyes and asked God to send me a vision of Jesus. At the time, I remember feeling that I needed this more than anything else.

Barry usually came home around midnight after his marathon of seeing patients scheduled every fifteen minutes for his thirteen-hour shift. I had rules concerning his return to our home. I did not want Barry to wake me up, as I got up early with Rami. I did not want him coming into our bedroom without taking a shower first. Being sensitive, I could feel the energy of so many patients all around him. Our bed would actually feel crowded. He would take a shower and then quietly come to bed. This happened over and over again, week after week.

To help him stay awake, Barry usually listened to his rock and roll cassettes during the hour ride back to our home. This particular night, he reached into his pile of tapes and put one up in front of his face. It was "The Messiah," by Handel. Rather than put it back and find a rock and roll tape, he chose to listen to this spiritual music during the ride home. He had never done that before, since the slowness of the songs would have normally put him to sleep, and he needed all the energy he could get after such an intense day. Yet, for some reason, Handel's famous masterpiece actually energized him on this night.

When he arrived home, he also ignored my rule of always taking a shower before entering our bedroom. He immediately came into our bedroom and kneeled down close to me just to watch me sleep. His heart was overflowing with love for me.

Barry's presence near me brought me out of a deep sleep. I opened my eyes and there before me was the vision of Jesus I had prayed for, made even more real by Barry's long curly hair and beard. But it was the unconditional love shining from his eyes that made the biggest difference. And then I heard these words inside of me:

"Love the beautiful feeling of Jesus which resides within Barry and comes through his heart."

I reached up and hugged Barry as he lovingly tried to explain, "I know the rules, but for some reason I was so strongly guided to come right in to be with you like this."

I said, "Barry, this was perfect. Thank you."

That experience has had a powerful impact upon my heart. Through loving Barry, I am also allowing my love for God and Jesus to come forth. I recalled the work of Mother Teresa in which she sees the Christ in each dying person that she tenderly cares for and loves.

I wish I could say that I love Barry with that kind of deep devotion all of the time. The truth is I don't, though I wish I could. But there are moments when I look at him and experience the presence of God. It only takes a few seconds like that to change the energy between us. Perhaps it is a look or a feeling of love passing between us that allows us to experience the higher self of each. And these moments of pure love shine like a beautiful light over us as we go about our busy days. However brief these moments of seeing the God in Barry, it is the highest gift of love that I can give him.

Chapter 33: The Miracle of Fatherhood

Barry: Tuesday evening! Lately, this has been my time to recuperate after twenty hours, between Monday and Tuesday, of running a county medical clinic and seeing patients. This particular Tuesday evening, I felt more burned out than usual. With a little bit of luck, perhaps my evening could be free of responsibilities.

I loved being a father! Sometimes I just needed a break, and this was one of those times.

Maybe it was a little sneaky, but I did it anyway. As I approached our house, I turned off the motor of our VW van, and glided noiselessly into our driveway. That way, the children wouldn't notice me, and I could slip out of the van for a "cooling out" walk in the woods ... by myself.

As I opened the driver's door, the living room curtain flew open, and two bouncing, smiling little people were enthusiastically pointing at me, wildly screaming, "Daddy's home! Daddy's home!"

My cover obviously blown, a sheepish smile on my face, I pretended, as best I could, to be happy to see my eight-year-old and two-year-old girls.

A moment later in the house, the bouncing children became hugging-each-of-my-legs-children, and Joyce greeted me warmly with a kiss. Then, before I could say anything, she said, "I'm so sorry, Barry, but I just got a call. There's an urgent meeting tonight at Rami's school, and I'll be late if I don't leave immediately. Could you please bathe the girls, read them a story, and put them to bed?" Then she noticed the pallid expression of fatigue on my face, and she apologized for being caught in a bind like this.

Of course, I understood, but that didn't help much. Then I looked down at the eager faces at each leg. "Let's play rough-house," begged the bigger face, and an immediate echo came from my other leg. Before I had time for any serious indulgence in self-pity, I found myself romping on the rug amid a chorus of squeals.

"Rough-house" consists of everyone jumping on daddy for as long as daddy can take it. Five minutes later, daddy decided that "chase" would be a little more humane ... for him! So "chase" it was. This is one of those gentle, loving games ... daddy plays the mean ogre who tries to catch, and viciously devour, the fleeing children. But alas, every time he catches one and is about to munch, the other child miraculously rescues the captive child right out from under the open jaws of the ogre. This goes on until at last, Rami, out of tender-hearted pity for her daddy the ogre, submits herself open-armed as a willing sacrifice. This transforms the ogre back into daddy, who then tenderly holds his two daughters in a loving embrace.

Somehow, I'm feeling better!

Now it's bath time, two little kids and one big kid in the tub, rugs moved aside and towels placed into position next to the tub "just in case" we splash. By the end of the bath, the three of us put our heads together in counsel to decide if there's more water in the tub or outside. Mira surveys the situation very thoughtfully before giving her two-year-old assessment: inside (usually).

I'm feeling better still!

Next, the bathroom cleanup committee is formed: three persons. Then the diapering-Mira-for-night-time committee: one person. Pajamas are donned: two persons, and we're ready for story-time. We cuddle together on the couch, and I open a carefully chosen book. I read the text, but there's always something very interesting to be said about the illustration that isn't quite said in the text.

After the story, I send Rami out to her "bedroom," beyond the curtain in the laundry room, and lift Mira into her crib. I lean over the rail to give her a good-night kiss, but a muffled voice leaks out around her thumb, "Daddy, sing me a song." So I sing her a song I used to sing to Rami when she was Mira's age, and it brings back sweet memories. Mira stops me in the middle of the song to say, "I love you, Daddy."

I look at her as if for the first time. Her eyes are no longer only the eyes of a two-year-old. She is on the border of sleep, and her eyes have taken on that fathomless depth of the real being inhabiting that little body. I relax into her gaze, and say, "I love you too, Mira. Go now and be with the angels."

As I watch, her eyes slowly close and, within seconds, she is asleep. I touch her gently in the middle of her chest and ask God to bless her through me. I ask the great Father-Presence to use me as His instrument in guiding Mira to adulthood and the emergence of her true nature. Then I give her a kiss on her forehead and tiptoe out of the room feeling uplifted and grateful.

I find Rami in her bed, her face lit up with a smile at my approach. She is still tucking in her teddy bear and dolls, each with their own pillow and blanket. I sit on the edge of her bed and sing her favorite songs. As I sing, I watch her shift into that sweet, peaceful, pre-sleep state.

Then she stirs, looks questioningly into my eyes, and asks, "Daddy, you weren't in such a good mood when you got home, were you?"

"You're right," I reluctantly answer. I'm always amazed at how tuned in she is to me.

"You feel better now?" she asks.

"Ten thousand percent!"

"Daddy, why do people get sad?"

I have to smile at the pensive look on an eight-year-old's face, and at my own day's predicament.

"We get sad, Rami, because we make things important that aren't really that important."

"What should be important?"

I say the first word that comes to me, "Love. Everything else in life, everything else we fill our days with, is less important."

Rami looks like she is hovering right on the border of sleep, yet she is more with me than when wide awake. While I marvel at this, she speaks again.

"Love is what God is made of."

I smile at her, nodding yes. Then I feel my heart welling up with love and tears come to my eyes.

"Rami, thank you for coming to live with Mama and me. You've blessed our lives more than you'll ever know."

All she says is "Daddy," but with such sweetness and love that I know she has heard my deepest feelings. She has taken my whole being into her, and has given me back the fullness of her own love and gratitude. Her arms reach up to me and we embrace for a brief eternity, then she lies back down.

She now moves through the transition into sleep. Her eyes are still open, but her breathing takes on that relaxed, sleep rhythm. I am amazed at how similar this is to being with a dying person, preparing her to leave her body so that her last moment on earth is one of love ... that this is the greatest gift I could give her. I remember often reading about the "halls of learning or wisdom," or the "temples of healing," places where a soul abides for learning or healing, whether in sleep or after death of the body. I have dreamed about these places, and sometimes have glimpsed them in my meditations. I am convinced of their reality.

Rami's eyes are now closed. She is asleep. And I know by the way she fell asleep that she has made it to her special temple, where she may be reviewing this past day, or looking ahead, seeing the higher view of her life, or studying with one of her guides, or perhaps a great master who, with infinite wisdom and love, reveals her destiny on earth.

I sit a long time on the edge of Rami's bed, trying to follow her soul's travels in my imagination. I am grateful beyond words for this privilege to serve as an earthly guide for these two amazing children, who will then go on to add their blessings to others in an ever-widening circle ... until love and peace fill this world.

And all this happened to a burned-out dad who was reluctant to put his kids to bed!

Joyce came home later, apologizing for making me take care of the girls when I was so obviously tired.

All I could say was, "Thank you for allowing me to have such a special evening!"

Then I gave her all the details.

Chapter 34: Anjel 1986

Joyce: Four years after Mira's birth, I again heard an unseen voice that was just as clear and strong as with Mira:

"You are to conceive again. This soul has a special reason for needing to come."

Our prayer that night before uniting our bodies was to serve God in the deepest way. We surrendered our own plan to a higher, divine plan.

Three days later, Barry and I said good-bye to ten-year-old Rami and five-year-old Mira, and to my parents who were to watch them, and journeyed to England to lead some workshops and attend a five-day retreat at the White Eagle Lodge. It was during this retreat that we both felt the full glory of the soul who had chosen to come to us as our third child.

When we returned to California, we told our girls about the new family member within me. Both girls became ecstatic.

Then severe nausea set in. The second, third, and fourth months of pregnancy were extremely difficult. I was nauseous pretty much every minute of the day, having to spend most of my time lying down. There were times when I felt completely discouraged by the physical symptoms. I tried to remind myself that a great gift ... the presence of a great being ... was certainly worth the hardship. But the nausea was so severe that I just couldn't feel the soul of our baby.

By four and a half months of pregnancy, I began to feel alive again. Our baby was starting to touch me lightly with its movement. An abundance of beautiful pregnancy dresses came from many loving sources. Our little red rented house underwent a major transformation as we squeezed out a small corner for the new baby.

Each of us held the secret hope of another little girl, and all but Mira felt that a boy would be just great too. Mira clearly wanted a sister. She rationalized, "We have all girl toys. Why buy more toys?" I knew she wanted to share her special dolls with the baby.

We wanted to have a mid-wife for this birth, to have more support this time. We knew a good midwife, Sharon, but not well, and knew she was extremely busy as a nurse-midwife in a local hospital and rarely took on home-births. We decided to ask her at a house blessing of mutual friends. There were many people present, but we found Sharon sitting on the grass, and bent down to hug her. After a few minutes of conversing, I asked her if she might consider taking me on as a home-birth client. She looked at me, smiled a little awkwardly, and said she would have to think about it. Just then, our attention was diverted by other friends who approached us, and we said good-bye to Sharon.

The next day, Sharon called. She seemed a bit nervous as she spoke, "Joyce, I have to apologize for acting strangely at the house-blessing."

I said, "I didn't feel anything strange. Maybe because there were so many people…"

"I need to tell you," she continued, "Nothing like this has ever happened to me before. When you asked me to be your midwife, a bright light appeared around you, and I heard the words, 'of course you will.' I felt myself almost go into a state of shock, and I barely managed to mutter the few words that I did. It was almost like the soul of your baby reached out to touch me … really to choose me.

At six months pregnant, a few days before Christmas, I was feeling unusually tired, so Barry took the two girls to a special Christmas program while I stayed at home to rest. During that time alone, while lying on our couch looking at our Christmas tree, I received one more message from this soul,

"I am a girl and my name is Anjel. I will be one of your angels in this life."

When Barry came home with our daughters, I told them the baby's name. Everyone liked it!!

Two days after Christmas, because Sharon couldn't hear the baby's heartbeat, she sent us to the hospital for an ultrasound. While I waited for the technician, I reached into my purse and pulled out a little package of "Angel Cards" from the Findhorn Community in Scotland. Each of the fifty cards has a picture of an angel with a corresponding word. I closed my eyes and picked a card. Then I opened my eyes to see the word, "gratitude."

Finally, the technician came in, did the ultrasound, and hurried out of the room without saying a word. Soon a doctor came in, repeated the ultrasound, and stated without any compassion, "Your baby has died."

Then, all but ignoring my sudden outburst of sobbing, he whisked Barry out of the room to speak "doctor to doctor."

The loss of Anjel was devastating to all of us. Extreme grief filled my being, and I was all set to fall into a tunnel of darkness when little Mira spoke, "Mama, I'll take a boy rather than no baby at all. Will that help?" Her innocence and purity touched my heart, and I couldn't help but smile.

In that moment on the exam table, I knew that I was to be grateful for my two healthy children. I thought about the angel card of gratitude, and sat up to hug and kiss the children, and to receive Barry's hug when he came back into the room.

Anjel had already become a part of our family, and we had all bonded with her, especially me. I went into a very deep grief that was helped only by caring for our girls each day. I could not understand why the guidance was so strong to conceive her and then have her die.

Lying in bed that night, my body ached from crying. Finally, I woke Barry and blurted out, "I'm desperate. I need some wise words."

He sat up in bed, understanding my profound need. He gently rubbed my back and tenderly smiled. I so dearly love Barry's fatherly smile.

"Why was I given so much assurance that the baby was alive?" I asked. "Is my intuition all wrong?"

Then the words I needed flowed from Barry's mouth:

"Your intuition could never have been more right. Anjel has always been alive within you. You were connected to the vastness of her being and presence, far more than to the physical body in your womb. That's why you have looked and felt radiantly pregnant in these past days, even though the little body was not alive.

"Anjel never needed to be born in a physical way. Her greatest need was to give her love to the world through us. She has been doing this all along, but this pregnancy has deepened her link with us. The creation of a physical body has anchored her consciousness within us both. It has been a tremendous leap for all of us.

"Beloved Joyce, Anjel has been born within us. We now have three children, two with physical bodies and one with a body of light. We have just as great a responsibility with our third child as

with the other two. We have the joyful responsibility of maintaining our connection with her. The work she will be doing requires that connection. In addition, we are like children and she, our mother. We now know a spirit guide, a being who is holding us in her loving embrace while she works through us."

These words helped us both that night, as well as in the difficult times in the months ahead.

Barry: The next day, December 30, 1986, we went to have Anjel's little body removed from Joyce's womb under general anesthesia. I waited out in the lobby with four very dear woman friends. We held hands and prayed and meditated. I had never participated in a more focused healing circle. Joyce later told us she felt held in loving arms the whole time.

Finally, the obstetrician beckoned me into a little room. Joyce was not yet awake from the anesthesia, but he wanted me to know all went well. He told me the little body was female, and then asked if I wanted to see her. I said yes, then followed him into another room. He went over to a counter, took the lid off a container, and reached gently inside, as if he were about to pick up a live baby. Before taking the body out, he turned to me and warned me that it wouldn't be the prettiest sight...

I was prepared to see a fetus somewhat shrunken and macerated from lifelessness in the womb, in addition to disfigurement from the surgical instruments used to remove her. I was not prepared to see a face that reflected the timeless wisdom of the ages, a face that was in every way ancient. The doctor placed her back in the box, closed the lid and, against hospital rules, handed it over to me to bring home for burial.

That evening, we went to bed after setting the alarm for 3:45am, so we could be awake for the first world peace meditation to be held worldwide at the same hour. In California, it was to be 4-5am.

At exactly 4am, while we were sitting in bed, leaning on pillows and preparing to start the meditation, neither of us feeling very peaceful or inspired, the door to our bedroom slowly and quietly opened. We knew it was Rami. Mira could not yet open a door quietly. She poked her head into the room and whispered, "I have an earache."

Joyce and I looked at each other and smiled knowingly. Joyce then turned to Rami and said, "Rami, maybe you're just feeling what's happening now all around the world."

Rami's face relaxed, and she said, "I guess I really don't have an earache." She smiled. Rami had been lying wide-awake in her bed, and felt an urgency to be with us precisely at 4am. She knew she needed a very good excuse to wake her parents up in the middle of the night. We're convinced her ear, probably because of her sensitivity to the amplified energies of so many people meditating all around the world, gave her a momentary twinge of pain to provide the necessary excuse.

Sitting in bed for that next hour, the three of us felt so happy to be together. We clearly needed Rami in that hour to help us, and help us she did. We strongly felt Anjel's loving presence in the room with us, giving us deep assurance of her nearness, and the gifts she was bringing into our lives.

Joyce: Three days later, we were scheduled to lead a workshop on the Hawaiian island of Oahu. Since I was physically unable to travel, I stayed home with my visiting parents, and Rami and Mira. I planned to join Barry a few days later for a small vacation and rest before we led a seven-day retreat at Kalani Honua on the Big Island.

The morning that Barry left, the milk came into my breasts. My body was confused and was producing milk for the baby. This was perhaps the hardest part of the whole experience. For three days, I had to deal with breasts tender and full of milk. As painful as this was physically, it was nothing compared to the pain it brought to my heart. Nursing had been such a highlight in my mothering experiences. It was now almost more than I could bear to have milk and no baby to receive it.

In this period of despair, Anjel's presence came to me all the stronger. Through her love, she gently took away the pain, and eventually the milk went away too. I never felt alone.

On the third morning of Barry's absence, he called from Hawaii. I burst into tears just hearing his voice. I missed and needed him so much, and wanted desperately to talk with him. But the connection was very poor and I could hardly hear him. He finally managed to communicate that he'd call me during a lunch break in the workshop.

That time came and went. There was no phone call. By late evening, I realized there would be no phone call. I felt terribly hurt and, in my extreme state of vulnerability, all of my old insecurities surfaced. I was convinced Barry was off in Hawaii having a grand time, totally oblivious of my pain. I pictured him laughing and joking, but also engrossed in such deep and meaningful work, but happy to have a break from my tears.

I started to feel angry. I was scheduled to leave the next day to join him, and I didn't even want to go. As I felt anger and distance from Barry, I could no longer feel the comforting presence of Anjel. During the following painful hours in which I battled with my feelings of hurt and anger, I realized I could only return to the grace of our baby's love when my heart could open to Barry. It was through our love for each other that she came to us originally, and it would be through my opening heart that I would continue to feel her blessing.

Going to bed that night, I opened my heart once again to my husband. I thought of him with love and tenderness. "How much Barry really needs me," I thought and, with that thought, came a beautiful vision of Anjel. It was as if she were standing at the foot of the bed, smiling down on me with a radiant glow. With my inner ears I could hear her sweet message to me,

"Let your attention always rest upon how much Barry loves you. Have the courage to see past the appearances and go straight to the love within his heart."

From her radiant smile, I knew she would be helping us to deepen our love, and I fell into a peaceful sleep.

I awoke to the sound of the phone ringing and heard my dad answer in his booming voice, "Hi, Barry. Yes, she's been waiting for your call all evening. Now she's asleep. What did you say? The phone lines were all down?"

Barry had tried to call. I smiled to myself as I drifted back to sleep.

The next morning, I said good-bye to Rami, Mira, Grandma and Grandpa. My parents, visiting from their home in Buffalo, New York, would watch the girls for the next two weeks. I boarded the plane with hundreds of happy people going on vacation to Hawaii. I sat in my seat listening to my little personal stereo. Each song and piece of music reminded me of the joy I had felt while pregnant. I couldn't stop the tears from flowing down my face. My friend, Margaret, whose fourteen-month-old baby boy had died a year previously, had warned me not to hold back the tears. "Tears help to wash away the sorrow," she wisely told me.

When lunch was brought, I turned to a couple sitting next to me and asked, "Are you going to Hawaii for a vacation?"

"You bet! We've been saving money for five years for this next week's vacation."

I glanced down and saw a mask and snorkel sticking out of the man's daypack, seemingly ready for immediate use after landing in Hawaii. Their excitement starkly contrasted with my reddened and puffy eyes.

"Why are you going to Hawaii?" they curiously probed.

I answered, "I'm going to lead a workshop with my husband."

I immediately realized my mistake when I saw the confused look on their faces.

The wife asked, "Mind if we ask what the workshop is about?"

I started to feel embarrassed, in the light of how much I had been crying, but I answered anyway, "It's called 'Living from the Heart.' We help people experience inner joy."

By the continued confused look on their faces, I wondered if I should've said, "We help people experience inner sadness!"

The husband finally blurted out, "How do you get people to come?"

I could easily understand their confusion. I imagined them thinking, "Boy, she needs to attend that workshop, not lead it!"

As the plane landed, I thought about my one request to Barry before he left, "Please meet me at the gate when I arrive." (In those days, loved ones could actually meet you at the gate.) Having to be confined to a wheelchair, and to feel so weak and helpless, made me feel so vulnerable. All I wanted was to be with Barry once again and feel his fatherly arms around me. In eager anticipation of receiving his warm hug, I was wheeled out to the gate and left there.

No Barry! My heart sank. I felt like a small, defenseless child dropped into a busy world with no protection. People pushed and shoved to greet loved ones. "Aloha" was called out again and again as flower leis were placed around necks in greeting. Everyone else seemed so eager and joyful.

Soon the crowds dispersed, and I was left in my wheelchair with no greeting or flower lei around my neck. The gate area felt desolate. Despite all my efforts, I couldn't hold back the tears. I felt abandoned and unloved! Dark thoughts invaded my mind and anger began to rise within me.

Then I remembered the vision of Anjel and her wise words,

"Let your attention always rest upon how much Barry loves you. Have the courage to see past the appearances and go straight to the love within his heart."

It took tremendous inner work and prayer to finally follow Anjel's wisdom. A moment later, I felt a flower lei slip down over my head and I heard the words of my breathless husband, "I'm so sorry to be late. I came an hour early to be sure I'd be here on time," he puffed out the words. "It's so good to see your beautiful face and finally to be with you."

Then he continued, "The ticket agent told me the plane was coming in at a gate a half-mile from here. I waited there dumbly, until I realized it was the wrong gate, checked the monitor, and ran here."

He was obviously sorry, and I realized this entire incident was perfectly orchestrated to reinforce the important lesson I needed to learn.

Wheeling me to the inter-island terminal for our next flight, we were greeted by three women who had been in the workshop with Barry. Each placed a flower lei around my neck and confided to me that Barry had spoken so often and so lovingly about me that they had to meet me.

Two days later, I was strong enough to walk again, but in my mind not strong enough to speak to one hundred twenty people as I hesitantly walked into the Maui Palms Hotel where a luncheon with a guest speaker is held each month. Barry and I were the speakers for the month.

It was now one week since the removal of our baby's body. Since that time, this would be the first group of people I would address, except for the small group of friends who had gathered for a memorial service the day after the operation.

An old friend called out from the crowd, "Joyce, congratulations on your pregnancy. When is the baby due?"

"This is going to be even harder than I thought," I groaned inwardly. I wanted to run away, so I turned to go back out the door. Barry, holding my hand, understood my fear but followed me anyway. I walked right into a smiling, pregnant woman. "Our babies are due on the same date," she happily said, unaware that my belly wasn't as big as hers.

With every bit of me, I wanted to leave that room, but I didn't. Instead, I retreated to a quiet corner of the room and said an urgent prayer. Then, miraculously, I felt surrounded by Anjel's loving presence just as strongly as when I was still pregnant, and felt her reassurance that I would be helped and guided every step of the way. Feeling strengthened, I turned and walked back into the group.

The atmosphere of the luncheon was that of a party. People were greeting each other again after the holidays. There were roars of laughter. I settled down beside Barry to eat my lunch, hoping we could remain unnoticed. Of course, that was impossible. We had many friends on Maui, and our books had always been well received there. The happy and well-meaning questions came, "Do you think you'll have a boy or a girl?" "It's wonderful you're going to have a third child." "It's great how you've kept your weight down during the pregnancy."

No one except Barry knew the heaviness of my heart. No one knew that, at any moment, I could start sobbing.

My heart throbbed wildly as a long and glowing introduction of us was spoken. I had never been so afraid of standing up and giving a talk. I feared that I would open my mouth to speak and start to cry uncontrollably for the rest of the time.

"And now I present Joyce and Barry Vissell!"

Cheers and applause broke out as Barry and I stood up and walked to the front of the room. I thought, "I don't think they are expecting what they are about to receive."

I somehow managed to step up on the stage and receive the microphone. I thought everyone could probably see my hand shaking. The room began to fade from view. "Oh, no," I thought, "My worst fear is about to manifest." I closed my eyes and asked God to help me in this, the most difficult talk of my life.

I finally found my voice and began, "I always speak the deepest feelings in my heart. Today, I hope you can bear with me through my pounding heart and shaking hands as I share my sorrow as well as my joy."

The energy in the crowd instantly changed from party atmosphere to intense quiet. I told the story of conceiving Anjel and then her mysterious death after six months. I was aware of everyone's rapt attention and their hearts opening in love, not only to Barry and me, but also to their own pain and grief. I told them about receiving the word "gratitude" as my key practice to keep me above the storm of emotion that continually threatened to submerge me. And finally, I told everyone how living with death in this past week had made me realize how important it is to reach out and appreciate loved ones each day. Death can come when we least expect it, so we must take every opportunity to give and receive love.

Barry led an inspiring exercise on appreciation, and then spoke about how blessed he felt to be Anjel's father. Our scheduled talk of thirty minutes was soon over, the most difficult as well as perhaps the most beautiful talk we'd ever given.

Soon afterwards, a man rushed up to us and said he could see a radiant figure standing over us and pouring her love down upon us. We indeed have a divine helper. Each person in the room was deeply touched.

Chapter 35: John-Nuriel 1989

Joyce: After Anjel's passing, I closed the door completely on ever wanting any more children. I was happy with Rami and Mira and never wanted to go through such a painful experience of having a baby die again. Barry scheduled a vasectomy to make sure no more babies would come. One day before the operation was scheduled, he looked at me and said, "How about if we are just very careful and trust in God." I agreed and he cancelled the operation. We were extremely careful.

However, when we would see little babies, my heart would yearn so much for another. As soon as the yearning would begin, however, I would remember the pain and instantly close my heart to any more children. Rami and Mira were such delights, how could I ask for more.

One summer night in August, a friend called to tell us his baby boy had just been born. I was really happy for him. After the call, Barry and I talked and wished that Anjel had lived. That night, we made love at a time that had always been a "safe" time for me, right when my period started. For many years this had always been the safe time when we did not have to use protection. Unknowingly, our son, John-Nuriel, was conceived that night.

Barry and I had been asked to be a part of a very large fund-raising event for the local Santa Cruz Waldorf School which, without help, might have to be closed. We were to begin the program, which featured well-known authors, Gayle and Hugh Prather, Jerry Jampolsky, Diane Cirincione, and Wally "Famous" Amos (of cookie fame). Over three thousand people packed the Santa Cruz Civic Auditorium.

Our talk was simple and direct, expressing our love and appreciation for children and family.

It had been a meaningful and successful evening, and the applause was loud and joyful. The feeling on-stage was one of victory and lightness. I felt carefree and childlike.

Suddenly, the clapping faded from my consciousness. I felt a light surrounding my being, and a sweet voice spoke to me from within:

You are pregnant with your fourth child. You are blessed and honored to carry this one.

The light faded. The clapping sound resumed. This could have been one of the most inspiring moments of my life. Instead, I fought against my heavenly messenger and wondrous news. At forty-two years of age, with two lovely girls on their way to independence and having had the experience of a baby dying in my womb, I did not want to be pregnant again. I felt like screaming, "NO!"

The clapping ended. People began hugging. Hugh came over and gave me a big hug. "That was a great talk you and Barry gave. I could really feel your love of children." He was quickly gone. I felt like a hypocrite.

Diane embraced me and warmly said, "I have read your books and, after tonight, I can even more sense your love of family."

I felt even more like a hypocrite. I was left standing alone again with my thoughts. How could this be happening to me? Again, all I wanted to do was scream "NO!"

Barry came bouncing over to me, a boyish look of exuberance on his face. "We've been invited to the Prathers for a party tonight. I know it's late, but let's go. It's been such a special evening."

"Barry, I'm having a hard time." I was struggling to find my voice. "Let's go home. I feel like I'm going to burst out crying."

He looked at me with concern. It was a big shift of energy for Barry, who was vibrating with excitement, but he said, "All right, let's go home." After all these years, he has grown used to a quality of unpredictability in our relationship.

On the drive home, I told him about my heavenly message and the news of a fourth pregnancy. Barry hopefully suggested I was pregnant with a new book or a new way of being. He kissed me, and I knew we could handle whatever came.

The next day, I found Barry in his humble laundry-room office busily working on our upcoming schedule. He was excited as I entered the room and urged me to sit down beside him. He proudly showed me our plans for the next summer. He had arranged a weeklong international family retreat in the French Alps. Then we were doing a tour of Germany arranged by the German publisher of our books. The grand finale would be a two-week workshop and tour of Russia.

Barry's eyes shone as he spoke, "It has taken a lot of time and energy, but this will be our first really big international tour. Finally, the girls are at the age where we can travel with them. We'll have a wonderful time!"

I looked at him with a pained expression and shared once again my revelation from the night before. Barry looked at me thoughtfully, "There's no way you could be pregnant. Your vision has to be about something else." We both understood that, on a physical level, there was an extremely small chance of me being pregnant.

"God works in mysterious ways," I reminded him.

"I know," he replied, "but how could a baby be coming when it's so clear to both of us that our work is just beginning to really reach out?"

I left the room wishing I had Barry's confidence that I was not pregnant. We both felt that God's will for us, a picture bigger than our intellects could grasp, was to reach out and touch more people. We had sheltered our two children at home for over twelve years. All four of us were now ready to expand, travel and have new adventures. Another baby absolutely did not fit into this picture. With such "reasoning," I ignored the early physical signs of pregnancy, believing I had a stomach flu. I helped Barry plan our upcoming summer tour, avoiding the intuition deep inside that we would do none of it.

Sometimes we don't understand the ways we are prepared for our next step in life. For us, this preparation came in the form of the death of our mother cat, Turn-Up, named because she seemed to only turn up for meals. She had given birth to four fluffy kittens. Ten days after they were born, she was killed in the middle of the night by a large roaming dog. We found the kittens in the morning and took them to our veterinarian, who told us they had little chance of surviving. He explained the many things we could do each day in an attempt to save the kittens. He concluded by telling us that even with the best of care, kittens of that age would have a tough time surviving without their mother.

We all felt that we owed it to Turn-Up to try our hardest. The four of us accepted the challenge, which proved to be more difficult than caring for a human infant. It took one hour to feed them all, and they had to be fed every three hours. Barry and I took on the night feedings. Barry was gracious enough to take on the "pee and poop" detail. That meant rubbing their bellies with a damp, warm cloth to simulate a mother cat's tongue. Otherwise, they couldn't pee and poop by themselves.

At first, the kittens grew weaker and weaker, then they gradually responded to our constant loving care. They began to grow and open their eyes. We all rejoiced at the miracle of their thriving.

One week after Turn-Up died, we needed to travel to Mt. Shasta to begin a weeklong whitewater rafting trip on the Klamath River combined with a workshop, and then a workshop tour of the Northwest. We were to be gone from the house for a month, so we had no choice but to take the kittens along. Our dilemma was to find someone we could trust to watch them during the week we were to be on the river.

Finally, a father and his ten-year-old son agreed to fill in for us for the week. We knew it was a great inconvenience to the father, but out of his love for us he had readily agreed. Our family breathed a sigh of relief. We knew the kittens would be well taken care of.

A week later, after the river trip was over, I knew for certain I was pregnant. The physical symptoms had become too strong to ignore further. As I opened to this fourth pregnancy, I heard inside:

Remember how important it was for you to find the perfect situation for your little kittens? You did not mind inconveniencing the father and son, as you felt the kittens' care was so important. The father, out of his love for you and his gratitude for ways you have helped him, accepted the responsibility. This is a small example of what God, your Higher Self, is now asking of you. This precious soul, your fourth child, needs specific conditions for his earthly sojourn. He needs what your family has to offer in order to fulfill his purpose upon the earth. We rejoice that he is with you. You will readily accept this gift out of your love for Spirit. The inconvenience you feel today is small compared to the blessing you will receive through mothering this soul.

Two days later, a positive test confirmed the pregnancy. A baby was due in spring. Even with the spiritual message given to me, and the reference to "he" was not lost on me, our family had some major readjusting to do. Four healthy kittens played at our feet, reminding us of the miracle of life.

Barry: Our next stop was Breitenbush Hot Springs Conference Center in the Oregon Cascade Mountains. This would be the first of what was to be many years of summer retreats there. We had read beforehand that Breitenbush had a strict no-pet policy, yet we showed up with our four very young kittens. We knew we were breaking their rules, but what could we do? We snuck them into our cabin and hoped for the best.

Sure enough, a staff member heard the faint mewing coming from our cabin, and investigated. She brought our infraction to the attention of the other staff, and finally to the man who was the founder and owner, Alex, who just happened to be a participant in our workshop.

Alex came to us, his heart wide open from the workshop, to hear why we decided to bring kittens to Breitenbush. We told him the story.

He took a deep breath, thought about the situation for a minute, then said, "Sometimes rules have to be broken."

The kittens not only stayed in the cabin, but several members of the staff volunteered to help take care of them.

Joyce: Barry took a deep breath and canceled the entire summer tour we had been so excited about and had worked so long to create. He canceled all travel plans for two years. We looked at other ways to earn our income. Providing for our family was going to be a real stretch. We began to think of expanding our already crowded two-bedroom home. Realizing there was no way, we just threw away a lot of nonessential stuff.

Each day, we surrendered more, and changed our outer circumstances to accommodate this next assignment, another soul coming to our family. Each day, our family sat together and meditated on God's desire for us. We tried to connect with God as our spiritual source, as the light within us, and our desire for the baby grew and grew. As our own plan began to merge with a higher plan for us, the inconvenience started to seem very small, just like the kittens.

As the months passed and I continued to throw away more and more possessions, I was amazed at how big a tiny two-bedroom house could seem. Barry refused all the fantastic travel invitations that came our way. Sometimes that was hard for him. The girls each prepared for what they would need to give up as a new baby entered their lives. All four of us discovered that we were being filled with a deeper peace through this process of substituting our personal desire for God's desire.

Spring arrived, and never had a family more excitedly awaited the birth of their little one. I planned to labor and give birth in our hot tub. Roxanne, who we considered to be the absolute best midwife in our area, was on board for the birth, even though she had never attended a water birth. Our research showed that labor in body-temperature water was significantly less intense. I was so looking forward to that!

I went into labor on May 1, 1989, spending many hours of relaxed labor in the water. Actually, too relaxed. Since labor was progressing too slowly for Roxanne, she suggested moving me into our bedroom. Easier said than done. I was nearing transition, and had to be practically carried into the house and into our bedroom. I felt like a beached whale, so at home in the water, but so uncomfortable out of the water. However, labor did speed up and, suffering as I was, I sped through transition and was ready to push our baby out.

I just couldn't stand being out of the water. I insisted on getting back into the hot tub. So the whole ordeal had to be repeated, my feet barely touching the ground as I was mostly carried out the back door, down the steps, along the sidewalk, and finally lowered into the water. The mermaid was once again in her element.

This time, being in the water did nothing to slow down the pushing phase of labor, but it made such a difference. I felt held and supported by the water, and by the Heavenly Mother.

Mira, at age seven, insisted she stay up for the birth. It was getting way past her bedtime, but we let her have her way. Even so, during the intensity of the final phase of labor, between pushes, Barry and I and Rami glanced over to see how Mira was doing. She was floating on her back on the other side of the hot tub, playing a little game by herself, completely oblivious to us. We all had to laugh at the incongruity of the scene.

Barry, meanwhile, had the brilliant idea of wearing a snorkel, mask, and underwater headlamp to better see what was happening underwater. I took one look at him and had the thought, "Our baby will come out and be greeted by an alien!" I insisted Barry take off his gear and just be present with us.

John-Nuriel was born at eleven in the evening. We were all in the hot tub in a little circle when his ten-pound body squeezed out into the water. We gently brought his face to the surface for air, while the rest of his body remained in the water. He was pale blue, somewhat limp, and was not breathing. Roxanne, who was leaning in to the hot tub, simply asked us to tell the baby how much we wanted and needed him. We did just that and, within seconds, he took a big breath and opened his eyes!

Oh, how much we wanted him! The canceled plans, the inconveniences, the lack of potential income, all seemed so trivial compared to the ecstasy of holding him in our arms. By stretching our lives to accommodate him, our hearts have been stretched and opened as well. His presence in our lives has blessed us each in a thousand ways. The "Nuriel" part of his name is Hebrew for "fire or light of God." We truly feel he has brought more fire and light into our lives and work.

Once, I was sharing with a group of women how, before my first three pregnancies, the souls of Rami, Mira and Anjel each had knocked loudly on the door of my consciousness. Each one of them made it clear that they wanted to be conceived. Five-year-old John-Nuri was busily playing in the same room and, evidently, was listening to our conversation. He suddenly announced, "I didn't bother to knock. I knew you were too busy, so I just came!"

John-Nuri was an energetic yet very sensitive boy. He loved us all very much and was close to each of the four of us. We soon learned that he had a fantastic singing voice and he started receiving the lead parts in many of the school plays and musicals. He also took up juggling and entertained us often in the evenings. He excelled in martial arts and volleyball and received the most valuable player for his position on the high school team. He grew to be 6'5" and, before we wanted or were ready, he was off to Lewis and Clark College in Portland, Oregon, on an almost full scholarship. He soon brought home his first real girlfriend, who we instantly fell in love with. We thought that perhaps they would marry as they were so close.

One summer evening, after his girlfriend had just left from a nice long visit, I was sitting with John-Nuri on a couch when he blurted out, "Mama, I'm gay."

A million thoughts ran through my head all at once, but fortunately I did the right thing. I wrapped my arms around him and told him how much I loved him. Then I told him I needed to get Barry from his office. The thought of telling his father made his body shake all over. Barry also did the right thing and hugged him and told him how much he loves him. The three of us sat on the couch and talked well into the night.

As I lay in bed that night, I felt so grateful for the two years that we had with Leo Buscaglia and all of his gay friends. We knew and loved gay men and women. We just had no idea whatsoever that our son was one of them.

John-Nuri does not like to be called "gay." He likes the term "queer," which is just a bit difficult for us to say given the negative connotation that word had while we were growing up. However, to honor him, I will say here that he is queer. He also likes to be called androgynous, as truly he is a combination of male and female in a male body. He also refers to himself as pansexual, to honor the multifaceted nature of sexuality.

He performs with his husband Isaiah, and their mission is to show the world that being different is beautiful. They are a huge success wherever they perform in this country and in Europe. They go to places in the mid-west that I thought would not receive them well. Our son tells us that they always have big crowds of mostly straight men and women, and all love them and ask them to come back. They are fulfilling a big need.

Several years ago, John-Nuri came to me and explained the mystery of why Anjel stayed for such a short time in her body. "Mama, I fully believe that I was Anjel. I needed to come to this earth and experience even for a very short time what being in a female body was like. I feel that the essence of Anjel lives inside of me."

Part 2

Even More Miracles

Chapter 36: The Intruder Miracle

On a Friday evening in May 2001, Joyce and I helped all the women get settled in for the first night of Joyce's annual weekend women's retreat at our "HomeCenter," as we like to call our property. Then we went to bed.

At about one in the morning, I felt myself being roused from a deep sleep. I opened my eyes and beheld in the dim moonlight a young man's face about a foot above my head. He was swaying slightly, intermittently leaning his weight on me, and there was the unmistakable smell of alcohol on his breath. The sight was so bizarre, and I had been in such a deep sleep, that I thought I was dreaming and closed my eyes hoping this ghost in our bedroom would somehow simply vanish.

This changed, however, when I felt his grip tighten on my shoulders. By now, Joyce was also awake. I realized this was not a ghost, but an actual person in our bedroom, and someone I had never seen before. Within seconds I was wide-awake, adrenaline pounding in my veins. At the same time, I could see the disoriented look in his eyes, the confused face of someone who didn't know where he was, so I didn't feel immediate threat.

I finally found my voice and asked as calmly as I could, "Do I know you?"

There was no response.

"What's your name?" was my second attempt at communication.

His only response was to mumble some incoherent words. I realized he was drunk, but wondered if he was also high on other drugs.

I felt a strange combination of fear mixed with the desire to help this lost young man. Joyce and I slowly sat up in bed, so as not to startle him. Then, while I tried to calmly communicate with the intruder, Joyce slipped out of the bedroom, crossed the hall into our daughter Mira's vacant bedroom, quietly locked the door, and then dialed 911. Unfortunately for her, she didn't see the lost expression on the young man's face, and couldn't tell if he was dangerous or not.

I got out of the bed, told the stranger I would like to help him, and got dressed. A strange wild look came into his eyes, and he bolted out of the bedroom, heading across the hall to the room Joyce was in. As he tried the locked doorknob, I tried to calm him down. It didn't work, and he next headed for our twelve-year-old son's room. He opened the door, ran into the room, jumped up on John-Nuri's bed and stood there with his shoes straddling our son's head. I was afraid John-Nuri would surely wake up with all this commotion. I firmly but still calmly commanded, "You can't stay in this room. You'll wake up our son. Come out now!"

He jumped off the bed, headed toward me, and suddenly put up his arms in an aggressive stance. I backed away saying, "I'm not going to hurt you." I could see he was getting paranoid.

Abruptly he turned and ran down the stairs. I immediately thought about the three women sleeping in our living room. I quickly tried the door to Mira's room, remembered that it was locked, and yelled for Joyce to call 911. I didn't know she had a police dispatcher on the phone who heard me yell, and asked Joyce if I was all right. His rapid-fire questions, designed for efficient emergency triage, did little to help Joyce's escalating fears. "Was that your husband? Is he in danger? Does the man have a weapon? Mam, do not unlock the door. Stay in that room and stay on the phone with me." Joyce started shaking uncontrollably.

I ran after the young man. I saw that he had run out the front door rather than into the living room. My relief was short-lived. He was running around the garage and up the stairs to Joyce's eighty-four-year-old mother's apartment. Joyce's dad was compulsive about locking the door but, since his passing a few years ago, Joyce's mother eventually completely stopped locking her door. The young stranger tried the knob. Miraculously, it was locked.

Standing at the bottom of the stairs, I again called him back. As he came down toward me, I could see his paranoia was getting worse by the minute. Although I again reassured him that I wasn't going to hurt him, he acted as if I was the enemy. He came at me to hit me but his intoxicated condition allowed me to get away from his swing. Our driveway was filled with cars because of the retreat. I thought it best to keep a car between us, and to keep him with me rather than in the house with the women.

A few minutes later, I heard sirens in the distance. I knew I had mere minutes to stall him. He was beyond all reason and control now. He chased me around the cars in those final moments in what must have looked like a scene from a suspense movie.

Finally, the first of four police cars raced up our driveway, sirens blaring and lights flashing. Within seconds the young intruder was subdued at gunpoint, handcuffed, and then roughly dragged off to one of the waiting cars. I felt relieved, shaken to my core, and profoundly sad for this young man who had gotten himself into so much trouble. We learned he was only eighteen years old, and was recently arrested for public intoxication and for attacking and breaking the hand of a sheriff's deputy.

Can you imagine our surprise when, the next day at dinnertime, there was a knock on our door and there standing on our front porch was this young man and his friend, who had come to apologize. The young man, who I will refer to as Bill, had spent the night in jail, had somehow gotten out on bail, and learned our address from the police report. We learned he had been driven by his friend to a party at our neighbor's house, where he "blacked out" drinking and wandered up the hill to our house. He had absolutely no memory of anything that had happened at our house. He listened with rapt attention and deep remorse as we narrated the full details. Joyce and I (especially Joyce because she did not know what was happening) were both still shaken and exhausted from a sleepless night.

Bill admitted to having a serious drinking problem, with both parents' alcoholics. As he left, he told us how touched he was by our love and caring. He was fully prepared to receive our hatred and vengeance. Because of his sincerity and remorse, we were drawn to hug him before he left. We pray that Bill will get the help he so desperately needs, in lieu of prison time.

Three weeks after our peaceful bedroom and lives had been violated, we were still not quite back to normal. The image of a strange face with an eerie, vacant expression less than a foot away, still haunted us both. Yet we couldn't help feeling that this whole experience was guided by a great spiritual power, that Bill was guided to us for some unknown reason. I feel I was given an opportunity to love in a truly difficult situation.

Because Bill came back to fully apologize, he made it easier for us to forgive him and make faster progress in letting go of the whole traumatic incident. We have often wondered how we would have felt if we had never seen him again. We are convinced this would have made it more difficult to open our hearts to him.

Chapter 37: The Lost Dog Miracle 2001

From the time I was a little girl, I have dreamed of finding a homeless dog and helping it to find a wonderful home. My chance came in 2001 when our family rescued a lost dog on the beach. We named the dog Lucy and she sure wasn't a prize for good looks. Our four Golden Retrievers barely tolerated this little fifteen-pound mutt, while our four cats were terrified of her. She didn't fit in our family and I knew we needed to find her a home. We placed ads in the local papers, hung lost dog signs at the beach and gave a description to the SPCA.

After ten days, Lucy had gained weight and looked better after frequent brushing, but not one call came for her. Our cats looked at me with pitiful glances, begging me to get rid of Lucy, as she chased yet another one around the house. I was beginning to despair that we could ever find Lucy a home. This isn't the way I had dreamed it would be when I got my chance to rescue a dog. Our twelve-year-old son commented that Lucy sure needed a magical moment.

Later that same day, I mentioned to my eighty-four-year-old mother, who lived next door, that I was afraid I would never be able to find Lucy a home. She thought for a moment and then announced, "My friend, Barbara, might want a dog. Her dog just died."

My mother immediately called her friend and described Lucy to her. Barbara didn't want a dog, but became excited, "My neighbor lost his dog ten days ago and I think she looked a lot like the dog you are describing. I'll walk over and ask him."

An eager call came an hour later and Barbara's neighbor drove to our house. "That's my dog!" the excited man rejoiced as he picked up his precious bundle. Lucy had run four miles from home, losing her name tag on the way. Her owner had checked every animal shelter in the county, and somehow, they had misplaced our listing. We stood there with tears running down each of our cheeks as we realized the unbelievable odds for this dog to be reunited with her owner. As he was driving away, he thanked us for caring for Lexy, a name that was so close to the one we had given her.

Chapter 38: My Near-Death Miracle 2009

It was Saturday, June 20, 2009, and Joyce and I had one more week until our daughter, Rami's, wedding. I had no idea that this day would shake my whole world. We worked to get our house and property ready for the anticipated 170 people. Our new refrigerator arrived and I emptied out all the food from the old one. In the back of the freezer, I found a piece of chocolate cake baked by our son months before, and couldn't resist tasting it. It was still delicious.

After the new refrigerator was filled and shelves adjusted, I made myself a cup of green tea, went into the office, and started working on the computer. I had only had a few sips of the tea, when I started feeling light-headed with a very strange "buzzing" in my head. At first, I thought I was hypoglycemic, or maybe the green tea somehow had an unusually large amount of caffeine, but really ... green tea! But the sensation felt very different than anything I had ever experienced. It was not at all unpleasant, just unusual.

Except it was getting stronger by the minute. The "buzzing" was now spreading throughout my whole body.

I got down on my hands and knees, touching my forehead to the floor, hoping to bring more blood to my brain. It didn't work. The strange sensation kept getting stronger. I thought, "Maybe I'm down on my hands and knees to pray for help, or to be closer to the earth." I did indeed pray for help.

Sitting on my chair again, ever the medical doctor, I wondered if I were having a stroke. Not your typical stroke that involves pain or paralysis, but an atypical one that was only affecting my sensations and not my muscles. I even thought about Jill Bolte Taylor's description of her own stroke in her book, *My Stroke of Insight: A Brain Scientist's Personal Journey*.

There was only one thing in the whole world I wanted to do – and that was to find Joyce. I stood up, not at all sure I could stand, let alone walk. I found I needed to will myself to put one foot in front of the other, but my balance seemed OK. I made it to the kitchen, found Joyce, and let her know I needed her help. It has often been difficult for me to ask Joyce for help, to lean on her strength and love, but in this moment it was a "no-brainer."

She took one look into my eyes and immediately knew something was very wrong. Although my pupils seemed normal, my eye movements were sluggish and my skin was cold and clammy. She helped me lie down on the couch, sitting close to me, and together we tried to piece together what was going on. My thinking faculties seemed fine, even hyper alert. Caffeine overdose was out of the question. Stroke was very unlikely, given the progressive quality of the symptoms.

Now my skin was becoming hypersensitive. The blanket Joyce had placed upon me felt like it was filled with lead. Even her hands upon me felt oppressively heavy, a clear warning sign. Normally, there's nothing I like more than Joyce's touch.

I kept returning in my mind to the chocolate cake. Poisoning by a neurotoxin seemed to be what was happening. But really ... chocolate cake? In the freezer? Then I wondered if John-Nuri had added something "special" to the recipe ... something that could be mind-altering. Our twenty-year-old son was at a party with his friends. Joyce called his cell phone and left an urgent message.

Even though it had been more than 35 years since our "experimenting" with psychedelics, I knew what I was experiencing was no "bad trip." There was no mind altering, no euphoria, no hallucinations ... just this intense physical sensation that was vibrating or buzzing without pain. And it kept getting stronger!

Joyce was on the phone, trying to reach a doctor friend. On the couch, I had the oddest sensation of starting to go to sleep without being even remotely sleepy. It felt like my body was shutting down internally and I, my real self, my conscious self, was somehow detaching from my body. I was starting to feel profoundly peaceful, more peaceful than I have ever felt. Letting go in that moment would have been blissfully easy, but another part of me understood that this could very well be my body's way of dying. I felt that, as intense as the poison was, I had a choice of whether to stay or leave. I even thought about Rami's wedding in exactly one week. I needed to be there. Rami needed me to be there. And I had so much more to give and experience in my own life.

I called out to Joyce. She got off the phone, only getting a message to our doctor friend. She came right over and sat close to me. I asked her to keep me engaged, to help me stay awake ... to anchor me to my body.

We talked about going to the emergency room, but it never seemed right. I really wanted to stay at home, surrounded by love and quiet. Some moments, I wondered if I was dying, so intense was the experience. Other moments, I felt I had the conscious decision to live or die.

My body started to shake and Joyce found more blankets to put on me. I couldn't tell if I was cold or hot. I just wasn't that connected to my body.

Joyce asked me to stand up. She may as well have asked me to climb Mt. Everest. It wasn't that I felt weak, or even sick. The difficulty was simply being in my body.

I somehow made it to my feet. Then she took my arm and asked me to walk with her. With great effort, I placed one foot in front of the other. She guided me outside onto our deck, to a chair in the warm sun. Joyce knows how much I love the sun, but it didn't feel good and, after just a few minutes, she helped me return to the couch.

John-Nuri arrived home and breathlessly entered the room. He assured us there was nothing unusual in the cake, only his love. I looked up into his loving brown eyes and asked him if he felt I was dying. In that moment, he felt more like a compassionate father than a son. I felt a great need for his love, and complete trust in his intuition and healing ability. He looked deeply into my eyes for what seemed to be an eternity, then smiled and said, "Daddy, you're not dying! It looks like you're just on a very strange trip!"

I felt bathed in the love of my wife and my son. I received an inner assurance that I would live. I just needed to now ride out the rest of the process. I needed to let my body do its miraculous job of detoxifying and eliminating whatever I had ingested.

As intense as this drama was, Joyce couldn't resist adding a moment of levity. She took both my hands in mock solemnity and spoke, "Barry, with the wedding next week, this would be a very bad time to die!" We both had to laugh, even for a short time.

It was then that I finally remembered something else I had tasted during my busyness in the kitchen. It was my home-grown kombucha. Widely revered for its immune strengthening properties, it looks like a mushroom but is really a symbiotic relationship between bacteria and yeast that is grown in a solution of sugar and black tea. The "mushroom" had been growing for several months, and I remembered sampling the solution about an hour before my symptoms started. It tasted normal. Luckily, I only poured myself about two ounces of the drink. Had I poured myself a full glass, you would probably not be reading this article right now.

My medical friend later told me, after much research and several calls to Poison Control, that my kombucha culture somehow became contaminated. Some stray organism invaded the mixture, reproduced itself, and secreted a neurotoxin that poisoned me. There have been other cases of poisoning with home-grown kombucha, including one reported death.

Hours later, upon returning from a trip, our daughters, Mira and Rami, arrived and added their love to the mix. It was unbelievably sweet to be surrounded by so much good energy.

I feel so different as a result of this experience. I have never felt so grateful to be alive. I received IV treatment to support and flush out my overburdened liver. Within 24 hours, I was 90 percent clear of symptoms, and after 3 days back to normal except for an occasional episode of nausea and lightheadedness.

I notice I take more time to give and receive love with friends and family. Being so close to death really forces me to appreciate life, to slow down and notice all the beauty around me, to be a better human being.

I am so aware of the fragility of our bodies. Two ounces of a drink placed me on the brink of a precipice. A few seconds are all that are needed to destroy a human body in a car accident. How much have I taken life for granted. I realize that every minute of life is precious. Every day holds the opportunity for more growth and love.

After officiating at the wedding ceremony, I became separated from Joyce while we were greeting friends and family. Joyce noticed the time. It was exactly one week since she sat on the couch helping me to stay in my body. Overcome with gratitude that I was alive, she ran to find me, and invited me to be alone with her for a moment. With the noise of celebrating in the background, Joyce and I held tightly to each other and gave thanks for more time to be together on earth, and to keep giving our gifts of love to the world.

Chapter 39: The Hand upon My Head

Joyce: One of my favorite things is to imagine a divine hand upon my head blessing me in my life and letting me know that I am cared for and loved. I do this especially when I feel insecure or stressed. Once, while in the emergency room with a badly broken leg and ankle, I closed my eyes and blocked out the flurry of other patients and medical staff and just imagined this otherworldly hand upon my head reminding me that everything would work out all right. Another time, right before I was to speak at my mother's memorial service, I also imagined this hand upon my head helping to calm my emotions and nervousness. When I remember to do this, I find that it works every time to help bring peace to my sometimes-troubled soul.

As far as actually feeling a divine hand upon my head, this only happened one time when I was a child being confirmed in our church. At that time, I clearly felt an invisible hand touching my head during the ceremony. Now, however, it is a spiritual practice to receive comfort by imagining that heavenly touch.

Since this practice has brought so much peace to my heart, we also try to give this experience to others. Usually, toward the end of every one of our workshops, Barry and I have people close their eyes in a silent prayer. We then use this opportunity to go around to each person and place our hands on their head to bless them and say a prayer for them. If it is a small group, we go together. For a larger group, we split up and each take half of the group.

In July, 2009, we were leading our annual "Shared Heart Summer Retreat" for singles, couples and families at

Breitenbush Hot Springs in Oregon. During the last morning's meditation, we asked everyone to sit with their eyes closed and offer a silent prayer. As is our custom, we went around and placed our hands on each person's head and said a prayer for them. This was a large group, so Barry and I split the room in half. I finished before Barry and went to sit in my chair in the front of the room.

Across the room, Barry was still tenderly placing his hands on someone's head and saying a prayer. I closed my eyes and, as I did so, I distinctly felt a physical hand upon my head and felt that I was being blessed in prayer. It was the most wonderful experience and lasted perhaps five seconds. When the hand lifted off my head, I opened my eyes and wondered how Barry could have possibly come to me so quickly. To my amazement, he was still far away standing over the same person. It was clearly not Barry who touched me.

I sat for a moment in awe. I was physically touched on my head in the most loving way by an unseen presence. For perhaps thirty years, I have been imagining a hand upon my head and, for the first time, I actually felt a physical presence touching me. My immediate thought was, "It is real!! We really truly are loved and watched over! This is not just something of our imagination."

Chapter 40: Miracle on the River 2012

Barry: Things can go wrong in the blink of an eye. One moment, all appears well. The next moment, everything can change. No matter how well we plan, we can't protect ourselves from life's upsets. It's not what happens to us, but how we respond, that matters the most. We can respond with disappointment and anger, or we can look for the miracles and divine interventions.

In July 2012, Joyce and I finished our Summer Retreat at Breitenbush Hot Springs and headed south to raft the Rogue River. Permits for this particular stretch, the "Wild and Scenic" Rogue, can be quite difficult to obtain. We weren't successful in the lottery, but lucked out scoring a cancellation.

One problem. When we got into southern Oregon, we encountered more and more smoke. At the ranger station to pick up our hard-won permit, the smoke was so thick it irritated our lungs. Still, the ranger on duty informed us that the forest fire burning down river was not bad enough to stop people from rafting. She said, "The two of you are the only ones hesitating to go. Everyone else has put in. If you cancel your permit, you will be blacklisted and not allowed to have a permit the rest of this year and next year!" In spite of her threat, Joyce and I had to listen to our inner guidance. We just couldn't go. We cancelled our permit.

Disappointed, we decided on plan B, the Klamath River in northern California. Not the wilderness of the Rogue, with a road following the river, but still beautiful in its own way. And we could breathe!

We set off in our twelve-foot raft and had a wonderful two days and nights on the river. On the third day, we approached a class III rapid named "Otter's Playpen." This was only our second time on this particular stretch of the Klamath, and the last time we came through I didn't remember having any problems. Now, the river level was low because of the drought year. The only route that looked clear was a narrow slot on the right side of the river. I shipped my oars (brought them into the raft) and entered the slot. I watched helplessly as the front left corner of the raft caught on the rock. Before I could react, the back of the raft quickly swung around to the right and we were almost sideways blocking the narrow channel.

Joyce and I were astonished by how fast our raft flipped. One moment we were enjoying a lovely river trip, and the next moment the raft was upside down in the river with the two of us dumped into the water floating behind the raft. I shouted for Joyce to swim to shore, then grabbed onto the boat and tried, in vain, to pull it to shore. It was way too heavy with all the gear, and the current too strong. As the raft and I approached the next class III rapid, Fort Goff Falls, only about a hundred feet away, I realized the danger and let go of the boat. After I watched the raft disappear over the lip of the falls, I turned to swim to shore and find Joyce. She was scared but safe, clutching her paddle in both hands.

I told her I would run after the boat, and she should come as quickly as she could. We both expected the raft would soon be caught in an eddy on the side of the river, and we would see each other in mere minutes. I learned later that this section of the Klamath had no calm stretches. I had no choice but to go after the boat. This involved running along the shore and, when the shore was too choked with bushes or cliff walls, swimming down the rapids.

About a mile downriver, I was sloshing along the shallow river shore when I happened to notice a tiny spot of blue between some river vegetation. Reaching down, I picked up my favorite water bottle. What are the odds that I would glance down at exactly that moment, and even see a tiny glimmer of blue! Clearly this was a miracle gift from God, since I was thirsty and, although I did not know it, I still had four more miles of arduous hiking, climbing, swimming, and bush-whacking ahead of me, during which I did not find one more item of loose equipment.

At one point, crawling on my hands and knees through a dense willow thicket, I came upon some fresh bear scat (i.e., poop). I thought to myself, just what I need, to come face-to-face with a bear and not even be able to stand up!

Meanwhile, Joyce walked a very difficult two and a half miles downriver along the highway, without seeing me or our boat. Scared, tired, thirsty, scratched and bloody, she came upon a lone house on the riverbank. She knocked on the door and was met by a woman who looked more scared than she was. Joyce started to explain our situation, but the woman shut the door and ran for her phone. She probably thought Joyce was some kind of crazy person, got scared, and dialed 911.

Joyce didn't know what to do, so she just waited outside the house. The sheriff's deputy, who soon arrived with sirens blaring, immediately saw that Joyce was not dangerous, invited her into his patrol car and began the search for me.

Five miles and two hours after the flip, I swam yet another rapid, finally entered the first quiet pool, and there was the raft, floating upside down in the center of the pool.

Meanwhile, the deputy, with Joyce in the passenger seat, had been searching along the river, occasionally stopping and calling my name into his loudspeaker. Finally, he gave up and was just about to request a helicopter when Joyce spotted me and the raft through the brush and trees. The very moment I pulled the raft to the left side of the river, the patrol car pulled down a dirt road to the right side of the river and out stepped Joyce, still holding her paddle.

Even though he was on the wrong side of the river to actually help, he stayed for the hour to make sure the two "senior citizens" unloaded and flipped their boat right side up. That was no easy task. It required multiple dives under the raft to untie all the gear, and then flip the boat over. Finally, when he saw us floating downriver, he took off in his car.

A few miles downriver, as we approached the first available takeout, there was our old friend, the deputy sheriff, waiting to make sure we made it in one piece. He patiently waited while we unloaded all our wet gear and food onto the beach, then drove me an hour out of his way up-river to our truck.

If we have eyes to see, life is a never-ending series of miracles and divine interventions. Yes, Joyce and I were both disappointed by the smoke on the Rogue River. Spending many more hours stripping our upside-down raft of gear, turning the boat right side up, floating around the bend to the next take-out, spreading wet food, sleeping bags, clothes, and other gear in the sun to dry, then packing everything up in our camper for the trip home, was not our idea of a vacation. Yet it's impossible to ignore how divine hands helped us every moment. Sure, life will flip you over from time to time. Your invitation is to realize that life's upsets can deepen your trust and faith, and allow you to see from a spiritual perspective.

Driving home from our aborted river trip, I checked my cell phone messages: "Hello, this is Rogue River Ranger Taylor. I'm calling to apologize to you and your wife for threatening you with blacklisting because you cancelled your trip. All the other people who put on the river the day you cancelled had to be evacuated. We've taken your name off the blacklist, and would like to offer you a permit for next year, any date you wish."

I smiled as I removed the cap from my blue "miracle" water bottle, and took a big drink.

Chapter 41: Miracle at Poggio Bustone 2013

It's October 2013, and Joyce and I are trudging up a very steep rocky trail near the top of a mountain high above the Rieti Valley in central Italy. We were about to lead a retreat in Assisi, but set aside this time for our own pilgrimage. We left our friend, Evelyn, down at the end of the road at the monastery of Poggio Bustone. The drive up the winding mountain road with sheer cliff drop-offs was plenty enough adventure for her. It's only 500 or so more feet of elevation to the top of the mountain, where lay a more primitive monastery. Right! Only 500 feet! Practically straight up the mountain.

About 800 years ago, Saint Francis also climbed this mountain. Only he did it barefoot and without a trail! It was a time in his life when he felt he could not go on with the work he was being called to do without feeling God's complete forgiveness. You see, his early life was filled with riotous living, drinking, partying, orgies and, even worse, fighting in battles against neighboring towns. Although there are no direct references, I am convinced that he must have experienced violence, even killing or wounding other men.

In his early twenties, he began to turn his life over to God, but he had to know he was forgiven for the unconscious actions of his former years. So he climbed this mountain, found a cave near the top, and sequestered himself away from the world to seek complete forgiveness. He was determined not to leave that cave until he knew for certain that he was forgiven. We don't know exactly how long he meditated and prayed on that mountain, but we do know that he finally received a clear message from God: *he was completely forgiven.*

Thus began a new phase in Francis's life. He no longer had to carry the heavy burden of his past transgressions.

Like most things and places of Saint Francis, the original cave has been transformed into a small chapel, and is referred to as The Place of Forgiveness. It's just too high and steep to be made into a "proper" cathedral. Yet it still retains a certain rustic simplicity and sacred feeling as a place of pilgrimage for the few hardy souls willing to make the trek.

And, like Saint Francis, Joyce and I were also climbing the mountain to seek complete forgiveness. We have often spoken about the unconscious actions of our younger years. I have always considered Joyce's misdeeds as "lightweight." Like once, when she stole a piece of fruit from a neighbor's tree, and her parents marched her down the street to apologize. We both, on the other hand, have considered many of my teenage acting out to be a bit more major, and some could have been punishable by prison time. I have stolen things, unfortunately a lot of things. I have been mean. I have engineered some "pranks" that have ended up nearly scaring people to death. I could go on, but perhaps you get the picture.

Tired from the climb, we arrived at the simple stone addition to the original cave. We opened the rough-hewn wooden door and entered the cool interior. We were alone. It would have been completely dark except for a shaft of light coming in from a tiny window up high on a wall. We found a place to sit on some rustic chairs in front of a crude altar, and began to ask for forgiveness.

Bottom line, both Joyce and I expected me to be sitting in the primitive chapel for a long time. Perhaps Joyce would feel forgiveness, and then she could do some sightseeing or sunbathing outside the chapel while she waited for me to finish my big ordeal.

That's not what happened! Instead, I closed my eyes, preparing to list off my offenses. Within minutes, I felt a wave of complete forgiveness for all my actions, almost like an ocean wave of divine energy washing over me!

My first thought was, "Wait. This was too easy! I haven't worked and sweated hard enough to earn complete forgiveness. I have just begun to go through my long list."

I couldn't deny it. I felt an almost overwhelming sense of God's unconditional forgiveness. I felt light as a feather with the divine assurance that nothing I have ever done could keep me from my worthiness for divine love. I felt like jumping up and dancing with joy!

There is a famous line from the *Course in Miracles*, "God does not forgive because He (She) never has condemned." I have been the only one condemning myself. The Divine Presence *is* forgiveness. Forgiveness can never be earned. It is freely given at all times.

So many of us, as children, have been misled into thinking we needed to earn our parents' love and forgiveness. If only I was better behaved, or did things right, or apologized more, then I'd prove my worthiness to mom and dad. We then make God into a higher version of our parents. This is futile. The Great Spirit loves us no matter what we've done. God sees all our actions, in the great experiment of free will, as a holy learning and growing process.

Joyce was, needless to say, very surprised to see me stand up and quietly leave the chapel after only a few minutes. Her first thought was, "Oh dear. The task is just too hard for Barry. He had to give up."

Sometime later, she finished her own process of opening to divine forgiveness, and came outside to console me in my failure. When she heard my experience of spontaneous forgiveness, she smiled and embraced me in one of her wonderful hugs.

Chapter 42: Miracle on Lake Tahoe

I pulled our nineteen-foot sailboat up to Lake Tahoe to experience sailing and camping on the largest alpine lake in North America. Yes, I was alone. I would have preferred that Joyce accompany me, but she wanted to stay home and help with our daughter, Mira's, newborn son. And I have a need for occasional solo adventures.

By the time I launched, I had only a few hours of daylight left. The wind had died down, so I started my outboard motor and headed toward a small beach I found on the map. I didn't get very far. The motor sputtered and died. I couldn't get it started again. When I pulled on the starter cord, the little flashing red light proclaimed "low oil." I forgot to check the oil level before launching. Did I have extra engine oil stored in the boat? Of course not!

A very faint breeze allowed me to inch into a private boat harbor and tie up to the only vacant mooring buoy as darkness was descending (a miracle in itself). I slept that night in the boat.

In the morning, I saw a boat leaving the harbor. Perhaps they might have some engine oil. I only needed a small amount, maybe half a cup, to allow me to start the motor. That would require asking for help, flagging them down by waving my hands, inconveniencing them, showing my helplessness.

I swallowed my pride, flagged them down, and asked the young man for oil. He didn't have any, but gave me a ride to the dock, where I could walk a half hour to a small convenience store. On the way to the store, I practiced asking for help/oil a few more times without success. I did notice, however, that most people were very nice, wanting to help even though they couldn't. They felt needed, and that brought out their best.

I bought a quart of engine oil at the store, walked back to the dock, got another ride out to my boat (more asking for help), and added the oil to my motor. I got it started, but just barely, and headed across the vast lake to an area of small, more hidden, pocket beaches. As long as I squeezed the primer bulb hard and continuously, I could keep the motor running. Obviously, the low oil was not the problem. There was something else wrong with the motor.

I kept waiting for the wind to pick up, so I wouldn't be so dependent on the motor but, alas, it was not to be. No wind the entire day! And hard to believe on such a huge lake!

My hands were cramped and exhausted from all the squeezing when I saw an isolated little beach, almost hidden from the rest of the lake. About a hundred feet offshore, the motor finally died. I pulled and pulled on the starter cord with no success. Finally, I jumped into the lake, holding a length of rope attached to the bow, and started pulling the boat to shore. Amazingly, a man on the beach called out, "Do you need any help?" At that particular moment, however, I was actually doing just fine, and enjoying being in the cool lake water. Another part of me silently added, "Barry, you just missed another opportunity to ask for help, whether you could do it yourself or not!"

The next morning dawned practically windless again and I decided to end my trip and get back to the boat ramp as soon as possible. I pushed off from shore and, while again inching at a snail's pace from the beach, tried to start the engine. Nothing! I kept at it. For three hours I pulled on that starter cord, trying every trick I could. I'm amazed the cord didn't break, leaving me in much worse condition. And all the while, I hoped the wind would finally come up. That was not to be.

I practiced asking for a tow from other boats that passed, but no one offered that level of help. I called a boat towing company that was happy to help, for $375! I told him I'd call him back.

Finally, it dawned on me. Not in all this time had I even had the thought to ask for divine help. I pray for divine help every day. I pray that Joyce and I can continue to be instruments of peace and love with our books and events. I pray that I can learn to trust God in all things, big and small. I pray for the well-being of our children and now grandchildren. But to pray for an outboard motor? Didn't even cross my mind.

Why not? Nothing is too small or insignificant for the angels, those heavenly helpers. I let go of the starter cord, placed my sore and cramped hands on the motor, and asked the angels for their all-powerful help. I sincerely asked, then gave thanks for their help. It took perhaps a minute or two. Then I pulled the cord once more.

The motor instantly roared to life. I had to laugh at the odds of that happening. I yanked on that starter cord maybe a thousand times with no success, said one prayer to the angels, and voila! What a lesson! I could almost imagine a group of angels sitting around just waiting for me to ask them for help, perhaps having this conversation,

"Any asking yet?"
"No, he's still pulling on that cord, trying to do it himself."
"How many hours has it been now, in Earth time?"
"Hey, wait. He's asking us for help. Finally! Okay, who wants to bless that motor?"

I sincerely hope I can once and for all learn the joy of asking for help, from people and from angels, from those I can see and from those I can't see. I hope I can remember how much joy it gives others to help me. And I hope I can remember that problem size doesn't matter, that I can feel my dependence on God and the angels in all situations.

Chapter 43: An Answered Prayer

Our Assisi retreat in October was looking to be very small, with only five participants. Barry and I had never done a retreat with so few people, but cancelling it was out of the question. Plus, we really wanted to go, as it is a highlight of the year for our own spiritual growth.

My dear friend Debbie is a devout Catholic, and she told me about a special room at her church that is dedicated to prayer. Our Assisi retreat was in two months, and I felt we needed at least one more person to make the retreat flow better. I felt that I needed to go to this special room that Debbie had told me about.

Sitting in this room, I felt a little out of place since I was not raised Catholic. While the others in the room were kneeling, I sat very quietly and prayed. I sincerely asked for one more person to be guided to the retreat. When I left that room, I had a very good feeling that, regardless of the number, the retreat would be just perfect.

At that very time, all the way in Australia, a Catholic nun realized that she had the possibility to be in Assisi from October 11-17. So, she typed into Google search, "Assisi Retreat October 11-17." Since those were our exact retreat dates, we were the first search result to pop up. She had never done a retreat that was not Catholic, and so she wondered if it was the right thing for her. At the time, she was visiting her childhood home with her eight siblings. As she is so loved in the family, all of her siblings became involved and started reading our many articles on our website. Finally, they concluded that it would be a good fit for her.

She emailed us and asked what we thought. At first, Barry was hesitant, as we had never had a Catholic nun in any of our retreats before. He said, "What if she only wants to sing and pray, and wants nothing to do with the personal growth work?" But I felt this was so divinely guided that I assured him it was going to be fine. In a Catholic church, I had prayed for another person and, of course, a nun signed up. I pictured that she would be in long black robes, like the nuns in Assisi. I have to admit, it was hard to picture a nun in our retreat, but I felt that we needed to trust.

This nun showed up in blue jeans and a flannel shirt with a large red heart necklace around her neck. She lives in South Africa and helps run a large home for eighty African children who desperately need help. Sister Sally turned out to be a very great light, and her presence in our small group filled the room with love, courageous personal growth work, and humor. Indeed, it was a very great blessing and answer to my prayer.

Of the ten Assisi retreats we had done up until then, this one was my favorite, and her presence was a large part of that.

Chapter 44: Two Blondes in the Back Seat

Barry: I was returning from a solo river trip on the Owyhee River in southeast Oregon. I was in my pickup truck, with the truck bed filled with river gear, and the back seat filled with our two older golden retrievers, Rosie, and her daughter, Gracie. Driving through Sacramento on busy Highway 80, with six lanes going each way, with a sinking feeling in my stomach, I saw the flashing lights of the Highway Patrol car behind me. I heard the loudspeaker command, "Take the next exit and pull over." Perhaps you know that sinking feeling: I'm about to get a ticket and I have no idea what I did.

Exiting onto a busy city street, I pulled over to the curb to await my fate. The police car pulled up behind me, lights flashing, but no one got out of the car. That seemed strange. Then, as I watched in the rearview mirror, a few minutes later a second car arrived behind the first, also with lights flashing. Then a third and finally a fourth car pulled in. It was beginning to look like a crime scene with all the lights and yes, I was beginning to wonder if I was the criminal.

With four police cars behind me, I suppose the policeman in the first car felt properly backed up, so he very cautiously got out of his car and slowly approached the passenger side of my truck. I saw him coming and powered down the front windows. Meanwhile, Rosie and Gracie, in the back seat, were sitting up and alert. The other police were now getting out of their cars and getting into support positions. It all seemed unreal.

Policeman number one arrived at the passenger side window, looked into the truck, focusing on the back seat, looked confused for a moment, then smiled and said, "Oh, they're dogs."

I said, "Officer, is something wrong?"

He said, "We got a 911 call from someone who was following you. They described a drunk driver in a white pickup truck with your plates, having trouble staying in the lane, with two little girls with blonde hair in the back seat. Looks like they were wrong about the girls."

Then he asked me, "Have you been drinking?"

"No," I answered.

"Are you tired?"

"Actually, no. I stopped about a half hour ago and had a nap."

"Why would the driver describe you as drunk, swerving all over the highway?"

"Officer, as you can see, I have a few snacks on the seat next to me. Reaching for food might, I suppose, cause me to move a few inches this way or that, but certainly not out of my lane."

"Would you mind stepping out of the truck for a sobriety test?"

In that moment, I reflected on my appearance. I had been driving or living in the wilderness for a week. I was unshaven. I had no idea what my hair looked like. And with the combination of my smell, plus the two dogs' river smell in the back seat, who knows what assaulted the officer's nose as he leaned in my window.

I got out and joined him on the sidewalk. He held up a finger and asked me to focus on it as he moved it from side to side. He was looking for nystagmus, one sign of intoxication. At one point my eyes left his finger to look into his eyes.

"Don't look at me. Just look at my finger," he barked.

What can I say? In my world, I look into people's eyes, not at their fingers.

Meanwhile, the police officers from the other three cars, some with partners, now stood watching. One officer asked my permission to pet Rosie and Gracie. Another one took a peek into my truck bed and said, "Wow, you're a rafter! I am too. Did you just come back from the American River?

While answering him, I happened to glance into the busy city street. There was a major traffic jam in all four lanes, with cars moving at a snail's pace, while every person in every car took a good look at the major criminal surrounded by police on the sidewalk. I imagined someone leaning out of their car and yelling, "Barry Vissell, is that you?!"

However, no one recognized me and it all ended well. The police officer cautioned me to drive carefully, and let me go. As I pulled away from the curb, I imagined all the officers having a good laugh at the two blond canines in my back seat.

And on the bright side, Rosie and Gracie did enjoy all the attention they got.

Chapter 45: Angels on the Road

If we only knew how many times we are rescued by divine intervention, we would completely trust this higher power. There would then be nothing to worry about – ever! Joyce and I had yet another powerful reminder of this truth – and divine miracle.

In honor of both of us turning seventy in May 2016, we rented our favorite house in Hana, Maui, for eight days, and had a wonderful vacation with our three grown children, one of our children's significant other, and our five-year-old grandson. Six weeks post-op from a partial knee replacement, it was a real joy for me to actually hike without pain for the first time in several years.

On the way back to the airport from remote Hana, we had a flat tire. No problem! Even at seventy, I was confident that I could change a tire in less than ten minutes. We had left an extra hour early just in case. I opened the trunk of the rental car, emptied out all our luggage, and lifted up the flap to expose the spare tire.

There was no spare tire! Instead, there was a small twelve-volt air pump and a can of "flat-fixer" that somehow attached to it. Our son, John-Nuri, who was in our car, figured out how to attach the "flat-fixer." I plugged in the pump and watched, satisfied, as the tire started to inflate.

Turning off and removing the pump, we heard the loud hiss and realized the flat was not fixed. "Okay, everyone back in the car," I ordered. "Let's see how far we can travel with the leak."

We were maybe forty-five minutes from the airport. I started driving. Five minutes later, the tire pressure was obviously too low to continue driving. I pulled over and we repeated the process, hoping the "flat-fixer" might work after a second try.

No luck! I got another five minutes closer to the airport. (Note to self: never, ever, rent a car without a spare tire!)

Now we recognized we were in trouble. John-Nuri's flight was twenty minutes earlier than ours, so we needed to reach our daughters, Rami and Mira, who were ahead of us somewhere in a separate rental car. We finally did, and they doubled back to meet us. I had the brilliant thought to check if their car had a spare tire. It did! But the tire iron did not fit our tire's nuts! No luck there!

John-Nuri squeezed into their car with his luggage, and off they went. Our children felt terrible leaving us on the side of the road. Joyce and I understood the reality that we very likely would miss our flight home. First, we called the rental car company to see if they could help. All they could do was refer us to a taxi company, who we immediately called. They said they could come get us in three hours. Great! We were told that we could leave the rental car on the side of the road and they would come and get it in a matter of hours.

Joyce: My main practice at this time is to try to see everything as an opportunity to trust more fully in God. When the tire went flat, I was sure that somehow the angels would come down and magically fix the tire or, at the very least, allow us to get to the airport. While Barry and our son were using the pump, I put my hands on the tire and prayed for a miracle. I visualized the tire surrounded in light. But, after all the attempts, it finally became apparent that this car was not going to get us to the airport.

Barry and I pulled all of our luggage out of the car and stood on the side of the road. We were both praying for help, and we must have looked rather pathetic, two senior citizens standing by their luggage, waving their hands and begging for help on the side of a very remote and winding road. Twenty minutes went by and not one vehicle stopped. It was now 12:10 and our flight was at 1:20. We were still at least 35 minutes from the airport, and knew the airlines had a strict policy. We would not be able to check in less than 40 minutes before our flight. We got a very sinking feeling inside that the plane with our family would leave without us, and we would have to wait until the next day, with no place to stay and no car to drive.

A rusty old white van pulled up with two Hawaiian men. It was a son, perhaps in his forties, and his elderly father. They listened to our sad story and agreed to take us to the airport. The son told us he doubted we would make it in time for the flight, but the father said, "Let's give it a try," and off we went.

We told them how grateful we were and the son said, "I've learned that all of life is meant to be lived in gratitude. Gratitude is the key to a good life." When we asked if we could pay them, the father said that the best payment would be to "pay it forward" and help someone else.

The town of Paia, which is normally very congested with traffic, was totally clear and we sailed right through what can take an extra half hour. The son knew of a short cut that was just completed. He miraculously got us to the airport one minute before the 40-minute deadline. The Hawaiians told us to run and we took off. The gate agents took our bags and again told us to hurry as fast as we could.

We were the last people on the plane, sweating and out of breath, but we made it. Our children were thrilled and surprised! As I sat in my seat and closed my eyes, I distinctly heard my inner voice quietly say, "Trust Me, I have your back!" This was yet another opportunity to trust.

Epilogue

Barry: Are miracles still happening in our lives? Every day!

Our lives have been composed of many thousands of miracles. Remembering them is a source of infinite joy. Accepting everything as a miracle continues to bless us to this day. And the gratefulness we feel as a result keeps us optimistic about our future, and the future of this world.

Our work in the world is all about helping people with their lives and their relationships; individually, as couples, or in our groups and retreats. Do we see miracles happen? Yes, often. Each person's heart opening to more love is a miracle to be celebrated.

Starting with the onset of the Covid Pandemic, which canceled all of our live events, we recorded a simple short weekly video containing an inspiring message and me singing one of the songs I have written, accompanying myself on the harmonium, a small hand-pumped organ, originally from India. Before each video, Joyce and I pray that our words and music can help whoever needs help. We don't have a huge following but, each time, we hear from a few people who tell us that the video they just watched was exactly what they needed. Is this a miracle? You bet. (You can sign up for these free videos at SharedHeart.org)

To be aware of the miraculous in life requires paying attention and being present. To notice life itself is to notice miracle after miracle. If you're waiting for fireworks, you can easily miss the constant stream of miracles happening right now. Even as I sit in my office room now, I am looking out my window at the infinitely varying shades of green in the foliage, the dark greens of a wisteria vine gone wild with reckless abandon, reaching out in every direction; the maturing silver maple tree beginning the amazing transformation of reds, oranges and yellows that signals autumn. The change of color is not static; it is ever-changing, even as I watch this miracle unfold.

Then there's the miracle this morning of sitting with Joyce, after our meditation and prayer time, and looking into her face and eyes, seeing the radiance of the Goddess shine through to me. During the day, as we pass each other in each of our activities, sometimes I miss out on this miracle. I don't pay attention or notice her divine beauty, or the little way she smiles at me, even in passing. But sometimes, even in our busyness, we stop and hug, and not a short hug but a real embrace. And then I remember and feel the miracle of two souls, joined in love for not just a mere fifty-seven years, but for eternity.

Joyce: Miracles can come to us in many different ways. Sometimes it is just a reassuring feeling and message that comes from within. Barry and I recently took a camping trip to Glacier National Park in Montana. It took us several days to get there and, during the long drive, I reflected on the fact that we were both seventy-five years old. Barry seems as active and strong as when he was a much younger man. I am definitely slowing down physically. We both love our work so much and really do not want to retire. Both of us have good strong minds and hearts and a deep willingness to continue. But the reality is there, "Just how much longer will we be able to continue?"

Barry noticed a trail along the way that would allow us to bring our two golden retrievers, Honey and Gracie. It was a very long trail and after an hour I decided to head back to our camper early as my knee was hurting me. Barry chose to hike to the end, which was fine with me. While I was walking back, I was reflecting on my age and the fact that I am slowing down, not able to do as much as I would like.

Suddenly I came to a place in the trail that was just so beautiful it took my breath away. I love autumn leaves and there in this spot were several magnificent trees in their full autumn colors of red, orange and yellow. The sun was shining through the leaves making them glow. And flowing around these trees was the sweetest little stream making magical noises. I stopped and was very still to hear and take in the beauty as much as I could.

And then I heard the "voice of guidance" that has been guiding me for my whole life. It is not a loud voice and does not come that often. There are no lights or sightings of angels, just a simple very loving voice. As always, the message was very comforting,

"Trusting me is now your full-time job and service in the world."

I felt that I do not even have to worry one bit as to whether I can continue to do the work that I love. Now my full-time job is to trust in all ways, and the work and my life will flow with trusting. This simple message is a guidance for the rest of my life, and it brought so much joy and comfort. Trust is my full-time job. This message is a miracle for me.

About the Authors

The Vissells' books have been translated into five languages. They lecture and have led over 20 workshops per year internationally to audiences who welcome their warm, relaxed and yet profound wisdom. Joyce and Barry have written a monthly column for over 40 years, "New Dimensions of Relationship," which they email for free to their subscribers. These articles also appear in about 80 publications internationally, and countless e-zines, websites (including their own), and blogs.

Ram Dass describes Joyce and Barry Vissell "as a couple who live the yoga of love and devotion." Marianne Williamson says, "I can't think of anything more important to the healing of our society than a connection between spirituality, relationship and parenthood. Bravo to the Vissells for helping us find the way."

Barry and Joyce are two people deeply in love since 1964, who have raised three children and "walk their talk." They are the authors of *The Shared Heart, Models of Love, Risk To Be Healed, Light in the Mirror* (also published as *The Heart's Wisdom), Meant To Be,* and *A Mother's Final Gift, To Really Love a Woman, To Really Love a Man, and Heartfullness.*

. A story from *Meant To Be* was made into a Sunday Night NBC Movie, *"It Must Be Love,"* starring real-life couple, Ted Danson and Mary Steenburgen.

The Vissells, since 1983, are the founders and directors of the Shared Heart Foundation, a non-profit organization dedicated to changing the world one heart at a time (SharedHeart.org).

Joyce and Barry live at their retreat center and home near Santa Cruz, California, where they counsel individuals and couples, and lead retreats and trainings when they're not travelling.

Go to **SharedHeart.org** to sign up for their **free heart-letter** and **free weekly video inspiration**, to read past articles on many aspects of personal growth and relationship, to see their event or workshop schedule, or to contact Barry or Joyce.

ALSO BY THE VISSELLS

THE SHARED HEART
Relationship Initiations and Celebrations
ISBN 0-9612720-0-7, 186 pages,
©1984, Ramira Publishing, $9.95

The Shared Heart was one of the first books to bridge the chasm between following a spiritual path and having a deeply committed love relationship. As the book says, "Loving one other person teaches you how to love all people."

"The Shared Heart is full of beauty and compassion, richness and clarity. Barry and Joyce plough through the hard and soft spaces of the journey with great inner strength and deep respect for reflective inner tuning." —*Ram Dass*

"From the perspectives of romance, marriage, making love, parenting, careers, spiritual initiation, and loss of a loved one, this remarkable couple exhibits insight, acceptance and transcendence, at the same time offering specific tools for the transformational process of love."
—*Yoga Journal*

MODELS OF LOVE
The Parent-Child Journey
ISBN 0-9612720-1-5, 320 pages,
©1986, Ramira Publishing, $12.95

Contributors include Jack Kornfield, Eileen Caddy, Leo Buscaglia, Jerry Jampolsky, Joan Hodgson, Jeannine Parvati Baker and others.

Our children need not fall asleep to the beauty of their heavenly state for twenty, thirty, or more years, at which time breaking the habit of material thought is very difficult. We can help them begin the awakening process from the day they are conceived, so that the bridge of consciousness between the two worlds is continually strengthened.

"This is a book we whole-heartedly recommend to first-time parents, to grandparents, and to everyone in between."
—Mothering Magazine

"Models of Love is more than a parenting book. It will bless your whole life!" **—John Bradshaw**

"This book is full of miraculous incidents and sacred moments of loving connection that will bring tears to your eyes."
—Whole Life Magazine

"What society needs most is a connection between spirituality and parenthood. Bravo to the Vissells for helping us find the way"
—Marianne Williamson.

RISK TO BE HEALED
The Heart of Personal and Relationship Growth
ISBN 0-9612720-2-3, 192 pages,
©1989, Ramira Publishing, $9.95

Not infrequently, we receive an email or a letter with the words, *"Your book has changed my life."* Almost without exception, the writer is referring to *Risk to Be Healed*.

"In this book, Joyce & Barry offer the priceless gift of their own experience with relationship, commitment, vulnerability, and loss, along with the profound guide to healing that comes from the core of their being and blesses us with gentle wisdom."
—**Gayle & Hugh Prather**

The Vissells, in their uniquely captivating and personally revealing way, extend another written offering to the world. *Risk to be Healed* is filled with stories from their own continuing growth, as well as the healing risks individuals and couples have taken in their counseling sessions and workshops. The book begins with the profound experience of Anjel's death in utero and her subsequent birth into the lives of the authors. Subject matter includes: risk-taking in relationship, the way of intimacy, the power of right livelihood, understanding pain, healing relationships with those who have passed on, addictions, appreciation, vulnerability, and simplifying our lives.

RAMI'S BOOK
The Inner Life of a Child

by Rami Vissell
ISBN 0-9612720-4-X, hardcover,
56 pages, full-color illustrated,
©1989, Ramira Publishing,
$13.95

"We have been taught for a long time that the entrance to God's presence is through the eyes of a child. Rami flings wide that delicious door of perception."
—**Rev. Stan Hampson, Past President, Association of Unity Churches**

"My hope is that all adults as well as children may benefit by the understanding and love that Rami shares in this delightful book."
—**Ken Keyes**

"Rami's book is a gift from an angel. The innocent beauty filling these pages brings me tears of joy. I wish children of all ages would read this book." —**Alan Cohen**

"Sensitively and endearingly written ... Rami's innocence and candidness is both moving and refreshing." —**Science of Thought Review, England**

"Of all the books I've reviewed, this one went right to my heart and made me cry quite wonderfully. Truly an angelic and marvelous work, and a gift to the child still within me. I put it on display with a sign: 'very, very highly recommended. 4 stars on the goose bump chart!'."
—**Richard Rodgers, manager, The Grateful Heart Bookstore.**

LIGHT IN THE MIRROR
A New Way to Understand Relationships
ISBN: 0-9612720-5-8,
©1995, Ramira Publishing, $13.95

Republished by Conari Press as
The Heart's Wisdom: A Practical Guide to Growing Through Love

"Light in the Mirror *is an expression of deep love and vulnerability, and the celebration of what commitment can be."* —**John Gray, PhD**, author of *Men Are From Mars, Women Are From Venus.*

"In Light in the Mirror, *Joyce and Barry Vissell share with deep tenderness and vulnerability the valleys and peaks of their relationship. They go on to share 'practical spirituality,' suggestions that will be most helpful to everyone finding their way home to the heart."*
—**Gerald Jampolsky, MD** and **Diane Cirincione**, authors of *Love is the Answer* and *Change Your Mind, Change Your Life.*

"We have always benefited from the gentle wisdom of the Vissells. Light in the Mirror *is one of the rare voices for sanity in the field of relationships."*
—**Gayle and Hugh Prather**, authors of *Notes to Myself* and *I Will Never Leave You.*

"If you had but one book to choose to renew your relationship, this should be the one." —**Small Press Magazine**

"Light in the Mirror is a must for anyone who yearns for better connection and more joy in their intimate relationships."
—**Napra Review**

MEANT TO BE
Miraculous True Stories To Inspire A Lifetime Of Love
ISBN 1-57324-161-X,

©2000, Conari Press, $14.95

"The true miracle of these stories is that they open your heart to your own miracle, for the miracle of love is within you too, and your story can be as magical as these. That is the healing message on Meant to Be, that is its wonder."

— **Neale Donald Walsch**, author of *Conversations with God*

"Few books make me cry, but this one did, many times. The best collection of heart-full stories that I have ever read!"

— **Mary Jane Ryan**, author of *Random Acts of Kindness*

"The Vissells now bring us deeply moving (and some very entertaining) true accounts of Love's presence in the lives of other couples. Meant To Be says to us all, 'Relax. There are no chance encounters.'"
—**Hugh Prather**, author of *Notes to Myself*

"These wonderful stories remind us of the miracle that love is, and the magical ways it comes into our lives. Meant To Be proves that, at the deepest levels, destiny is always at work in our lives."
—**Susannah Seton, author of Simple Pleasures**

A Mother's Final Gift
How One Woman's Courageous Dying Transformed Her Family
ISBN-13: 978-0-9612720-3-6,
©2011, Ramira Publishing, $14.95 US

As we gave my mother her final gift on honoring her dying process, she gave us her final gift of opening a window into eternity and allowing us to have a peek.

"*A Mother's Final Gift* is the story of one courageous woman – Louise Viola Swanson Wollenberg – and of her tremendous love of life and family, and her faith and resolve. But it is also the story of her equally courageous family who, in the process of rising to the occasion and carrying out Louise's long-held final wishes, not only overcame so many stigmas about the process of death but, at the same time, rediscovered what it means to celebrate life itself. This book not only touches the heart in a very powerful, poignant, and joyful way, but reading it was life-changing for me. In writing this book, Joyce and Barry Vissell, and their children, mentor us through an experience that many of us were afraid to even think about it. Louise looked at death as her greatest adventure. So should we all. The title of this book is indeed *A Mother's Final Gift* but, in truth, this story is an exceptional gift to every person who will read it." – **George Daugherty**, Emmy Award-winning producer, director, and conductor

TO REALLY LOVE A WOMAN
ISBN-13: 978-0-9612720-7-4,
©2018, Ramira Publishing, $15.95 US

"Read this book if you want to have a more loving, intimate, understanding and vulnerable relationship with the special person in your life." –John Gray, PhD, author of *Men are from Mars, Women are from Venus*.

"To Really Love a Woman and To Really Love a Man are backed by the powerful work the Vissells have been doing decade after decade in helping couples thrive and see the highest in one another, fueled by the beauty and success of their own partnership." –David Feinstein and Donna Eden, authors of *The Energies of Love*

This book will show you how to:

- Really make love with her
- Become vulnerable with her
- Trust her in the deepest ways
- Take care of the relationship as much as she does
- Uniquely appreciate her
- Resolve conflict with her
- Identify and love the inner mother as well as the inner little girl
- And much more

TO REALLY LOVE A MAN
ISBN-13: 978-0-9612720-8-1,
©2018, Ramira Publishing, $15.95 US

"The Vissells challenge us to let our imagination be big and to reach down deep to expand our repertoire of ways we show love. It's a detailed, practical, and inspirational guide for those who aspire to become great lovers and to bring maximum delight to their partnership." –Linda Bloom, co-author of Secrets of Great Marriages.

"To say that Barry and Joyce Vissell are masters of love is not an exaggeration. Not only is their own marriage a model of the kind of relationship most of us would like to have, but they teach us what real, lasting love is all about." –Jed Diamond, PhD, author of The Enlightened Marriage: The 5 Transformative Stages of Relationships and Why the Best is Still to Come

This book will show you how to:

• Uniquely appreciate him
• Trust him in the deepest ways
• Become vulnerable with him
• Really make love with him
• Find out what he really wants and needs
• Resolve conflict with him
• Identify and love the inner father as well as the inner little boy
• And much more

HEARTFULLNESS:

52 Ways to Open to More Love
ISBN: 9781708957384
Copyright © 2020 by Ramira Publishing
$15.95 paper; $5.99 Kindle
Only available on Amazon.com

This book contains writings and stories that all illustrate the many facets of heartfulness. For this book, we have chosen 52 of our writings that most illustrate heartfulness. That's one per week. Our goal is to lead you into your heart. Our goal is to give you a feeling experience of the heart in its many dimensions. We could say each piece will make you feel good. And this may be true. But each will also challenge you to grow in spiritual awareness, for there is often a certain risk that must be taken before the heart can open. Sometimes we need to leave our comfort zone to really live from the heart.

"Heartfullness is unique among the Vissell's line of books because there are short 2-3 page inspirational chapters with a theme related to what it is to live from the heart, enjoyable to read in the evening when one wants inspiration. The stories always relate to a personal experience, and often are little gems that delight the reader. Read and enjoy this beautiful little Kindle book for wonderful stories from two masters in the Heartfulness movement." – Carolyn D. Cunningham

Made in the USA
Las Vegas, NV
12 November 2023

80720145R00215